Grit and Hope

Grit and Hope

A YEAR WITH FIVE LATINO STUDENTS
AND THE PROGRAM THAT HELPED
THEM AIM FOR COLLEGE

Barbara Davenport

UNIVERSITY OF CALIFORNIA PRESS

University of California Press, one of the most distinguished university presses in the United States, enriches lives around the world by advancing scholarship in the humanities, social sciences, and natural sciences. Its activities are supported by the UC Press Foundation and by philanthropic contributions from individuals and institutions. For more information, visit www.ucpress.edu.

University of California Press
Oakland, California

Library of Congress Cataloging-in-Publication Data

Names: Davenport, Barbara, 1945- author.
Title: Grit and hope : a year with five Latino students and the program that helped them aim for college / Barbara Davenport.
Description: Oakland, California : University of California Press, [2016] | "2016 | Includes bibliographical references and index.
Identifiers: LCCN 2016006126 (print) | LCCN 2016007272 (ebook) | ISBN 9780520284449 (cloth : alk. paper) | ISBN 9780520284456 (pbk. : alk. paper) | ISBN 9780520960077 (e-edition)
Subjects: LCSH: Reality Changers (Program) | Hispanic American high school students—California—San Diego—Case studies. | College applications—California—San Diego—Case studies.
Classification: LCC LC2688.S25 D38 2016 (print) | LCC LC2688.s25 (ebook) | DDC 371.829/680794985—dc23
LC record available at http://lccn.loc.gov/2016006126

Manufactured in the United States of America

25 24 23 22 21 20 19 18 17 16
10 9 8 7 6 5 4 3 2 1

For Reality Changers' students and graduates:
they are the heroes of this book and of their own lives

Contents

Author's Note

I am deeply grateful to Reality Changers' students, especially the seniors and alumni who were the focus of the story, who have been remarkably generous with me. At a time when they were intensely preoccupied with applying to college and the work of transforming their lives, the seniors were always willing to talk about themselves and their hopes. The alumni were equally helpful, offering a longer-term perspective on Reality Changers' impact on their lives. From every student I talked with, I learned lessons of courage and tenacity and giving back. The more I came to know the students and graduates, the more I saw how hard they worked over years to change their realities, and the more deeply I admired them. They are the heroes of this book.

The book could not have happened without the help and goodwill of Chris Yanov and Reality Changers' staff and volunteers. It's a significant commitment to allow a writer to hang around your program, talk to everyone, and watch everything you do. I told Yanov what I wanted to do, and he didn't flinch; from the beginning we had a handshake deal. He allowed me full access to the program—on bad days as well as good ones—to his blind spots as well as his inspired vision. He always had time to talk and always had patience with my questions, which must have seemed endless. His openness was an act of faith and generosity that made the book possible.

Jenn Garner, program designer, and Grace Chaidez, program manager, were always willing to offer their perspectives on the program. They provided valuable insights and helped broaden my understanding of the program. Thanks also to Debbi Leto, who developed and ran the Senior Academy, to Martha Berner, the tutor who found so many scholarships, and to Marshela Salgado-Solorio, vice president for events and communications. I'm grateful for the many conversations about the program I had with all of them over the course of writing the book.

In every interview, I was impressed by how deeply the staff and the volunteers cared about the program and how hard they worked to support its goals. They valued Reality Changers because they recognized that here was a place where they could bring their caring and make a difference in students' lives and, inevitably, in their own. The quality of everyone's care infused Reality Changers so that it was a college-readiness program that often felt like family.

Books have multiple midwives. Margaret Metzger, my dear friend and a superb teacher, believed in my project before I was sure of it. Her encouragement sustained it and me during its early gestation. Caitlin Rother offered a number of helpful recommendations as I was writing my proposal; I'm glad that I listened to her. In the writing's later stages Isabella Furth provided reassurance and sound editorial advice in equal measure; both were invaluable. Her confidence in the project, her good cheer, and her sure editorial hand saw me through. Miles Corwin and Arthur Salm offered thoughtful reviews and recommendations, which have made it a better book. At a critical point, Roberto Gonzales provided encouragement and pointed me to readings that enlarged my understanding and strengthened the book. My editor, Naomi Schneider, guided me from proposal to finished book with tact and patience. Her vision enabled this book to become a reality.

My wife, Benita Berkson, believed in me from the beginning. For years she tolerated the time this project required—in observation and interviews and writing—and the unevenness of authorial temperament, with her usual good humor and grace. This was an invaluable gift. Thank you.

Cast of Characters

Some of the individuals profiled in this book:

SENIORS, CLASS OF 2009

Daniel Merced
Kimberly Palafox
Jesse Sanchez
Robert Silva
Karina Vasquez
Fernando Carrillo

UNDERCLASSMEN

Eduardo Corona
Santiago Milagro
Marlon Silva

FOUNDING MEMBERS

Suzana Lozano, RC '05
Jorge Narvaez, RC '05
Jonny Villafuerte, RC '05
Perla Garcia, RC '06

STAFF

Christopher Yanov, founder and director
Grace Chaidez, program manager
Jennifer Schadler, program designer
Debbi Leto, Senior Academy/College Apps Academy

Several students requested that their actual names not be used, and this request has been honored.

Introduction

On a winter night in 2002, Christopher Yanov sat with a handful of eighth and ninth graders and college-student tutors in the Iglesia Presbiteriana Hispaña (Hispanic Presbyterian Church). The one-story cinderblock building in Golden Hill, near San Diego's downtown, looked more like a fortress than a church. Iron grillwork protected the windows; the door was a slab of hardened steel.

Yanov and the tutors and students sat on folding chairs around two tables in a room that faced the street. The kids settled into doing their homework, and the room was quiet, punctuated with occasional murmured consultations.

Reality Changers was eight months old and had a census of twelve, six boys and six girls Yanov had recruited at Ray A. Kroc Middle School, where he worked as a substitute teacher. Students were expected to come every week, but attendance was spotty. Tonight just six showed up. He wasn't sure the program was going to fly.

A rock clattered against the bars. Heads snapped up from books. Another rock crashed on the bars, so hard the glass rattled. A direct hit would shatter the pane. Salvo after salvo of pebbles followed, clanging against steel and glass.

Then the shouts.

"Kiss-ass schoolboys! Little pussies!

"How come we're out here and not in there!"

"Hey, Chris! You forgotten your friends?"

A brown face pushed between the bars and pressed against the glass. "Chris! You only talking to the smart kids now?"

The tutors looked at Yanov, eyes wide. They were freshmen from University of California, San Diego, worlds away from the iglesia; they hadn't bargained for this. The younger kids shot sidelong looks at each other and tried to look cool. One of them, Perla Garcia, knew the guys outside; she wished they'd go home. Jorge Narvaez kept his head down and pretended to read. He hoped they'd be gone by the time he had to walk to the bus stop.

"Just ignore it and keep on working," Yanov told them. "They'll get bored and quit."

"Losers! Wait'll you get out here. We'll fix you, pussies!"

The rocks kept clattering. The shouts got louder. Kids stopped even pretending to study.

Yanov rolled his eyes and exhaled with exasperation, stood up, and walked out the front door in his shirtsleeves. The night was cold; in the light from the street lamp he could see his breath. He stood a shade under six feet, shoulders squared, chin high, dark hair and beard cropped close.

A dozen eighth and ninth graders stood under the street lamp. All of them lived in the neighborhood and most went to Kroc. Their heads were shaved, and they wore the cholo uniform of baggy jeans that dragged on the sidewalk and oversize black nylon jackets. He'd invited every one of them to join Reality Changers.

They'd have to bring their grades up to a 3.0 grade point average in order to join. Come to meetings every week, for tutoring and work on study skills, and hear lessons on values and life skills. Instead of being in a gang, they'd be part of a group where everyone was aiming for college, and where kids helped each other. If they stayed with the program through high school, he guaranteed, they'd get into college and they'd have the scholarships they needed.

He'd worked especially hard on Jonny Villafuerte. Jonny lived across the street from Yanov, a few blocks east of the iglesia. He was a sweet, soft-looking boy with a shy smile and lush, dark hair that fell over his forehead.

His notebooks overflowed with drawings of cars and characters from video games and words in bulging, kinetic letters. Yanov knew him from honors algebra, but lately he'd seen him at the coral tree in the courtyard at Kroc, where the guys who were on the way to joining a gang hung out. The Lomas26 gang ran the streets in Golden Hill, and they were leaning on Jonny to join. Last fall, he'd shaved his head and started dressing like them. Yanov hoped that he hadn't made up his mind. If he didn't get to Jonny soon, Lomas26 would.

Now, here was Jonny, throwing rocks. "Hey, Chris, no fair," he yelled. "You didn't let us in!"

"You guys know you're invited," he said. "You just got to get your grades up."

"Aw-w, man."

"Kids inside did."

"We know you better. You're our guy. You should just let us in."

"When you get your 3.0, we'll be glad to have you. Tonight's not a 'no,' it's a 'not yet.' See you around." He waved and walked back into the church.

Rocks rang the bars like chimes. The kids and tutors were rattled, and not much homework got done that night. The tutors chalked up the meeting as a loss.

Yanov couldn't stop grinning. Those guys wanted in. He knew he had something.

.   .   .   .   .

Christopher Yanov heads an innovative college-readiness program called Reality Changers that, over the course of the last fifteen years, has altered the possibilities for disadvantaged youth in San Diego. Its students come from the city's poorest, most violent neighborhoods. Some are citizens; some are undocumented. They aren't cherry-picked high achievers: many enter the program as academic underperformers or chronic truants or as gang affiliated. Yanov looks for what he calls "outsize personalities," students who have the capacity to lead, are good communicators, and are highly motivated. Reality Changers not only provides academic tutoring but also helps students cultivate resilience, curiosity, the ability to collaborate, and perseverance.

Students maintain at least a 3.0 grade point average and 90 percent attendance to stay in the program. Reality Changers' constitution, written by its first students, prescribes that members have no involvement with alcohol, drugs, gangs, or sex. They must participate in at least one school activity or club or play a sport; practice public speaking and compete in in-house speech tournaments; and contribute fifty hours to community service each year.

Driven and charismatic, Yanov is himself an outsize personality. Even as a college freshman he was looking for a grand quest. At nineteen, he moved out of his dorm room at UC San Diego and into an apartment in Golden Hill to start his own gang-diversion program at the Iglesia Presbiteriana. He went to law school to become an advocate for the cholos he worked with, but flunked out because he spent more time running with them than studying. Two quests, not much success.

While substitute-teaching in a tough urban middle school where gangs ruled the courtyard, he saw that many of his students had as much innate ability and determination as the middle-class kids he'd grown up with. What they lacked were aspects of family and social support that middle-class students take for granted: an ambitious vision of what they could accomplish, the experience of being held to high standards, and a milieu of peers and adults who validated their ambitions and helped them reach their goals. If he could build that kind of scaffolding around his students, they'd stay in school, work harder, and aim for college. He was sure of it. This would be his quest.

At twenty-two, Yanov started a program to provide the scaffolding that would help students like his get to college. He'd never studied adolescent development, never taken a course in education or social work or psychology, never worked for an organization that served disadvantaged youth. But his tool kit included some important skills: He was fluently bilingual and had an impressive ability to connect with high-risk adolescents. From years of hanging with gang kids and then substitute-teaching, he'd built a deep understanding of what they needed, what worked with them, and what didn't. He started with three hundred dollars and the use of a room at the Iglesia Presbiteriana. On *Wheel of Fortune,* he won enough money to support himself and his fledgling program for two years. When that money ran out, he kept Reality Changers afloat by sheer determination, charisma, and seven-day work weeks.

Reality Changers now serves more than five hundred students a year and is the leading provider of scholarships among mentorship organizations in California. Its alumni go on to study at Berkeley, UCLA, UC San Diego, and all the other University of California undergraduate campuses, at twelve California state universities, at Dartmouth and Duke, at Northwestern and Columbia and Harvard. Yanov still lives in Golden Hill in the apartment he moved into when he was nineteen. He draws a modest salary and drives an eleven-year-old pickup truck. Reality Changers is his quest and his life.

I spent a year studying Reality Changers close up—hanging with the students, probing Yanov's sensibility, and interviewing staff, volunteers, and family members. I wanted to understand how the program works and how it makes a difference for its students. I also wanted to learn whether this program devised by a twenty-two-year-old could become a model for the rest of the country. I found that Reality Changers works because it demands more of its students, academically and behaviorally, than they believe they can achieve, and it provides the scaffolding that helps them do it.

The elements of its scaffolding are an ambitious vision of what students can attain, intensive academic tutoring, and equally intensive teaching of the values and behaviors that are essential for personal and academic success. The scaffolding provides a strong sense of family and a long-term commitment to students, from eighth grade through high school and beyond. From the day they join, students see their own aspirations reflected in the wall of photos of all program graduates, wearing their college sweatshirts. They see juniors and seniors taking Advanced Placement courses, seniors writing college applications, and program alumni who have gone on to college returning to talk to them. They're surrounded by living proof that kids just like them can do big things. The message from other students is: *Yeah, it's hard, but we're doing it, and you can, too.*

Behaviors and attitudes like self-control, resilience, curiosity, perseverance, and helping each other—what psychologists call noncognitive traits—are taught every week and cultivated in community service work and other program activities. Students eat together at the weekly meeting, and parents provide dinner. Tutoring takes place in groups of six to eight, with a volunteer tutor for every two students, and students stay in the same group all year. They feel held in the program's embrace, and they invariably say that the feeling of family is what they like best about the program. Like family, Reality Changers commits for the long haul: students can start in eighth grade and continue through high school graduation. The program charges no fees.

Hanging out at Reality Changers, I brought my perspectives as a psychotherapist and a parent. I trained first as a clinical social worker and then at the Chicago Institute for Psychoanalysis, where I studied child and adolescent psychotherapy. I worked for more than twenty years with adolescents and their families, first in the Midwest and then in San Diego. In my work and in helping my own daughters through their teens, I developed a particular interest in launching, the developmental era when adolescents navigate from the smaller arenas of their families and high school to make their own place in the adult world. Launching is a critical period, because the capacities and deficits that adolescents bring to this passage, how high they aim, the roads they take and those not taken will shape the rest of their lives. The work unfolds over a number of years, and the tasks change with time. The journey is the adolescent's own, but how each individual meets its demands is determined both by her own capabilities and deficits and by how well the scaffolding supports her.

Launching is hard developmental work for all adolescents; it's significantly harder for students who start from a place of severe social and economic disadvantage. For undocumented youth, the work of launching is even more complicated, because their efforts to assume adult roles and privileges—working, driving, voting—are blocked by laws that prohibit them from taking steps that their native-born peers take for granted. Immigration scholar Roberto Gonzales observes that "for undocumented youth, coming of age is itself a turning point: it begins the *transition to illegality*. Laws aimed at narrowing the rights of those unlawfully in the United States prevent these youths from participating in key adult rites of passage. The result is a stalling, detouring, and derailing of the life-course trajectories of thousands of young adults every year" (emphasis in the original).[1]

As disparities in income and opportunity between haves and have-nots become increasingly stark, I've grown concerned about how they affect youth growing up on the have-not side of the gap. I was looking for a way to explore the subject of adolescent launching and inequality when I found Reality Changers. I wanted to find out how much difference a strong program could make. How effective was its scaffolding in helping students launch themselves? How well could the program make up for lifetimes of economic and social disadvantage? Which realities in students' lives could Reality Changers help them change, and which ones remained stubbornly unchanged? These were among the questions I brought to my conversations with students.

Those conversations quickly got specific: What it's like to shift from selling dope at school one semester to taking Advanced Placement classes the next. How to keep yourself motivated when your parents don't understand what you do, or don't care. If you're used to making yourself invisible because you're undocumented, and then you get admitted to a college on the East Coast, do you travel by plane and risk being arrested at the airport?

In the chapters that follow, I will take you into the lives of some of San Diego's most disadvantaged and most determined students as they work against prejudice, cultural deprivation, and poverty. The year I spent with Reality Changers was a year of drama, of painful failure and surprising triumphs, and of growth toward students' goals in unpredictable ways. My aim is to show the lives they lived and the realities of launching from a place of significant disadvantage.

Around the country, a host of programs aim to help disadvantaged youth get to college, and as I followed Reality Changers I compared it to some of the most successful ones. The largest is the Harlem Children's Zone, which serves twelve thousand children in a historically African American section of New York. With an annual budget of $85 million, it operates its own preschools, charter schools, and health clinics and runs wraparound parenting and job-readiness services for parents of young children. Its vision is nothing less than to change the expectations of a generation of parents and children, so that school achievement and going to college become the norm.[2]

Many highly effective programs maintain a narrower focus, often within school systems, working with the schools' credentialed teachers.

OneGoal identifies excellent teachers in seventy public high schools serving large percentages of low-income students in Chicago, Houston, and New York. OneGoal trains its selected teachers to work with a cohort of disadvantaged students from sophomore year to high school graduation, with the goal that each one will get into college, succeed, and graduate. Like the Harlem Children's Zone, OneGoal seeks to change a culture: through teachers' advocacy and the example of students' success, OneGoal aims to make host high schools more supportive of students' efforts to get into college, as well as to spread that culture throughout the community.

The Barrio Logan College Institute in Barrio Logan, a historically Mexican neighborhood of San Diego, starts third graders in its after-school tutoring program. Its program begins with the assumption that its students' success is directly tied to parents' conviction that college is attainable and to parents' active involvement in promoting that success. Children and parents apply to the institute together, and parents must commit to helping the program for thirty hours each year. Staff are all first-generation college graduates, all bilingual. Barrio Logan College Institute works with students through middle school and high school, and keeps in close touch with its graduates through their freshman year of college. The program is small—its largest graduating class was fourteen seniors—but it boasts a record of 100 percent college enrollment.

Among the most successful programs, I found many of the same elements that Yanov built into Reality Changers: support from mentors, a positive peer culture, high expectations for students, and a commitment to teach grit, resilience, and self-discipline along with academic skills. What distinguishes Reality Changers in the college-readiness landscape are Yanov's intuitive approach to program development, the strong sense of the program as family, and the idiosyncratic tone and tenor of its meetings.

College-readiness organizations are generally run by educators and researchers who develop their programs from the top down, designing interventions based on research in child development and cognitive psychology. Yanov designed his program from the streets up. He'd never read the research. What he knew was the lived realities of the gang kids he worked with in Golden Hill and of the students he taught in crowded, aging city schools. He drew on his deep experience of adolescents and neighborhoods, of what kids needed, how to connect with them, and what worked. The model he built was lean enough to work with the austere budget of his start-up years, straightforward enough to be implemented by volunteers, and focused on the single goal of helping students get to college. The program he built from his own experience uses methods and practices that are strikingly consistent with what other programs have derived from research.

Yanov's substantive innovation was to make Reality Changers a family whose members share common goals and help each other achieve them. The program's students need this family. For many, excelling in school isolated them from their peers and cost them friendships. Setting a goal of college meant taking different, harder classes, studying more, and having less time to hang out with friends. Reality Changers' expectation that participants would avoid alcohol, drugs, and gangs further widened the distance between them and many of their peers. Students described friends who'd known them since grade school accusing them of being too good to hang out with them. One student was pressured to join a gang; and when he refused, gang members beat him up and stole his shoes. Doing what it took to get into college pulled Reality Changers' students away from the peer groups where they'd belonged during adolescence, the time in their lives when children want desperately to belong. Yanov designed Reality Changers as a place to belong, where students could find peers who shared their culture, their goals, and as in a good family, caring adults to support and mentor them.

To grow students' experience of belonging, he introduced Congress, his name for a simple, surprisingly powerful ritual that starts every small-group study session at every weekly meeting. The student who is that night's leader approaches each group member in turn, shakes her hand, and asks her to state her week's high and low and her prayer request of the group. At the beginning of the year, students' responses were glib ("I went shopping on Saturday," "I have an algebra quiz tomorrow"), but over time their responses revealed much about their lives. They spoke of a car broken down, a father's injury on the job, a grandmother's illness. In less than ten minutes a week, Congress builds connection and caring among students and between students and tutors. Yanov tells new tutors, "Congress is the thing that makes Reality Changers different from all other tutoring programs. We aren't here just to raise our grades. We're a family."

His stylistic innovation is the tone and tempo of meetings. Yanov has a lifelong fascination with game shows, and he modeled Reality Changers' weekly meeting on game shows' upbeat format, with himself as the smooth-talking, audience-revving emcee. A difficult vocabulary lesson, an announcement of next week's community service opportunity, praise for a student who has answered a question—all are presented with hyperbolic enthusiasm and exhortations to applaud. Meetings got boisterous and sometimes felt hokey, but Yanov knew that he needed to keep things lively and keep his young audience engaged. Let them stomp and cheer and have some fun and they were more likely to tolerate the hard parts.

I report the story that I tell in this book from more than two hundred interviews with Reality Changers' students and their parents, program alumni, staff, and volunteers, conducted over a span of six years. For a full year I came to the Tuesday night meeting in City Heights every week, six to nine o'clock. I ate dinner with students, volunteer tutors, and staff, and I sat in on every component of the program, including the Senior Academy, Congress, study sessions, and the lessons. In these I was, for the most part, a silent observer sitting in the back, watching, taking notes. Yanov has always invited visitors to meetings, and students were accustomed to their proceedings being watched. I took part in some activities, like conversation over dinner or participating in Congress, when I was asked to, situations in which declining to participate would have seemed awkward to students. Conforming to group conventions felt more important to the project than maintaining a conventional reportorial reserve.

As I identified the students that I wanted to follow, I talked with each one about my intention to write about Reality Changers and asked whether they would be willing to talk with me about their experiences. I assured them that they were free to refuse, and if they agreed to be interviewed they were free to decline to answer any of my questions. I promised that I would show them what I'd written and they could request changes or deletions. In most reporting situations, subjects are not offered the opportunity to edit what's been written about them. Adolescents are a different story: they speak with less self-censorship than adults, and often without an appreciation for how their words might be used. As Pulitzer Prize–winning writer Madeleine Blais puts it, "When you are dealing with children it is different from dealing with adults and it is that simple."[3]

With students, I left the choice of where to meet up to them. We met at Reality Changers' offices, in their homes, and, as they grew more independent, in coffee shops and shopping malls. My questions were open-ended, designed to help me get to know the students and gain an understanding of their goals and hopes, the challenges they faced, and how they met them. I asked questions like: "How did you get connected with Reality Changers?" and "What difference has the program made in your life?" and let the interview flow where it might. Since the initial year, I've stayed in touch with students and staff, interviewed them further, and followed their progress.

I've also benefited from the work of writers and researchers who've studied the barriers that disadvantaged youth face and how they make their way. Three writers' works have been particularly useful. In *How Children Succeed,* Paul Tough reviews current research about noncognitive traits such as resilience, curiosity, tenacity, self-discipline, and cooperation, and their influence on children's academic and social success. He provides a good review of research by the psychologist Angela Duckworth on grit and self-control. She and her colleagues found these traits are critical: they determine, more than intelligence, how students fare in school as well as in work and relationships. Yanov built explicit lessons about these traits into Reality Changers programming, and as the seniors navigate their route to college, the most successful ones are those who've worked to cultivate these traits. Tough lays out the research. The stories of Reality Changers' students offer vivid portraits of how these behaviors make a difference in their lives.

Roberto Gonzales, of the Harvard Graduate School of Education, calls the situation of undocumented youth "the most poignant civil rights issue of our times."[4] His paper "Wasted Talent and Broken Dreams: The Lost Potential of Undocumented Students" is a powerful indictment of federal immigration policy. His review of the legal barriers and the contradictions within immigration policy alerted me to their ruinous consequences for undocumented students and helped me make sense of my own observations. His new book, *Lives in Limbo,* documents in painful detail the ways that being undocumented derails youths' efforts to move into productive adulthood. In telling the undocumented students' stories, I've used his perspective to examine the overt and the insidious ways their immigration status undermined their efforts to launch and throttled their dreams.

Miles Corwin's *And Still We Rise* is part of the rich narrative literature about disadvantaged youth and the adults who work with them. Corwin, a reporter for the *Los Angeles Times*, followed a class of gifted and talented African American seniors at an inner-city Los Angeles high school and charted their personal disasters and their efforts to get to college. He wrote during a period when affirmative action in college admissions was threatened, and he made a strong case for its ability, if not to level, then at least to improve, the profoundly uneven playing field on which disadvantaged youth compete. Affirmative action was no longer a consideration in California admissions when I came to Reality Changers, and for the program's seniors the college admissions playing-field remained severely uneven. Undocumented students faced even more forbidding obstacles. I've written about those obstacles and the doors that close to these students when they leave high school.

Although each of these writers implicitly recognizes launching as the developmental work of adolescence, in *Grit and Hope* I've made its importance explicit. I've used launching as a framework to explore how both students and the program met the demands of the year, and how their successes and their shortfalls shaped them. Both the students and Yanov were working intensely in preparation for launching: the students intended to launch themselves toward college and a world of wider possibilities; Yanov, toward transforming Reality Changers from his personal quest to a sustainable organization with national visibility. The developmental perspective enriched my understanding of what I saw and helped me tell both aspects of Reality Changers' story with greater clarity. Conceptualizing the program as developmental scaffold and launchpad enabled me to examine how well it supported its students in their efforts to build a better future for themselves.

Organizations, like people, go through developmental stages; and like people, they face imperatives to launch. The structures and practices that serve an organization well in its earliest years may, as it grows, become less useful, even stumbling blocks. Communicating plans and expectations and hearing everyone's concerns become a different task as an organization expands and more staff come aboard. Seeing Yanov's and the program's difficulties during the year as part of the task of launching into the next stage made much of what happened more intelligible.

The story I tell in this book opens in late August as the new seniors recommit to the high-stakes gamble that has defined their lives since they joined Reality Changers. They're betting that their years-long, flat-out effort with Reality Changers will pay off, that they will get into college and have the scholarships to pay for it. They feel that their lives are at stake. They're right. How they launch themselves this year—not just where they're admitted to college but also how they take on the work of getting there—will resonate throughout the rest of their lives.

The story unfolds through the school year, in chapters that follow five seniors and four of Reality Changers' original students. Three of the seniors are citizens; two are undocumented. They labor long past midnight on their application essays in work sessions with Yanov that are a Reality Changers ordeal and tradition. They struggle to keep focused on their goals in the face of family upheavals and family indifference; one struggles simply to get enough to eat. Through the winter and spring, as college acceptances and rejections roll in, they scramble to find scholarships; and they learn that, for all that the year has demanded of them, it's only their first step. Launching's a long game.

The four original members, including two who were studying in the Iglesia Presbiteriana Hispaña the night the boys outside threw rocks, are also launching this year, as they prepare to graduate from college. One student's plans have been complicated since he fathered a child in high school. For another, two quarters short of graduation, the sequelae of childhood deprivation and trauma derail her. A third graduates from college, yet already sees doors closing because he's undocumented. A fourth succeeds beyond her wildest imaginings. Their stories reveal how much a good program can help students change their reality and how the intractable realities of private trauma and public policy undermine their efforts.

Another skein of stories, interwoven with the students', reveals Yanov's and Reality Changers' evolution throughout a year that he's called the most difficult in the program's history. As he attempts to transform Reality Changers from a project he's run from two file cabinets in his apartment into a model with national standing, he's forced to look at the program through his employees' eyes and face problems that threaten to derail all that he's built.

The school year ends fifty feet above the ground on a June night at the Scholarship Banquet. On the roof of a parking garage, where sweeping views range west to San Diego Harbor and east to the mountains, Reality Changers celebrates students' accomplishments. Seniors' parents, city council members, and program donors are all honored guests, but for Yanov the most important audience is the younger brothers and sisters and cousins who look on wide-eyed. They are Reality Changers' extended family and the program's future.

An epilogue follows up with the seniors and the founding members as they're finishing college and launching into their adult lives. Students call their experience in Reality Changers life-changing. They say it raised their own expectations of what they could do and opened opportunities that, without the program, they would not have known existed. Reality Changers gave these students the tools they needed and the confidence that they could succeed—resources that their families often could not, and their schools often did not, provide them.

Most disadvantaged students are not so fortunate: across the country, public schools, especially in large urban districts, fail to provide scaffolding for the students who need it the most—the high expectations, mentoring, and support services. The country has grown substantially more diverse over the last three decades, and no institution has felt the impact of that diversity more than urban school districts. In some districts, more than one hundred languages are spoken at home. These students, who are immigrants and the children of immigrants, come to school with a burning desire to improve their lives. Their parents may be highly motivated to help them succeed, yet many lack the education to provide the scaffolding their sons and daughters need: while about 8 percent of children of U.S.-born parents have parents who have not graduated from high school, about 26 percent of children of immigrants do. For children of Mexican immigrants the number rises to nearly 50 percent.[5]

These parents care just as deeply about their children's futures, but less education and the lack of familiarity with academic expectations leave them seriously disadvantaged in helping their children with school. In *The Long Shadow*, a longitudinal study that followed a cohort of urban youth and their families from first grade to age twenty-eight, Karl Alexander and colleagues show how significantly families' socioeconomic status (SES) influenced their children's ability to make use of school. "Higher-SES parents are good role models and effective advocates of their children's interests. They seek out safe neighborhoods, good schools, and favorable program placements within those schools. No one of these acts is itself determinant, but together they help move higher-SES children along the path to success. By contrast, lower-SES children labor under the burden of cumulative disadvantage imposed by their location in the SES hierarchy. Their parents want them to succeed in school and after, but most lack the means to help them do so."[6]

American public schools' historic mandate has been to help bridge this gap, to use teaching, academic counseling, social modeling, and social integration to help immigrants assimilate and step onto the escalator of social mobility. The increasing diversity of incoming students makes this task ever more complex. Schools are seeing more students with more diverse backgrounds struggling with all the challenges that bedevil new immigrants. The task is a challenge even for the most robust and well-funded schools.

Robust and well-funded schools are not the ones most immigrant students attend. Because public schools are largely funded by each school district's property tax base, students' educational opportunities are determined by their zip codes. Immigrant students in the poorest neighborhoods need the most skilled teachers, the lowest student-teacher ratios, and the richest array of supports. And yet their schools generally receive the least of these essential resources, a historic trend that the country's recent long recession has only exacerbated.

The size of school counselors' caseloads is a troubling case in point. In middle school and high school, much of counselors' work involves helping students learn, individually and in group sessions, about educational and career possibilities; choose the courses they need; and evaluate colleges and other post-high-school opportunities. They model how to navigate the system, stay on top of deadlines, investigate opportunities, and deal with unresponsive bureaucracies. More intangibly, their engagement with and expectations for students provide young people with the confidence that they can succeed and that their dreams can be achieved. Strong counseling can provide a crucial piece of scaffolding, especially for students whose parents are unable to do so.

Students are most likely to feel their counselors are helpful when they have a personal relationship with and easy access to them. The American School Counseling Association's recommended caseload for middle and high school counselors is 250 students. The national average school-counseling caseload is 477. In California, the average caseload now exceeds 940, the highest in the country. A counselor with 940 assigned students cannot be available to them in a timely way and may not even know students by name or face. The kind of interactions that students need with their counselors simply do not happen. A few students in these schools will find their way to programs like Reality Changers, which can provide what they need: informational and supportive services, high standards and expectations, and long-term nurturing relationships with adults. The rest will find no help, and much of their potential will be wasted, at grievous cost to themselves and their country.

The underfunding and underresourcing of urban schools is one of the most troublesome issues facing the nation. Its consequences are profound and far reaching: how well or poorly we educate our newest Americans, and how we support or fail to support their launching into productive adulthood, will mark our economy and our society for years to come. Rubén Rumbaut, a leading scholar of immigration, notes that almost 30 percent of the 68 million young adults age eighteen to thirty-four in the United States today are either foreign born or of foreign parentage. He adds, "A key to the future of California and to that of a nation being transformed by immigration will be how the rapidly expanding generation of young adults of immigrant origin is incorporated into its economy, polity, and society."[7] The task starts in public schools: the country, and especially its urban school districts, must find the resources and the methods to meet this challenge.

Some of the most promising solutions are coming from innovative non-profits like Reality Changers, and education leaders are taking note. Former U.S. secretary of education Arne Duncan has visited Reality Changers twice, and he's called it "absolutely a model, not for the city, not for the state, but for the country." Yanov is already engaged in scaling up the model, expanding the core Reality Changer's program (now called College Town) to serve a larger number of students. In addition, he and his staff have developed a college-readiness program for students in their junior and senior years, called College Apps Academy. This program, derived from Reality Changers' long experience in helping seniors choose colleges, write their applications, and search for scholarships, provides support for any student who needs it during this crucial year.

Yanov is also expanding the reach of his organization through an ambitious partnership with San Diego Unified School District. Under their agreement, the district, the largest in California after Los Angeles Unified, will provide Reality Changers with a building in City Heights, San Diego's largest immigrant community. Reality Changers will use this facility to offer College Town, the core four-to-five-year program, to one thousand students from schools all over the county. Both Yanov and San Diego's superintendent of schools, Cindy Marten, acknowledge that even this scaled-up program will reach only a small fraction of San Diego Unified's students who need such services. But both see the project as an important incremental step toward addressing the inequality that pervades American education. It will create a large enough cohort of students that their outcomes can be studied within the district, around the state, and very likely across the country. Its results will show what can be done, challenging the district and other school systems to rethink what is possible and work toward even better solutions.

In his typical visionary fashion, Yanov describes the impact he hopes to create with College Town: first an influx of one thousand enthusiastic, high-achieving students—many from immigrant families, many of them poor—into the city's largest immigrant neighborhood. And these students, inspired by Reality Changers' high standards and ambitious vision, will then flow from City Heights back to their own schools and communities bearing new hope for their futures and extending those powerful currents to their own families and neighborhoods. Yanov's vision is nothing short of a wholesale change in culture and expectations. He envisions students and parents across San Diego expecting more from themselves and from their schools. Ultimately, he hopes, disadvantaged students graduating from high school and going on to college will no longer be an unusual event but will become the new norm—in City Heights, in Golden Hill, and in every underserved neighborhood of the city.

Helping the newest Americans launch into productive adulthood is at once a national imperative and, for every student working to launch, an urgent personal task. The stories of Reality Changers' students show that our least-advantaged youth can succeed when we both ask more of them and provide the essential scaffolding to help them meet these expectations. Reality Changers has shown that it can help individual students succeed. Its partnership with San Diego Unified can show the way for urban schools to help all their students.

1 Across the Water

A teacher affects eternity. He can never tell where his influence stops.

Henry Adams

Fifty students churned around the ferry landing on San Diego Bay, laughing, scuffling, fist-bumping, hailing friends they hadn't seen for days. They chattered in English and Spanish, sometimes shifting in midsentence, the girls' voices rising and falling, the guys' rumbling an octave lower.

"Hermanita, ven. I've got something to tell you."

"Ooh, you're here. No sabía si vendrías."

"Dude. Que pasa?"

The girls wore tight miniskirts or cropped pants and, over them, royal blue scoop-neck T-shirts with the silhouette of a young woman in a mortarboard and gown against a city skyline and, underneath, the words *Reality Changers*. Their hair was piled in curving mounds on top of their heads or tumbled over their shoulders. They wore elaborate eye makeup and their earrings danced as they hugged and giggled; earbuds dangled from their necks, and cell phones were everywhere. The boys wore baseball caps with high crowns and broad, flat bills and baggy cargo shorts that ballooned past their knees. Their dark hair was gelled into baroque waves or shaved to an eighth inch of dense bristle. They, too, wore the Reality Changers T-shirts, with a boy in gown and mortarboard.

The following Monday was Labor Day, and school would start the day after that. Reality Changers' last outing of the summer always started with a ride on the ferry across San Diego Bay to Coronado Island.

Chris Yanov stepped out of his pickup. In cargo shorts and a Reality Changers sweatshirt, he looked like an older version of the students. The difference was the weight of responsibility settled permanently on his shoulders. Kids began swarming around Yanov, hugging, jostling, their hunger to connect with him palpable.

"Hey, Chris, where you been?"

"Chris, I got something I gotta talk with you."

"We gonna go now, Chris? We been waiting for you."

"What's happening man, how you doing?"

He bumped fists and watched as Grace and Jenn and Jonny, his young staff, handed out ferry tickets and herded students up the gangplank. They had it all covered. He didn't need to do a thing. After the years when he'd had to cover every base and solve every problem himself, it was a relief to show up and just watch things happen. A relief that left him at a loss: if he wasn't running the show, he didn't know what to do with himself. From the top of the gangplank, Jenn shot him a grin and a thumbs-up. He smiled a weak half smile and shrugged.

He pointed to two guys, signaling them to come with him to the upper deck. They followed him like puppies.

The huge marine diesels groaned; the ferry eased away from its mooring and turned 120 degrees toward Coronado. Out on the bay, the air was cooler. Sailboats glided across the ferry's path, and a V of brown pelicans cruised alongside, their wings just inches above the water.

The long arc of the Coronado Bridge lay off the boat's port side. The bus that brought the students to the landing could have driven across the bridge and delivered them to Coronado in half the time it took the ferry to cross. Yanov made this annual outing on the ferry for the pleasure of being out on the water on a summer night, and because for some students the Coronado trip would be the first time they'd ever been on a boat. Yanov understood the power of symbols to make a strong impression on his students, most of whom, when they joined Reality Changers, couldn't have told him what a symbol was.

Coronado Island is the northern end of a peninsula where the navy maintains an amphibious base, an air station, and home port for several aircraft carriers. The ferry docks at a town of prosperous homes and immaculate, tree-lined streets that evoke a Hollywood vision of 1950s America. Admirals come to Coronado to retire, and tourists come to enjoy its small-town feel and its downtown of upscale boutiques and restaurants and antique dealers. Closer to the ferry landing, souvenir shops, burger stands, rib joints, and a park with formal plantings and a fountain greet the tourists.

Yanov gathered the students on the Coronado dock. "Okay, listen up. You've got an hour to get something to eat and look around. Take a look over there. That's the park. Be in the park by seven o'clock."

Students headed off in search of fast food. After they ate they walked around the park's fountains and manicured flower beds, and as the sun sank they gathered and sat on a grassy berm near the water. From here they could look across the bay to San Diego's downtown skyline, where the city's lights twinkled like promises.

Yanov stood on a bench facing them and handed out awards for achievements from their week at Forest Home, a camp in the San Bernardino Mountains. The week's theme was "Be a Hero," and the camp awards were plastic discs on gauzy black ribbon, a star on one side, the word *Hero* on the other, ten for a dollar at the ninety-nine-cent store across the street from Reality Changers' offices. He presented awards for the best speech, fastest mud racer, likeliest to die of laughing, friendliest, most helpful, cleanest bunk, most gel in hair. He named every student, recognized something special about each one. The kids laughed and teased each other, memories of their week burnished by their medals.

The sky deepened to purple, and a fingernail of a moon drifted in and out of clouds. Yanov handed out the last medal and stood silent. Giggling and talk trailed away. The kids leaned toward him. His voice was low and strong.

"We've come across the water tonight to mark the end of our summer. We cross over the water to symbolize the separation between our summer and the year ahead. Tonight on Coronado we're still in summer, remembering the fun we've had, the friendships we've made. This summer we've kicked back and enjoyed ourselves.

"When we cross back over the water, we'll hold on to our memories and our friendships, but some parts of summer we'll leave behind, like sleeping in and taking it easy. When we step back onto the dock, we step into the school year. We'll get serious.

"Every one of you has important work to do this year. How you do your work will make a difference for the rest of your life. What you do this year will permanently shape who you become and what you achieve.

"You all know this year's theme: 'What's Your Message?'

"For you freshmen: This is where it starts. This year you begin to make your mark. You build your foundation in academics and in your character. At school. In your family. In your neighborhood. This year you'll get clear what your message is, and how you'll use your message to take a stand, live your commitment to yourself, and become a model for others.

"Sophomores: This year everything counts. College admissions officers will look at your sophomore grades. You're building the message about yourself that your peers, the people in your school, and those admissions officers will see. Think about the message you want to send. Think how you'll live that message.

"Juniors: You're starting the most important year of your life. The workload kicks up, and you'll have to step up to meet it. The quality of your work, the grades you make, and the way you serve your community, including your peers, will make the difference in how you're seen at school, how colleges see you. Know your message. Live it every day.

"Seniors: It all comes together this year. All that you've done, the message you've crafted, and the legacy you've built. In just six months, 180 days from now, you'll know where you'll be spending the next four years of your life. You have serious work to do this fall. Make your message clear. Make it count.

"The question now, my heroes, is . . . what will you do? How will you meet the challenges you're facing? You'll answer that question every day this year, and how you answer will write the story of your life. We're here to support you in becoming the hero you can be and making this year the best in your life."

The kids sat lost in their own thoughts. One by one they stood up and walked toward the landing in the dark, thoughtful and slow, as though they were coming out of church.

2 Senior Academy

I don't know how I'm going to do all that and do the stuff you're talking about, too.

Robert Silva

Daniel Merced's father pulled off the freeway onto University Avenue, the main street through City Heights. University Avenue ran through blocks of tiny, sagging bungalows with blistered paint and apartment buildings of crumbling stucco. In San Diego's punishingly expensive housing market, immigrants from Mexico and Somalia, from Thailand, Guatemala, Ethiopia, and fifty-six other countries came to City Heights for housing they could afford. The California Correctional Authority also knew about City Heights; it placed so many parolees here that the neighborhood was known as the parole capital of Southern California. Anything you'd want to smoke or snort or shoot was for sale on University Avenue. The murder rate was the highest in the city.

City Heights was familiar territory to Reality Changers' students. Many of them lived here. For the others, it looked like their own neighborhoods—the small houses and crowded apartments, guys hanging out on the corners, friends whose lives were going nowhere. Trouble could happen in daylight, in plain view, right on University. Sergio, a junior with a broad chest and powerful arms, who looked like he could handle anything, talked about walking eleven blocks on University from wrestling practice to Reality Changers. He said, "My head's on a swivel. I have a different

23

feeling for every block, and I watch my back the whole time. When I finally get here, I feel like I can breathe."

Daniel's father drove past 43 Produce, where Mexican papayas the size of footballs were stacked out front, and past the grocery that sold halal meats. In front of Café Doré, old men sat in white plastic chairs and studied their mah-jongg tiles. Café Doré sold banh mi, Vietnamese sandwiches of chicken or any of six different cuts of pork on a baguette, with pickled carrots and cilantro and daikon; and at the GiroMex counter, you could send your money order to Mexico or Honduras. At the bar next door a soccer game was always playing on the TV in the dark interior. Somali women in headscarves and caftans that covered them to their shoes and men in dashikis and in guayabera shirts shared the sidewalk with kids in gangsta clothes and earbuds.

They passed the Mid-City Church of the Nazarene, a big white stucco building with a red tile roof. The church distributed food on Tuesday afternoons, and Daniel saw two hundred or more people—Asian, Hispanic, African, Anglo, African American—waiting in a line that stretched past the church's facade and more than a block down University. Hunger came in every color and nationality.

His father turned onto Thirty-Ninth Street and turned again, into the drop-off area behind the Workforce Partnership Building, where Reality Changers had moved this summer. Across the street, kids younger than Daniel lounged outside the Kwik Corner Liquor Store, smoking and passing a bottle in a paper bag. The lights in the roof's overhang were yellow fluorescents that gave brown skin a greenish cast and turned white skin gray. Smears of blackened gum were stuck forever on the sidewalk, and the grass between the sidewalk and the street was flattened and brown, littered with cigarette butts. Kill enough afternoons outside the Kwik Corner and you'd believe your life was as blighted as the grass.

Daniel threw a glance over his shoulder at the kids and hurried into the building. The Workforce Partnership Building was new, built to provide office space for nonprofits. It was four stories of no-frills design: neutral colors and hard surfaces, materials that could be cleaned easily. Its public areas were small and poorly lit. A security guard's desk dominated the small lobby; the rest of it was a waiting area in front of the two elevators.

Daniel was solidly built, with dark eyes and skin the color of caramel, and a smile that could light up a room. His wiry brown hair was still wet from swim practice, and he wore his favorite T-shirt, one that read: "Building a Championship Is an Everyday Thing." He'd been up since five that morning, and he figured, after RC finished that night, he'd still have a couple of hours of homework.

On the third floor, he pinned on his Reality Changers name tag and headed down the hall to the Senior Academy room, where the seniors met, separate from the underclassmen. It was a computer lab with gray commercial carpeting, rows of oyster-colored monitors and keyboards on faux wood-grain tables, and low-end office chairs. To the seniors, accustomed to sagging couches at the iglesia and working two to a computer, the new digs looked great. Everyone got their own computer with a broadband connection, more than many of them had at home. Chairs that rolled were cool. They arm wrestled and played bumper cars in their chairs and checked each other out on Facebook, but they weren't feeling cool. Senior year was when Chris promised that their hard work would pay off and the doors of college would swing open. Now they were starting their senior year and they didn't have any idea how they'd get to college. They felt as young and clueless as their first day at Reality Changers.

Debbi Leto, who ran the Senior Academy, greeted every student by name and welcomed them all. She was a pretty blonde woman in her fifties with the confident air of a sports mom. She'd volunteered at Reality Changers for five years, and she'd known most of the seniors since they were eighth graders. She had a master's in Asian history from Berkeley, and she'd launched her own two daughters to college. She was warm and caring and bossy. She'd ask hard questions and badger the seniors as much as necessary to get them to do what they needed to do.

"It's how we do it as much as what we do," she said. "Kids see that we're paying attention, watching to see that they're doing what they need to do. And that they're getting the help they need."

Preparing for and running Tuesday night's Senior Academy; following up during the week with seniors' questions about their applications; taking phone calls, especially from the girls, who saw her as a second mother; riding herd on guidance counselors and admissions departments who lost documents or otherwise dropped the ball; and consulting with Jenn

Schadler, who ran the Thursday night Senior Academy—Debbi figured that she gave Reality Changers about thirty hours a week.

"My parents didn't go to college, and my brother and sister didn't go," she told the seniors on this night. "My parents didn't see the point. I'm the only one in my family. I drove down by myself from LA to go to UC San Diego. I know that I wouldn't be the person I am today if I hadn't gone to college."

She introduced the three other tutors: Alli, her daughter, a paralegal who'd tutored as long as her mother had, and Walt and Martha, retired teachers with decades of experience in college applications. All of them were volunteers. Tutors for the underclassmen were mostly college students, but Debbi insisted that the seniors needed the most experienced and skilled tutors. She and Alli and Walt and Martha knew every aspect of the application process, and they'd seen every pothole and washout and hairpin turn that could crop up on the road to college.

"We have a lot of work to do this year," she said. "We've given you your senior profile to complete." She reached into the rolling file box stuffed with folders for every student and held up the five-page green form.

"Remember this one? It's in your packet. You need to fill it out this week. This. Week. It'll help Chris and your teachers and anyone else you ask to write a recommendation for you. You'll also need to register for your SATs.

"Everyone should have opened a Gmail account. If you haven't, raise your hand and we'll help you do it tonight. You need to start learning your way around the Cal State and UC websites and get started on those applications. Some of you are applying to private colleges, and you'll need to work on the Common App. You've got essays to write. They'll take up most of the fall. Chris'll be in later to talk to you about the essays."

Daniel pressed his palm against his forehead. He was taking Advanced Placement classes in physiology and English lit. Two-a-day swim practices Monday through Friday. Already there weren't enough hours in the day.

He'd been eight years old and had spoken no English when he arrived in San Diego from Veracruz with his parents and his big sister. Their tourist visas expired years ago. Now his father bused dishes at Chevy's and his mother was the super for the building in North Park, where they lived. He rode the bus forty-five minutes to Scripps Ranch, an elite public high school where the parking lot was filled with BMWs and SUVs, and his classmates spent spring breaks in Europe. In his AP classes, his was often the only dark face. He swam varsity breaststroke and freestyle, and he'd won a gold medal at the national Junior Lifeguard competition. He wanted to study biochemistry and go to medical school.

His grades were good enough to get into Berkeley or UCLA, but he was undocumented, not eligible for a Pell Grant, the federal grant for low-income students, nor for a Cal Grant, California's financial aid for students at state universities. In several years' time, the California legislature would pass the DREAM Act (Development, Relief, and Education for Alien Minors), which would allow undocumented students who met criteria for in-state tuition to apply for Cal Grants; but this fall, undocumented students like Daniel couldn't get any state or federally funded financial aid.

He didn't have a Social Security number or a driver's license. He'd hardly traveled outside of San Diego County—too many border patrol checkpoints. He was pinning his hopes on private colleges that could offer him a full ride. If his essays were good enough, he'd be going to one of those places. If they weren't, this time next year he'd still be living in his old bedroom and riding the bus to San Diego City College.

Debbi reeled off the tasks in a matter-of-fact tone. "Once your applications are in, you'll need to file the FAFSA, the Free Application for Federal Student Aid, and start searching for scholarship money. If you're not eligible for federal aid, let us know so we can help you start looking for private funds. There are a lot of deadlines, and you'll need to be here every week to get things done in time."

The chairs had stopped moving. The seniors' faces were still.

Debbi looked at them, then said, "You guys are looking kind of swamped. Let's go around and everybody say what you're worried about the most. Jesse, you want to start?"

Jesse Sanchez's single mother cleaned houses to provide for him and his younger brother. She made seven thousand dollars a year. Before he joined Reality Changers, he'd figured that after high school he'd live at home and get a job to help out his mother, and also take some classes at San Diego State. Now he was aiming for an Ivy League school. He'd played football through his junior year and he loved the game, but he didn't go out this fall because he wanted to devote all the time necessary for working on his application. He was handsome, with dark, liquid eyes and black hair that he slicked straight back. He said, "What if I don't get in where I want to go?"

Heads nodded and there were murmurs of *Um-hmm.* Hearing other kids talk about the same fears that tormented them was somehow comforting for the seniors. Spoken out loud, their fears felt less awful, more manageable.

The comments kept coming.

"We've all got our regular schoolwork, and a lot of us are taking AP classes. I don't know how I'm going to do all that and do the stuff you're talking about, too."

"I don't want to disappoint my parents. They work so hard and try to help me every way they can. I'm scared I'll let them down."

Karina Vasquez said, "I'm worried about essays." She clutched her notebook to her chest, and bent her head over it, her luxuriant black hair tumbling over her hands. She was small and slender, and when she talked to adults she looked at the floor, her voice so low it was hard to hear. She'd taken every AP course her charter school offered and had kept her A average. She wanted to study psychology. Like Daniel, she was undocumented. Her guidance counselor gave her a list of private colleges she should apply to. The only one she'd heard of was Stanford. Private colleges made you go for interviews. Just thinking about interviews made her stomach churn; she wouldn't know what to say. Good essays could help her, but what could she write about her life that someone at a fancy private college would want to read?

She had been two years old when her parents left Durango, in Mexico's central plateau, and rode the bus to Tijuana, where they walked across the border into San Diego County. They planned to work and save their money until Karina was ready to start school. Then they'd move back to Durango and buy a house. Fifteen years later, the family lived in a one-bedroom apartment in Chula Vista, between San Diego and the international border, where her parents slept in the living room and Karina shared a bedroom with her two younger brothers, born here. Her father worked in construction. Her mother took care of other people's kids all day.

Another student spoke: "I'm worried about next year, about living away from home. Last summer at Academic Connections was the longest I'd been away from my family, and I was really homesick."

And another: "The year's just started, and already I have so much to do."

"You're right; you do have a lot to do this year," Debbi said. "Remember that you'll have help at every step. Walt and Martha and Alli and I are your support team. We'll be here every week, all year, to show you what you need to do and help you do it."

She knew how to build the scaffolding they needed.

"We're in it together here, like family. When you have a success, you'll have this whole roomful of family cheering for you. We also share things about ourselves and sometimes about our families. It stays here.

"I'll say it again. What we say here stays here."

Yanov had walked into the back of the room while she was talking. He lounged against the door frame, listening.

Now she nodded to him and said, "Chris is here."

Twelve heads turned.

Yanov's job tonight was to make the seniors understand that they must write the best application essays they were capable of. He looked at them for a long moment, then spoke in an urgent baritone. "Your college essays are the most important documents you'll ever write. The essays you write this fall will change your life. Your essays will determine where you'll be this time next year.

"Writing an essay is like peeling an artichoke. You strip away the outer layers, work your way down to find your heart. You'll find more than you knew was there.

"It's like peeling an onion, too: there's gonna be tears."

He pulled a red ballpoint from his pocket and slashed the air. "You'll bring me your essay, and it'll come back to you red and bloody. Marks all over the page. You'll rewrite more than you ever knew you could. I'm gonna push you harder than anybody's ever pushed you.

"You all know Miguel Cerón. He's at Harvard now. When he brought me his essay the first time, I gave it back to him with just about the whole thing crossed out. He couldn't believe it.

"Believe it. It'll happen to you."

This was how Yanov talked: their task was demanding and dangerous, a mortal struggle requiring high courage and fierce commitment.

Robert Silva watched the clock and wished Chris would finish. The aroma of posole, pork stew with green chilies and hominy, drifting from the kitchen made it hard to pay attention. At his grandmother's there was never anything for breakfast; he drank water in the morning to fill his stomach. Lunch today was a ninety-nine-cent bag of Doritos. Dinner most nights was baloney and tortillas, sometimes just rice and tortillas. He'd lost ten pounds since his father threw him out in June. He figured he didn't have a shot at the UCs. His junior year grade point average was 3.9, and he'd probably do as well this year; but for his first two years it was south of 2.0. Any Cal State campus he could get into would work just fine. Somewhere out of town, he hoped.

He had other things on his mind besides applications. His mother had started chemo again, and he hadn't seen her, or Angel, his baby brother, for two weeks. He was walking the Susan G. Komen Three-Day, and he needed to collect pledges.

"When we get down to the deadline those last couple of weeks, we'll be working late," Yanov warned. "Friday nights. Saturdays all day. Saturday nights. One Saturday night last year we didn't quit 'til three in the morning. From now to New Year's, forget about weekends. You've got essays to write."

Kimberly Palafox thought about essays and wished her parents could help her. Neither had finished high school in Mexico, and their firstborn's dream of going to college looked to them like a waste of time and money. When she talked about college, her mother's eyes went dull and she didn't say anything. Her father hardly spoke to her these days. She used to be his favorite, but he was drinking more and he didn't want anything to do with her. Her main ally was her sister Theresa, a year younger, also in Reality Changers. Kimmie was stocky, with thick, dark hair that fell to her shoulders. Behind her glasses her eyes sparkled. Her parents knew she was applying to college, but only Theresa knew how much she wanted to go to college in New York City.

This class was starting its senior year as the country plunged into the longest and deepest recession in eighty years. A month after tonight's meeting, Lehman Brothers, a 158-year-old investment bank and pillar of Wall Street, would close its doors and declare bankruptcy, taking down with it large chunks of college endowments. Through the fall and winter the financial news would only get worse. By spring, as the seniors focused on how they would pay for college, they would be scrambling for a piece of a much smaller scholarship pool.

Tonight they didn't know any of that.

Tonight felt the way Reality Changers always did. Chris and the tutors told you what you needed to do, it was ten times harder than you'd expected, and twenty times more work, and you were scared you couldn't do it. In college prep and AP classes, you were in with kids who read way more books and took special courses at camps you didn't know existed, whose parents could buy them anything they wanted. In your 'hood, kids bragged about flunking a class and laughed at you when they were going out partying and you stayed home to do schoolwork. You got called faggot and worse, and sometimes got beat up, for doing well in school.

The seniors understood the choice: do what Chris and the tutors said, or end up like their older sisters and brothers or cousins.

College glimmered, less than a year away. Between them and college and the futures they wanted stood those essays. The prompts were enough to make them wonder what they were doing here:

Describe the world you come from—for example, your family, community, or school—and tell us how your world has shaped your dreams and aspirations.

Tell us about a personal quality, talent, accomplishment, contribution, or experience that is important to you. What about this quality or accomplishment makes you proud, and how does it relate to the person you are?

Writing's a daunting enterprise for most adolescents, even more so if you're writing in a language that's not your first. The seniors spoke English all day at school; it was the language of the world they wanted to enter. But it was the language of outside, not the language in which they flirted and swaggered and dreamed. English felt solid and thick on their tongues. How could they write in English about their lives and their deepest hopes?

They didn't know how they would write the powerful essays Yanov told them they must, or how the year would change them. All they knew tonight was that, for them, Reality Changers and the Senior Academy were the only game in town.

3 Looking for a Home

Once I was in it, nothing else really mattered.

Chris Yanov

On a Sunday morning in the fall of his freshman year at UC San Diego, Chris Yanov got up early, pulled on jeans and a sweatshirt, and slipped out of the dorm. He pointed his truck up the ramp to I-5, the interstate that runs like a spine the length of California, from its northern state line all the way to the international border with Mexico. He drove south, toward downtown San Diego. He was looking for a church that held services in Spanish. A highway sign read "El Centro"—literally, "the center," and the Spanish term for "downtown." He drove east for ten miles before he figured out that the sign wasn't directing him to San Diego's downtown, but to the small desert city of El Centro. He turned around and made his way back to campus.

The next Sunday and the next, he was back in his truck, learning his way around his adopted city, finding the neighborhoods where immigrants from Mexico and Central America lived, and visiting churches. He'd studied Spanish in high school, and now, in San Diego, half an hour's drive from Mexico, he wanted to become more fluent. Later, he understood that he was looking for more than a place to improve his Spanish. He grew up in Camarillo, a comfortable town an hour up the coast from Los Angeles, where his parents both taught high school and it was a given that he'd go to college. In Camarillo, he said, he felt no sense of place, no practices or traditions that defined him. The culture he saw while growing up with his Mexican friends, and in the Mexican village where his church youth group built houses, was much more appealing: celebrations were more colorful, the food was more interesting, and there was a deeper, warmer commitment to family. A Spanish-speaking congregation could be his entrée to this culture.

At the Iglesia Presbiteriana Hispaña in Golden Hill, a world away from UCSD's leafy North County campus, he found what he was looking for. Golden Hill is a mesa that rises from the east end of San Diego's downtown. From the mesa you can look west to the harbor and south to the hills of Mexico. In the 1880s, wealthy San Diegans built homes there for the views and the ocean breezes that cooled the mesa. When Yanov found Golden Hill in 1996, it was two neighborhoods, divided at Twenty-Fifth Street. West of Twenty-Fifth, closer to downtown, the restored Victorian mansions and Craftsman bungalows with well-kept yards were home to young professionals and prosperous retired couples who parked their Volvos and SUVs on the broad avenues.

East of Twenty-Fifth, houses of the same era stood in disrepair, porches sagging and paint peeling, divided into single-room apartments and rented to laborers and the occasional artist. Others had been torn down and replaced with apartment buildings, where families lately arrived from Mexico lived, sometimes twelve or fifteen people crowded into a cousin's or an uncle's place. Old Toyotas with oxidized finishes and pickups with crumpled fenders, their plates from Baja and Michoacán, lined the streets. Two blocks of Twenty-Fifth Street served as the commercial district: a liquor store, a fruit stand, two small groceries that carried products from Mexico, a taco shop, and a by-the-slice pizzeria. On side streets, a nail salon, a ninety-nine-cent store, a barbershop, and a video store. A union hall had been part of the neighborhood for decades, along with a nursing home and a heating and air-conditioning business. Drugs changed hands on the street, and the Lomas26 gang claimed Golden Hill as its turf.

At the corner of Twenty-Seventh and B Streets stood the Iglesia Presbiteriana Hispaña, a mission of the San Diego Presbytery with fewer than twenty-five families and a struggling youth group. Services were in Spanish and people welcomed him. One of his first Sundays there, in the middle of the service, a woman walked into the sanctuary, her head barely visible above the enormous arrangement of lilies and gladioli she carried. She stomped up the center aisle, knelt, set the fountain of blooms on the altar, then stood and faced the congregation. "Hoy es el aniversario de la muerte de mi hijo Pablo." Today is the anniversary of my son Pablo's death.

Pablo had been shot in a gang fight. In high school Yanov knew guys who joined gangs, and he didn't get it. He saw their loyalties narrow, their ambitions wither. They ditched school, quit as soon as they could. The waste of their promise sickened him. Here at the iglesia, there were kids, girls as well as boys, doing the same. Maybe there was work for him to do here.

He came to services every Sunday, and Tuesday nights he came to the Cena Obrera, the workers' dinner. He told Tom Simpson, the iglesia's pastor, that he wanted to help kids stay out of gangs. Simpson welcomed him with some reserve. He'd seen young Anglos with good intentions come to places like this and burn out. He suggested that Yanov work with Jóvenes, the iglesia's youth group. Yanov jumped at the offer. Emily Content, who also volunteered with Jóvenes, remembers that Yanov "was amazing at making things happen. He did the weekly meeting, and then he'd organize outings, like softball games and barbecues. Everyone was welcome. Kids started bringing their friends. He didn't have any special skills or training, but he put in incredible amounts of time and energy."

Guys from gangs in Golden Hill City Heights started showing up at Jóvenes. By the following summer, attendance at Jóvenes was about half church kids and half gang kids. Yanov liked the mix; he believed it helped all the kids to get to know each other. Some church members were a lot less enthusiastic; they didn't want their church known as a place where gang kids were welcome. They brought their concerns to Pastor Simpson. He heard them out, and backed Yanov, saying that what the young man was doing could be a good thing and might bring more families to the church.

After his freshman year, Yanov stayed in San Diego for the summer quarter and spent even more time at the iglesia. He started hanging around at the taco shop and the basketball courts in the park with the cholos, the sixteen- and seventeen-year-olds with baggy pants and shaved heads. Sometimes they were glad to see him; sometimes they ignored him or shoved him around. Once when several of them were messing with him, he put up his hand to protect himself and got stabbed in the palm. Still he invited them to Jóvenes, and they came. He talked to them about staying in school and about the risks and downsides of gang life.

Yanov was doing what adolescents do as they launch: looking for a home, for his place in the world. Most college freshmen look for their home through friendships and campus organizations and campus social life; but compared to the intensity of the world Yanov found in Golden Hill, college life seemed like pretty weak tea. He worked hard at his courses, he was friendly with the people in his dorm, and he joined pickup soccer games, but what happened on campus just didn't interest him. He didn't join any clubs or groups, and he didn't care about campus politics. He didn't drink, he was uncomfortable at parties, and he didn't date much.

He was on a different mission. By his own description he was a skinny white college boy from the suburbs who couldn't even take a punch in the arm without wincing. He needed to prove to the guys at the taco shop that he was as tough as they were. If he wasn't, he could forget their ever listening to him. He also needed to prove it to himself. He dressed like the cholos in baggy jeans and oversize white T-shirts, and he shaved his head the way they did, down to a quarter inch of bristle. When he walked around Golden Hill, he imitated the way they scanned the street for trouble, eyes darting, looking for police or rivals wanting a fight. He learned not to hang out in front of houses or apartments at night: too easy a target for anyone driving by. He drove with them in his truck and got stopped by cops. He went to the hospital with them when someone got beaten up. He didn't drink or use or drugs or deal, didn't shoplift or beat anyone up. Hanging with the cholos was the hardest thing he'd ever done. With them, things really were a matter of life and death. It was the scariest, most exciting time of his life. The "action-packed days," he called the time. "Every time the phone rang, it was something. Once I was in it [with the cholos], nothing else really mattered."

Sociologist Victor Rios followed a cohort of forty Latino and African American adolescent boys in Oakland, California, who had been arrested, served time, or were on probation. In *Punished: Policing the Lives of Black and Latino Boys,* he eloquently documents the ways in which police, probation, schools, and community centers form a seamless network that he

calls the youth control complex, which promoted the hypercriminaliza-
tion and punishment of these young men. For years they have been "har-
assed, profiled, watched, and disciplined . . ., before they had committed
any crimes. Eventually that kind of attention led many of them to fulfill
the destiny expected of them."[1] The cholos Yanov hung with had traveled
this path since they were in middle school.

They liked having Yanov around, but nothing he said or did offered
them an alternative to the way they lived. Nothing moved them to change.
They stayed in gangs and still quit school as soon as they could. The guys
still got into fights with rival gangs and fought with sticks and knives, still
got busted for burglaries and small-time dealing. Six of the twelve girls got
pregnant in a year's time and quit school. Yanov could talk about staying
in school and be their event planner if he wanted, but he hadn't made
them an offer that would convince them to change.

He moved out of the dorms and rented an apartment in Golden Hill, a
few blocks from the iglesia. He liked living in two worlds that were so different; each provided a retreat from the other. He declared a double major
in political science and Spanish literature, but he built his life in Golden
Hill. "I got my education at UCSD," he said, "but the streets were where
I learned about life."

The adults around Yanov were less enthusiastic. The provost of his college looked at his new address and invited him in for a talk. She told him
she was concerned for his safety and urged him to move back on campus,
or at least to a safer part of town. He thanked her and said he felt fine
where he was. His parents worried that he spent so much time down in
Golden Hill and so little on campus. On the phone his father said, "We're
worried that you're not getting a real college experience."

Yanov countered, "I'm not getting *your* college experience, but I'm very
happy with my college experience."

He loaded up his schedule, went to school year-round, and graduated
with honors in less than three years. Next, he started at California Western
School of Law in San Diego. He'd seen so many of the cholos get arrested,
sometimes just because they were in the wrong place at the wrong time.
They couldn't make bail, couldn't pay for a good lawyer, and ended up
with long prison sentences that robbed them of their families and drained

away their youth. If he were a lawyer he could make a difference. See that they got a fair shot at justice. He bought two suits so he could look like a lawyer. He rode the bus across town to Cal Western, where his classmates were aiming for corporate suites and Wall Street. The bus ride was a passage between his two worlds, the people on the bus his daily reminders of why he was going to law school.

He read Malcolm Klein's *American Street Gang*. The University of Southern California sociologist had studied gangs and gang prevention programs for thirty years, and in *The American Street Gang* he upended much of the field's received wisdom. Klein reported that most gang-prevention efforts, whether by police or by social agencies, were in fact paradoxical: they actually strengthened gang culture. He described dedicated interveners who worked solo, building relationships with gang members. In every instance he studied, Klein found that the intervener became the gang's focal point, and his meetings with them actually promoted the gang's cohesiveness. Group activities intended to offer an alternative to gang culture in fact built attachments within the gang. Yanov groaned. Klein's description of gang workers' efforts sounded like what he'd been doing. Klein was telling him that the work he'd poured his heart into for three years was at best naive and, at worst, seriously counterproductive.

Another deeply unpleasant surprise exploded on him that year. He'd expected that law school wouldn't be any harder than UCSD. He hadn't reckoned on the tsunami of reading that crashes over first-year law students. Five hundred pages or more most weeks, no papers, the course grade determined only and entirely by the final exam. At the end of the first semester he failed one course and his grade point average was sixty-eight. The dean invited him in for a talk. If he wanted to stay in school, he'd need to raise it to seventy-seven or better for the second semester.

Between January and May he nearly lived in the law library. In May the dean called him in for another talk. His second semester grade point average was seventy-four. Not good enough. He wouldn't get credit for the year. If he wanted to stay in school, he'd have to repeat all his first-year classes.

There was no way he'd slog through Contracts and Property again.

Law school was over.

Time out.

For nearly four years now, he'd worked to help the kids in Golden Hill step away from gangs. He even endured Contracts and Property to help them get a fair shake. The cholos didn't change, and according to Klein's research, all his work may have made things worse. And now he'd flunked out.

He'd never failed at anything. Now it looked like he'd failed at everything.

He needed some time to think.

He registered with the San Diego Unified School District as a substitute teacher. Subbing would be a no-brainer. He could support himself while he figured out what he was going to do with his life.

While he was shooting hoops with the cholos, he mentioned that he'd be subbing in the fall. A couple of little brothers on the sidelines heard him, and they said, "Hey, Chris, come to Kroc. That's where we go."

At Ray A. Kroc Middle School, named for the founder of McDonald's, the student body spoke twelve languages and gang wannabes controlled the school's courtyard. Barbara Samilson, the principal at Kroc, described the climate when she arrived as "nine hundred kids looking to see where the fight's going to be." Samilson had seen students run off a lot of substitutes. "Chris was an amazing young man," she remembered. "He could handle a classroom from the get-go. He had a good relationship with the kids. They trusted him."

Kroc students hadn't seen a sub like Yanov. Tough-looking dude, buzz cut, always wore a suit and tie. Spoke Spanish like a native. It sounded weird, Mexican slang coming out of his white-boy mouth. He took his lunch to the in-school detention room, where the gangbangers shuffled in, tough guys with shaved heads laughing, cursing, thumping each other on the arm. No backpacks, no binders, no homework. He talked to them about staying clean from drugs and gangs. He told them they could go to college. They stuck their feet out in the aisle, folded their arms across their chests, and narrowed their eyes to slits.

It was like talking to the cholos. Nothing he said changed the realities of their lives. Years later, watching *The Wire*, Yanov saw Duquan, an African American youth who's isolated in the projects, ask, "How do we get from here to the rest of the world?"

That how it was with the tough kids at Kroc. They knew that the rest of the world, including college, was out there, but they didn't know how to get to it. He wanted to help them get there. He'd wanted to help the cholos, and what he'd tried didn't work. He needed to figure out what would work. Make the kids at Kroc a better offer.

4 Inventing Reality Changers

How do we keep this kid who's walked through our doors from ending up in a coffin?

Chris Yanov

It was a good assignment. Mr. Carson, who taught math at Kroc, would be out for a week. Yanov would have the same classes, the same students, five days in a row. Mr. Carson's lesson plan for his substitute was to show the film *Stand and Deliver,* a piece of it each day, with some time for discussion at the end of the period. All week long Yanov watched Jaime Escalante challenge his students at Garfield High in East Los Angeles. Escalante told them they could learn calculus. He'd tutor them. Even more valuable than his tutoring was the gift of his confidence: he believed that they could do it. Yanov looked at the kids in Mr. Carson's classes and thought about what Malcolm Klein found in *The American Street Gang:* at twelve and thirteen, kids might posture tough, but they were still so much more reachable than they'd be three years later.

Yanov sat after school in the teachers' lounge among the welter of dirty coffee cups and dog-eared file folders. He thought about how he could make his students a better offer, one they'd want to take up. Preaching about the downsides of gangs wasn't going to cut it. He had to have something positive to offer them.

A real chance to change the realities of their lives.

A bridge to the rest of the world.

His confidence that they could do it.

He picked up a napkin left from somebody's takeout and wrote: "Reality Changers." He liked the sound of it. Agentes de Cambio. Even better in Spanish. He folded the napkin and tucked it in his briefcase.

The plan he laid out to Pastor Simpson was simple and wildly ambitious. Start with four eighth graders. Make it invitation only; he'd pick the students he wanted. He wasn't looking for the smartest kids or the highest achievers. Those kids were already on their way; helping them do better wouldn't prove anything. The kids he wanted were the ones on the fence, already in the youth control complex's sights, close to joining a gang or already in one. He was looking for big personalities, kids who could be leaders. If they were the oldest kids in their families, so much the better. Their parents expected them be leaders for their younger siblings; they could set an example and lead those siblings straight to Reality Changers.

He'd look for kids with staying power. They'd need it. They'd have to come to Reality Changers every week, year-round, and work on English vocabulary, writing, and public speaking. Being able to speak well in front of groups could be a game changer, just as calculus was for Escalante's students: teachers and other decision makers would notice them. Confident, well-spoken kids would be harder to underestimate or write off.

As Yanov was inventing Reality Changers in the Kroc teachers' lounge, Angela Duckworth, then a graduate student in psychology at the University of Pennsylvania, was thinking about traits that could predict success for kids in school. Her research over the next decade would establish the central importance of what she calls grit, which she defines as "perseverance and passion for long term goals."[1] Yanov talked about determination and staying power. The street-level visionary and the MacArthur Foundation fellow both got it: students' capacity to lock onto a goal and stay with it through setbacks and over the long haul was critical to their success.

The program should feel like family, Yanov decided. Kids would eat dinner together, with parents providing the meal. There'd be a monthly meeting with parents, which he'd do in Spanish, and he'd tell them what was happening in the program, what it was trying to help their sons and daughters accomplish. He'd answer their questions. Tell them about college and what their kids needed to do to get there.

He'd recruit college students as tutors; they were close enough in age that students could see their own futures in them. He'd bring in speakers, community leaders, especially Latinos and Latinas who'd made it to the rest of the world. He'd make community service a requirement so students would have the experience of being givers and helpers, not just recipients. They'd have to commit to having no involvement in gangs. Instead of joining a gang, they'd belong to a group where everyone was aiming for college and people supported each other. No drugs or alcohol allowed. Staying away from them decreased the likelihood that kids would do dumb stuff and get arrested. No sex. The year that six girls in Jóvenes got pregnant and quit school still haunted him. He had no illusions that every Reality Changers student would graduate a teetotaler and a virgin, but he'd set the bar high. Make them think.

Stick with his program all the way through high school and he guaranteed you'd get into college. Get into college, and he guaranteed you'd have a scholarship to pay for it.

When he started Reality Changers, his not knowing the research on poverty and school achievement probably worked to Yanov's advantage. Several decades of research document the fact that poor children enter kindergarten well behind their affluent peers in mathematical skills, language skills, and interpersonal skills. Greg Duncan and Katherine Magnuson write, "Children from different social groups enter school with very different skills and behaviors. Comparing children in the bottom and top quintiles of socioeconomic status (SES), we show that low-SES children are 1.3 standard deviations lower than high-SES children in their kindergarten-entry math skills, nearly two-thirds of a standard deviation below in teacher ratings of attention skills, and one-fourth of a standard deviation worse in terms of teacher-reported antisocial behavior. None of these gaps shrinks over the course of elementary school, and in the case of antisocial behavior, the SES-based gap nearly doubles."[2] The eighth graders Yanov recruited were from families in the bottom quintile. He didn't know how hard narrowing those gaps would be.

For eighth and ninth graders, college was light years away. If they signed on to his program, then no matter how much grit they had, they needed short-term goals to aim for. UC San Diego had just launched Academic Connections, a three-week summer program for high-achieving high school students. Students lived on campus, took a college-level course, and earned one unit of college credit. Most of the kids at Kroc had never set foot on a college campus. Three weeks of living in the dorms, taking a course, and having the run of the campus would open their eyes. Academic Connections charged twenty-five hundred dollars per student. Yanov had no idea where he'd get the money to pay for it. He didn't know how he'd fund college scholarships either, but he had four years to figure that one out.

Pastor Simpson gave him the use of a room in the iglesia and told him he should try to bring in as many kids from the congregation as he could.

Yanov started Reality Changers to help his students at Kroc, but in the winter of 2001 he needed Reality Changers as much as they did. His picture of himself was that of a young man with big ideas and a bright future, a guy who aimed high and made big things happen. Four years of work with the cholos and nothing to show for it had put a big dent in the picture. Flunking out of law school blew it up in his face. He'd failed a piece of his personal launch; now he needed to do something big to restore that picture of himself. Helping his Kroc students was a high-risk, high-reward proposition. If he could help kids like them get to college, he'd be doing something that really mattered. He'd really matter.

Throughout the winter and spring, he talked to more than twenty students. Jorge Narvaez, one of the first students he approached, remembered Yanov's invitation.

"You do drugs?"

"No."

"You drink?"

"No."

"You had sex?"

"Yeah."

"I'm starting a program for kids who want to go to college. You interested?"

Reality Changers started with four boys and four girls. The program's funding was a three-hundred-dollar donation for Jóvenes.

As he was starting Reality Changers, Yanov applied to the master's program at the University of San Diego's new Joan B. Kroc Institute of Peace Studies. It was an interdisciplinary degree focusing on conflict resolution, international affairs, and ethics. After the debacle of law school, he needed to do something intellectually demanding—prove to himself that he had the chops.

He also applied to compete on *Wheel of Fortune.* He'd watched game shows since he was a kid, and he loved it when he answered the questions before the contestants did. He admired the hosts for their upbeat personae, their ability to keep things moving and keep their audience excited. *Wheel of Fortune* was his favorite. If he could get on the show and win some money, he could be more selective about subbing assignments, as well as have some time to read and study. The same month he started Reality Changers, Yanov drove to the Del Mar Fairgrounds north of San Diego and joined several thousand other people at an open call for *Wheel of Fortune.* He'd shaved his head that morning and hadn't thought to wear a cap. Now he stood with the other hopefuls under a blistering sun for more than two hours. What a bust, he thought driving home; all he had to show for the day was a sunburned scalp.

In July he went to two funerals on the same day, one for a student he'd taught at Kroc, run over in an intersection by a driver who fled the scene, the other for a cholo who'd come to Jóvenes and who was shot in a gang fight. Both were fifteen.

The *Wheel of Fortune* producers called him back for a smaller group audition.

In August, one of the cholos buried a knife in Yanov's palm. The next day he took the first group of Reality Changers students for a week of camp in the San Bernardino Mountains.

In the fall he went back to subbing and to scouting students for Reality Changers. He talked with students and their parents about their becoming the first in their families to go to college. That was what the program was about. But his private vision of his purpose was simpler, raw as the life he'd lived with the cholos: "How do we keep this kid who's walked through our doors from ending up in a coffin?"

Planes crashed into the World Trade Center and the Pentagon. His classes in peace studies now felt more urgent. In October the producer from *Wheel of Fortune* called: could he come to Los Angeles for a final audition? Driving to Los Angeles, he told himself he was nuts to pass on a hundred dollars for a day of subbing just to chase this stupid dream. The producer called back that night and said, "You're on the show next Friday."

He drove to Los Angeles the night before and slept on the couch at his brother Keith's apartment near UCLA, where he was a student. His mother, who hadn't missed a day of teaching in ten years, took the day off so she and his father could come to the studio in Burbank to watch him. Keith would join them after his class. Filming started at ten in the morning. When Yanov made it to the bonus round, he turned to scan the studio audience. He didn't see his parents or Keith.

He won $23,200. Nearly twice what he'd earn in a year of subbing. After the show, Keith found him and told him he'd had a voice mail from their mother. All she'd said was that their dad was in the hospital in Camarillo.

That morning his father had suffered a massive stroke. Chris and Keith found their father in the ICU with tubes attached to him and wired to machines that beeped. He recognized them, but he couldn't move or speak.

Yanov took a leave of absence from subbing and moved home, into his old room. Each morning he drove to the hospital and stayed through the day and into the evening with his father. "It's something I learned at the iglesia," he said. "When someone you love is in the hospital, nothing's more important. You don't just visit; you go there and you stay."

The World Series started. The Diamondbacks, the Arizona expansion team that was just three years old, had made it to the series. They were playing the Yankees. Yanov and his father watched every game together. Yanov cheered and his father blinked his eyes, the only movement he could make. The D-Backs won the first two games. The Yankees rallied and swept the next three; it looked like the series was over. The D-Backs roared back and won game six, fifteen to two, tying the series at three and three. They won the seventh game, a game and a series for the ages.

His father died the next day. He was sixty-four. Yanov didn't know until then that his grandfather, his father's father, had also died of a stroke, also in his early sixties.

Five years earlier Yanov had come to San Diego, a college freshman searching for a home and a path for his life. Now he was a man, tempered by failure and loss. In the midst of his losses, he'd found the work he wanted to do. He felt the clock ticking on his life. "Before my dad died it was: 'Why not do Reality Changers?'" he said. "After he died, suddenly it was: 'I've got to do this. I don't know how much time I have.'"

5 Dangerous Enough

If you're dangerous enough, you can make your dreams
come true.

Perla Garcia

Perla Garcia stood five foot nine, her full figure spilling out of a white T-shirt and baggy black overalls. She wore hoop earrings, heavy eye makeup, and brown lip liner, and her curly black hair tumbled over her shoulders. At Kroc she made herself the leader of the tough girls. She liked to scare kids. She'd see a girl looking at her in the hall and she'd get up in her face: "Why you looking at me! I hear you talking! You want to fight?"

She got into a lot of fights. Spent a lot of time in the principal's office.

She hung out in the school courtyard with kids who were in Lomas26, the gang that ruled the streets in Golden Hill, where she lived. Lomas26 posted up on corners and beat other kids up just for walking by. They tagged and shoplifted and sold rock and probably a lot of worse stuff she didn't know about. She knew kids in another gang in Serra Mesa; they never spoke its name, and neither did she. She'd talked with those kids about joining. If she was part of their gang, nobody would mess with her.

Kids who were in gangs told her about getting jumped in. It was ugly. Some night, she wouldn't know when, the gang would come for her. Walk her to some dark place and jump her, every girl in the gang punching, pounding, and stomping her for the longest minute of her life. She'd cover her head and tuck herself into a ball and hold on until they were done.

Once she was jumped in, she'd be part of a true family that would have her back forever. There'd be no getting out. "You don't get out of the gang unless you're dead," she explained. "You can try to change your ways, but you're marked, and they pull you back in."

She needed family. She used to have her brother, Antonio. He was ten years older, and when she was two he carried her on his shoulders, rode her on the handlebars of his bike, and took her with him when he hung with his friends. When she was four and Antonio was fourteen, a guy from another gang shot him. He recovered, and then he had to do payback. He went after the guy and shot him, and the guy died. Her adored big brother disappeared, and her family didn't tell her what had happened. He was in Centinela State Prison, doing fifteen years. Centinela was in the Imperial Valley, an hour-and-a-half drive from San Diego, but for Perla it might as well have been on the moon. Her family visited him once a month but didn't tell her that they visited, never talked about him when she was around. When she was nine, he was transferred to Donovan Correctional Facility, a maximum security prison near the Mexican border. She visited him there with her family once, but no one would talk about what he'd done.

In grade school she was a good girl and a good student, a teacher's pet. By sixth grade she was angry all the time. Good girls got pushed around at school, and their own families lied to them. Being good wasn't getting her anyplace. At home things were hard. Perla's father injured his back at the shipyard and couldn't work. He drew disability, which wasn't much money compared what he used to make. Her mother worked at a laundry and earned less than eleven thousand a year. There wasn't always money for food; some days they didn't eat.

Her father started drinking in the morning. By afternoon he was lurching around the house, swinging his belt and yelling obscenities. Once he walked in when she was taking a shower, pulled back the curtain, and slapped her with his belt. She was scared and angry, and she punished him the only way she could: she stopped talking to him. For nine years she acted as though he didn't exist.

At Kroc she was in the lowest math and English classes. The new sub was a white dude in a suit and tie. He was tough and serious. His first day he made them write an essay about their lives. The next day he asked her to stay after class.

"Perla, I read your essay. It's very good. You should be in a better English class."

She couldn't say anything.

"What are your goals?" he asked her. "What's your dream for yourself?"

"I haven't got any." She couldn't tell Mr. Yanov that her goal was to get jumped into Lomas26.

"You need to think about it."

"I went home that day and cried and cried. This guy really cared. Maybe I did write good. Maybe I had a chance." The day before, she'd known where her life was going. Get jumped in: that would take care of a lot of things. Now this guy was asking her to think about her future, and she wasn't so sure.

The next day, she asked him, "Am I allowed to go to college?"

He arranged for her to transfer to a better English class. That was huge. In her new class, kids listened to the teacher and did their homework and didn't fight. It felt so much better, the way school was for her before Kroc. She started doing her homework. She quit going to the courtyard. The gang kids hassled her, said she thought she was better than they were and called her bad names. She hung tough.

When Yanov started Reality Changers, he invited her to join. Every Tuesday she walked over to the iglesia and worked with Miguel, her tutor, who went to UC San Diego. Every week Miguel called her the day before the meeting to be sure she was coming, and again a few days later to see how she was doing with her homework. His calls made her feel cared about. She wanted to do everything that he and Chris expected of her.

She was studying in the iglesia the night Jonny and his friends threw rocks at the windows. She knew Jonny. He was an okay guy; she hoped he'd get his grades up and join.

She and the other students wrote the Reality Changers' constitution. They wrote that members should treat everyone with respect. She watched how Chris and the tutors treated people at meetings, and she decided she'd do like that at Kroc. She started with her teachers. She thanked them when they helped her and said hello to them in the halls. They smiled at her and said hello back. Even teachers she'd never had a class with said hello and knew her name. She stopped messing with kids. No more trash talk, no more fights. It surprised her how much better she felt.

"I knew there was a white light inside of me," she said. "It was covered by my family, until I got to Reality Changers."

At home there was always a lot of yelling, her father the most, but also her older sisters and her mother. The yelling gave her headaches, and in high school she looked for ways to not go home after school. She played soccer and joined the biology club and worked in video production. Sophomore year she had a 3.5 grade point average, and that summer she got to go to Academic Connections. In the class Law, Politics, and the Supreme Court the students did mock trials, and she won all three of hers.

Things got worse at home. Her father was drinking more, and he said terrible things to her and her sisters. He fought with her mother and called her bad names. He threw the turkey on the floor at Thanksgiving, and one Christmas he hauled the tree outside and burned it. She wanted to do for her family what Chris and Reality Changers were doing for her: show them a better way. When she was sixteen, her father was at home one day drinking, and he ordered Abby, her sister, who was just thirteen, to bring him more beer. When she didn't, he pulled her out of her room and started choking her. Perla ran to pull him off Abby, and he grabbed her neck with both hands and tried to strangle her. She got loose, he left, and she called the police, who came and took a report.

That scared her mother and her sisters, and they blamed her for making trouble. It hurt her that they blamed her, but she wasn't sorry she did it, since after that her father had to go to anger management classes and Alcoholics Anonymous. He stopped drinking and he didn't yell as much as he used to, and the day she left for college he knelt in front of her. "I made your life a living hell," he said, "and you lived through it. I beg you to forgive me."

She spoke to him for the first time in nine years.

Her first week at UC Riverside, she sat in her dorm and thought, "I'm in college. Is this really me?"

Part of "really her" was a strong sense of fairness. Her roommates, best friends from high school, told Perla their rules: no friends visiting in the room, no playing music, lights out by nine. She gritted her teeth for six weeks and cooperated. Then one night, well after midnight, she marched into the room with three friends, cranked up her boom box to full volume, and started dancing and singing.

Perla flipped on the lights. Her roommates sat up in their beds, mouths open.

"Oh, hi! These are my friends. Want to dance with us?"

"Get them out of here right now and shut off that music!"

"I pay for this room too," she said, "and I'm gonna have a say in what the rules are."

The next day the three of them talked about new rules. Before the year was out they were friends. Remembering, Perla smiled. "I taught them something."

.   .   .   .   .

The seniors were sweating over their FAFSA applications the night Perla showed up at the Senior Academy. She was a junior at UC Riverside carrying nineteen credits, majoring in sociology and minoring in theater. That night she was radiant, amazed at what she'd accomplished. She felt more hopeful about herself than she ever had and grateful to be where she was.

"Sometimes I still can't believe that I've made it," she told the seniors. "I'm working really hard. I like when I have a deadline; it helps me focus. The harder my courses, the more reading and papers I've got, the better I feel."

She was working out, she'd lost weight, and she loved the way she looked. After she graduated she'd enlist; the army recruiter told her she could go to officer candidate school to develop her leadership skills. After the army she'd use her GI benefit to go to law school.

Her family seemed to be in a better place. Antonio was out of prison and living with their parents, even talking about going to community college. Her sister Abby was in Reality Changers now.

She said, "If I hadn't joined Reality Changers, right now I'd be thugging it out in a gang."

Later in the year she met Alex online. He was an engineer, ten years older, and he shared custody of his son and daughter. She liked that a lot: a guy who stepped up to be a good parent. They were just friends online, and then they met. Things got more serious, and she moved in with him. For a while, being with Alex was everything she wanted. She got up at four thirty to fix his breakfast and had dinner ready when he came home. She cleaned his apartment and picked up his kids after school. She joked that she was playing house, but she was doing much more than that. Taking care of Alex and his kids was a way to make a good family for herself, the kind of family she'd never had. It made her feel taken care of, and it met a deep need. She let go of her friends from school and made Alex and the kids her whole life; and when it was time to register for the next quarter, she didn't.

Later, when she talked about that time, Perla said it might be hard to see why she left college when she'd come so far and had a full scholarship. College was hard work, but she could do it. This other part of launching, having enough hope and courage and staying power to stand on her own, was so hard. The longer she was on her own, the more painfully she felt how thin her inner resources were, how much she hadn't gotten while growing up. She'd lived all her life on a psychological starvation diet. She'd been able to pump herself up for a while, but now she desperately needed someone who cared about her and would stand by her. She wanted to believe that Alex would be that person.

Things started to fall apart. He complained about her cooking, the same food he'd loved before, and told her she was fat. He accused her of flirting with other guys and cheating on him. His best friend groped her; and when she told Alex, he blamed her and called her a whore. The worse he treated her, the more she did to show him what a good girlfriend she could be. The price of what she needed went through the roof, and the more she paid, the clearer it was that he wasn't who she needed him to be.

She took a long time to decide what she'd do, and then she registered for the fall quarter. She rushed Alpha Phi Omega, a coed community-service fraternity, and on the final night of rush the pledges elected her pledge class president. The upperclassmen told them they had to plan their major service class project right then, that night. They worked and talked and planned; it was dawn when Perla came home, exhausted and happy. Alex was furious and accused her of cheating on him. They fought and he stomped out, but she followed him and begged him not to leave her. He told her they were through. She cried for two days, then decided that being through with Alex was just fine.

She called that quarter "an amazing time of my life." She kept herself busy, too busy to think about Alex, working every day on Alpha Phi Omega's service projects. She carried a full academic load and made a 3.8 grade point average. She felt powerful. She didn't need him, she could do this on her own. She needed just three more quarters to graduate.

Winter quarter, she started strong, then her father called. Antonio had been in a knife fight. He'd been stabbed, badly, and now he was in the ICU, unconscious. "Come home, *mija*," he told her. "Your mother and I and your sisters are here. Your family needs you." She slumped against the wall. No matter how far she went, how well she did, she'd never escape her family's drama. They always sucked her back in. She didn't have anyone but them, and she felt so weak.

Her father called every day. Her sadness about Alex bubbled up now, and it was nearly unbearable. She cried every day for the relationship she'd hoped for with him and had never had. She couldn't concentrate, couldn't think, couldn't write her papers. She felt her resolve draining away—she couldn't hold on to the confident, strong woman she'd been last quarter, or the proud Reality Changers alum who'd talked to the seniors. She shuffled through the quarter and barely passed her courses.

The next quarter, she registered for classes and then withdrew. What was the point if she felt this bad? She couldn't remember that she'd ever felt any other way, and couldn't believe she'd ever feel better. She put on her false happy face and told everyone that she was taking a break, but she stayed on in Riverside and drank and partied every night. "I gave up on myself."

Two quarters short of graduating, Perla left college and moved home, telling her parents she was taking a break. They were glad to have her back and didn't ask questions. She felt ashamed, stupid, and weak. She got a job and started seeing a guy. She knew it was a rebound relationship, that he wasn't right for her, but she just needed some fun and some time to figure out what she was going to do.

Then she found she was pregnant.

She was angry and disappointed in herself and ashamed. She couldn't marry the guy; he and she both knew it wouldn't work. Midway through her pregnancy, she decided that this baby was what she had, and that she would be the best mother she could be, taking care of her baby in all the ways that she hadn't been taken care of. Her daughter, Salma, was born healthy and beautiful, and Perla poured all her love and energy into taking care of her. She didn't know where her own life would go.

6 Uphill

"I want to shut down that stuff and have a different kind of year."

Robert Silva

Robert Silva didn't have time for essays that fall. Since school started, he'd been getting up at five in the morning; any later and he wouldn't have a shot at the bathroom. Since June he'd lived in a garage with his grandparents and his Uncle Santiago, and now they'd been joined by his sister and her boyfriend and their year-old daughter. Robert and Santiago shared a windowless room that barely accommodated their two beds. Everyone used the bathroom in his Uncle Rick's house in the front. The garage didn't have heat, and at five it was cold. Robert wrapped himself in a towel, sprinted to the house, and showered fast.

His grandmother didn't have enough food for him to have breakfast, so he drank water to help himself feel full. Robert believed that what you look like is who you are, and so every morning he ironed his clothes for the day on the kitchen table. When he set out for school, his T-shirt was smooth, the shirt he wore unbuttoned over it was crisp, and his cargo shorts had a sharp crease. His dark hair, sleek with gel, was combed straight back.

He walked two miles to school. Mornings were easy, straight downhill. Afternoons were another story. In September in San Diego, the Santa Anas blow in, hot desert winds that bake the city under a deep blue, cloudless sky and drive temperatures into the nineties. Today, as he walked out of Abraham Lincoln High School at four o'clock, the air shimmered above Imperial Avenue and the asphalt in the street was soft. He felt the burning sidewalk through his sneakers.

He shifted the strap of his laptop bag on his shoulder. The strap and his shirt were soaked with sweat. His textbooks were crammed into his backpack; between the books and his laptop he was carrying more than twenty pounds. He was taking AP history, AP English, and AP economics. It was a load, but his grade point average from his freshman and sophomore years was so bad he needed those AP grades. He didn't use the laptop that much at school, but he carried it every day. "It was like my shield," he said. "If I looked and acted like business, I'd be about the business."

He had always been lean, but since he moved in with his grandparents he'd lost close to ten pounds. His pants hung on his hipbones, and his shirts ballooned around his chest. His cheekbones stood out, and his dark eyes burned from deep under his brows. In the mirror he looked handsome and fierce, but he'd have traded handsome and fierce for a few good meals.

He was doing the Three-Day in November, the Susan G. Komen Three-Day Walk for Breast Cancer. He and Grace Chaidez had signed up this summer. To be part of the walk he had to raise twenty-two hundred dollars in pledges. He wore a pink ribbon to school every day, and he talked to students and teachers about his mother and asked for contributions. It surprised him how many people cared. He had a ton of homework every night and college applications he should be working on, but this fall the Three-Day mattered the most.

His mother had been given her diagnosis seven months earlier, in February of his junior year. He had come home from school and found her in the living room, lying on the couch, sobbing. She had breast cancer, stage 4. When she was getting preliminary tests before chemotherapy, her pregnancy test came back positive: she was almost three months pregnant. She wouldn't consider an abortion. Her doctor gave her a 30 percent chance of living through the end of the year.

Everything got crazy. His father started drinking a lot and stayed out late most nights. Robert would hear him stumble in at three or four in the morning—Robert's sister Carol figured their dad had a girlfriend. His mother lay on the couch, exhausted from the chemo. Robert vacuumed and did the chores she was too tired to do and cooked for her and Marlon and Cathy, his younger brother and sister. Weeknights he stayed home because Marlon and Cathy needed to have someone there for them, and his mother was usually asleep. Late at night he'd hear his father walk out.

Robert had been in Reality Changers since the eighth grade. When Yanov told him the rules—keep a 3.0 grade point average, no gangs, no drugs— Robert said no thanks. His mother made him join anyway. "Just go," she said. He did, but not very often. Chris kept him in the program even though he broke all the rules and pissed away so many opportunities. His first two years of high school, he ditched as often as he went, never cracked a book. School was like breakfast, he said: sometimes you felt like it, sometimes you didn't. It was a place to hang out with his friends, sell a little dope, find out the buzz. His backpack was weightless back then, the only thing in it the weed and the rock he sold. He got into so many fights with guys and shouting matches with teachers that he lost count of his suspensions.

Sophomore year he got into it with his math teacher and shoved him into a bookcase. The principal requested expulsion. Yanov came to the hearing and told the hearing officers that Robert belonged to Reality Changers, and that 100 percent of the Reality Changers kids who stayed in school went to college. Robert was amazed. He hadn't shown Chris anything but a snotty attitude, and here was Chris showing up to save his ass.

He transferred to Abraham Lincoln High School, one of the city's oldest high schools, reopened after an extensive remodeling. He liked the notion that he and Lincoln were both starting fresh. He told Grace this year was going to be different. No more smoking weed, no more dealing. She'd heard it before from Robert, but this time he told her to write a contract, and he signed it. She pinned the contract on the bulletin board in her cubicle. He saw it every week. She must believe he could do it.

First week of his junior year at Lincoln, a security guard stopped him in the hall to check his backpack. Robert said no, the guard grabbed his arm and they shoved each other around the hall. Then he was sitting in the assistant principal's office while Mr. Moore, the assistant principal, slowly leafed through Robert's disciplinary folder. Finally he looked up and said, "I see that you were recommended for expulsion."

Robert lunged forward in his seat. He'd set this fool straight.

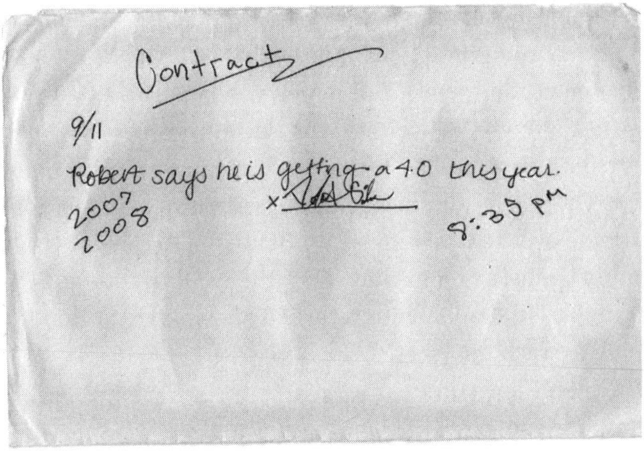

Figure 1. Robert Silva's contract to earn a 4.0 grade point average.

Then he stopped. I've been here before, he thought. Today I'm going to do something different. He sat back in his chair. He said, "Mr. Moore, I want to apologize. I want to shut down that stuff and have a different kind of year here."

"It was amazing," he remembered. "I didn't even have to mean it. I just said it, and it changed everything." That moment in the assistant principal's office was when he saw the power of the changes he was making.

He lost his bad-news friends, brought his books home, and did homework every night. He got A's on quizzes, A's on his midterms. He took speech and found he liked talking to groups. He joined MEChA, the Chicano student group. School became a different place for him. He'd slipped out of what Victor Rios and others have called the "criminalization scenario," in which adults saw him as untrustworthy, potentially dangerous, requiring intrusion and control.[1] He'd been stigmatized like that since middle school, cut off from beneficial interactions with teachers, not considered for more challenging classes or opportunities. Now his counselor signed for him to take AP classes. He was a young man with ideas and promise, someone adults wanted to encourage. Teachers and kids knew who he was. For Robert, the difference was like moving from smog and diesel exhaust to fresh mountain air.

Most weekends he did service projects with Reality Changers, then volunteered to be community service coordinator. He felt like somebody who could really make a difference. Fall semester he made a 4.0.

Even with his mom's cancer and his dad's weirdness, he made a 3.8 spring semester. Grace said that was amazing, and that he'd delivered on his contract. The night in June when things blew up between him and his dad, she'd come over to take him out to Benihana to celebrate. They were hanging out in the living room when his father walked through, on his way out for the night. He saw Grace and turned and snarled at Robert, "When are you going to wash the truck?"

"I'll do it when I have time."

"Don't give me that shit."

"I didn't mean anything. I'll do it as soon as I have time."

"You need to wash that truck."

"Pops, why are you being so ignorant about what I'm saying? I'll do it as soon as I can."

His father ran at him. Robert dodged and sprinted out into the front yard. His father followed, shouting, "You give me shit, I'll rip your fucking jaw off your face."

Robert turned and planted himself. "Okay. Bring it. Let's see what you got."

His father was much taller and outweighed him by forty pounds. He crossed the yard in two strides and stood close to Robert's face, arm hauled back, fist clenched.

Before he could swing Robert slammed his fist into his father's mouth. His father staggered back and stared at his oldest son. He pulled off his belt of thick brown leather, three inches wide, a solid brass buckle. He swung the belt over his head and walked toward Robert, the big buckle humming inches from Robert's face.

"Don't touch me with that thing or you'll be sorry."

"Motherfucker, I'll teach you."

"You going to teach me shit?"

"Get the fuck out of here. You don't live here any more."

Robert looked at his father and shook his head.

His mother stood in the doorway. She turned to Grace and said, "Can you get him out of here?"

He and Grace drove off, and went to dinner. Afterward she drove him home, and she waited while he stuffed his clothes into garbage bags and said good-bye to his mother. Then she drove him to his grandmother's.

There wasn't much to eat at his grandmother's, mostly bananas and baloney sandwiches. Sometimes his mother brought over a pot of beans or a stew, but Robert was always hungry. He got to take a break from the garage when he went to Academic Connections. Since he didn't own a suitcase or a duffel, he walked onto campus with his backpack and laptop case over his shoulder and his clothes and everything else in a garbage bag. For three weeks he lived in the dorm and took a course in urban anthropology. Some of the white kids complained about the rooms and having to share a bathroom. For Robert the campus was a resort. He had a room of his own for the first time in his life. He ate in the dining hall, three meals a day, as much as he wanted.

His baby brother, Angel Ali Silva, was born in August, tiny, red-faced, with a head of thick black hair and a high, strong cry. The first time Robert held him, Angel wrapped his fist tight around Robert's finger. The strength of his grip surprised Robert. He vowed that he would hold on to his baby brother just as hard as Angel held on to him. Taking care of Angel and his mother mattered more than anything. He wanted to see Angel every day, and he wanted to come home. His mother begged him to apologize to his father. He felt bad about throwing Robert out, she said, and if Robert would apologize he'd let him come home in a minute. Robert wouldn't do it. His father was the one who should apologize.

The heat was fierce today. He'd walked only halfway up the hill and already he was lightheaded. At his grandmother's, all there'd be to eat was beans. He was worried about his mother. He hadn't seen her or Angel for a week. His grade point average from his two previous years was killing him. Maybe no college would let him in. He could fill out the applications and write his heart out in his essays, and they could just look at his record and say forget it.

He knew a guy who lived around here. He could score a joint right now. Sit down on the curb. Blow everything off.

If he didn't keep walking he'd be thirty-five and still living in a garage.

7 Doing RC: How It Works

Others may choose to accept reality. God willing, we choose to transform it.

Reality Changers Statement of Purpose

Grace Chaidez sat at one end of the big open cubicle she shared with Jenn, talking on her phone to Jocelyn, a sophomore. When Grace had called her yesterday, Jocelyn said she had a ride to the meeting tonight. Today at four thirty, she didn't. Grace stared at her lists of students and tutors, trying to figure who could pick her up. Each week she called every student the day before their meeting, reminding them to come, making sure they had a ride. She'd started in the summer as program manager, describing herself as the "day-to-day, keep the program running, person." The calls, ninety-eight calls over three days, every week were one of the ways she kept things running. She also arranged community service opportunities; supervised Jonny Villafuerte, who'd thrown rocks at the Iglesia and now was the dean of students, and several interns; and subbed for tutors who couldn't make it. She worked with students whose grade point averages dropped below 3.0, did some publicity, and represented Reality Changers at the downtown Kiwanis Club.

She was twenty-five, two years out of college, the first person in her family to go to college. She remembered that, in Fresno, where she grew up, she saw her uncle's diploma from Berkeley hanging on the wall of her grandmother's bedroom. She wanted one of those. She went to Berkeley, and in San Francisco she met Hector Chaidez, who was in the navy. In time they got engaged, and when the navy transferred him to San Diego, she transferred to UC San Diego. She planned to be a nurse until, for a sociology course, she did an internship at Reality Changers. Before her internship was over, she volunteered as a tutor. The next semester she changed her major to sociology. In three years of tutoring, she'd formed close relationships with students, especially girls, who saw her as an older sister and mentor. She was short and her voice was soft, and it was easy to underestimate her until she started talking about students. Her knowledge of their lives was encyclopedic.

Robert Silva ambled into the cube and hugged her. Pacing and waving his arms, he talked nonstop about the Three-Day, the sixty-mile Susan G. Komen Three-Day Walk for Breast Cancer that he and Grace would do together in November. Grace was his strongest relationship at Reality Changers, the person who punctured his excuses and shored up his hopes, especially since his mother's diagnosis of breast cancer. Long before he believed he could go to college, before he believed his future could be anything more than that of a dropout and small-time drug dealer, Grace believed in Robert. Yanov, he could blow off; Yanov was a white guy. He couldn't blow off Grace. Her father was a mechanic and her mother worked at Burger King, and Grace graduated from college.

Marlon, Robert's little brother, hung back at the edge of the cube. He dressed like Robert, in an ironed T-shirt and baggy shorts. He acknowledged Grace with a curt nod and a scowl. Marlon was a freshman, new to the program this year. He'd lived through the same upheavals as Robert: his mother's cancer, his father's drinking and absences, Robert being thrown out the house, and in August, their new baby brother, Angel. Robert was already committed to changing his life when things in the family fell apart. Marlon was just trying to keep his chin above water. Reality Changers was Robert's place; Marlon didn't know yet whether it could be his. He didn't know whether he wanted it to be.

From the other end of the cubicle, Jenn looked up at him and smiled. "Hey, Marlon, I'm glad you're here. I could use your help getting the room set up for tonight."

Setting up meant unstacking sixty chairs—for forty students, twenty volunteer tutors and staff—and arranging them in rows in the community room next to their work area. The room was a common space, used by all the building's tenants; at the end of the evening the chairs had to be folded and restacked. At the iglesia, Reality Changers had had a dedicated room, where students draped themselves on tired couches, and where the college banners and photos of seniors holding scholarship checks covered the walls, reminding students of what they could do. This community room, with its plastic chairs and empty white walls, felt as soulless as a bus station.

Juan and Luis and José, sophomores, all wearing earbuds, spilled into the room, laughing shoving, punching each other. José's and Luis's heads were shaved and Juan wore his dark hair slicked back and curled on the back of his neck. All three wore baggy jeans and oversize T-shirts and trucker caps backward. On the street or at school, it would be easy read them as trouble, kids you'd need to watch. Victor Rios has documented how easy it is for teachers, youth workers, and police to categorize Latino and African American youth, boys especially, as bad, potentially criminal, even when they're nothing worse than boisterous.[1] The neighborhoods that Reality Changers' students live in, the friends they hang out with, and the schools they attend make them candidates for these negative assumptions. The assumptions come with severe costs, especially at school. If administrators and teachers see a student as heading for trouble, precious opportunities for growth—placement in better classes, trusting relationships with adults, a sense of belonging—don't happen. The ways they're seen by adults infect youths' own vision of themselves and contribute to their feeling unvalued. One of Reality Changers' most powerful tools is the confidence shown by staff and volunteers that all its students can do well in school and go to college. When students talked about how Reality Changers helped them, they mentioned that confidence. Perla, one of the program's first students, said, "They always thought I could do it. They helped me believe I could."

In *Keepin' It Real,* her study of academic disengagement among poor Black and Latino youth, sociologist Prudence Carter describes the significant tension her young subjects felt at school between their own ethnic cultures and sense of identity and their schools' rules and values, emblematic of the dominant white culture. No matter the ethnic and racial makeup of their student body, their schools valued white language (i.e., standard English), behavior, musical tastes, styles of dress, and models of decorum. Black and Latino students felt that their own cultures were not valued or respected. Boys particularly were likely to be seen as trouble-makers headed for bad ends. Carter observed three ways that minority students responded to the tension. Some were "noncompliant believers" who amplified their differences from the dominant model, challenged their teachers, and flouted the schools' rules and standards. "Cultural mainstreamers" assimilated the behaviors and style of the dominant cul-ture in order to fit in and improve their academic prospects. "Cultural straddlers" met social and academic expectations at school yet maintained much of their own culture and the respect of their peers.[2]

Reality Changers' students, especially eighth and ninth graders, talked about these tensions at their schools; and even when Latinos were the majority of the student body, they often felt themselves outsiders. Reality Changers was important to them because it was a place where they felt like they belonged. Their peers there held the same hopes and dreams and pushed against the same barriers. Program staff and volunteers, many of them white, looked beyond students' baggies and backward caps, their slicked-back hair, and their not-so-standard English. They understood that these were ways that students asserted a vital ethnic and cultural identity, and that these externals did not detract from students' commit-ment to working and learning. Even as the program promoted academic achievement, self-control, and working for long-range goals, it respected students' Latino culture, and its stylistic expressions, as sources of strength and self-esteem.

Reality Changers' lessons and behavioral expectations respected stu-dents' dignity and helped them achieve within the existing school struc-ture. Behaviors were presented as the skills and tools that would help them get where they wanted to go. Although staff and volunteers did not use explicit terms such as Carter's in describing how students might keep their balance at school, in honoring students' ethnic identities they encour-aged cultural straddling and the cultivation of multicultural competence. The students who were most engaged at school had clearly mastered those skills.

"Hi, guys," Jenn said. "How about some help setting up? Juan, can you bring in the whiteboard; and Luis, would you get the binders from our cube? And put away your phones, guys."

Luis and José rolled out the racks of three-ring binders, each binder with a student's name lettered down the spine, arranged alphabetically so students could find their own binders and—at six o'clock, start time—staff could glance at the racks and see who was there and who was missing. Every binder held a copy of the Reality Changers constitution and statement of purpose, along with sheets of lined paper.

Jenn was twenty-three, newly graduated from San Diego State. Like Grace, she'd worked as a volunteer tutor; she knew the students and the program. Her title was program designer, and her assignment was to write what she called "Reality Changers in a Box," an operations manual that would document the process and the rationale for every practice that Yanov had developed over the last seven years. She also helped new students who were having difficulty connecting with the program, and she recruited and trained a roster of 125 volunteers, mostly college students, who served as tutors and mentors for the three sections. She led Thursday night's Senior Academy and supervised the two other site directors.

Alma, a freshman in short shorts and a deeply scoop-necked T-shirt, begged Jenn to let her use her computer—"Just ten minutes, that's all, I promise"—to finish her homework. Silvia wanted to talk to Jenn about her friend who'd been hassling her. Juan and Luis were arm wrestling on the countertop.

"Okay, guys, take it somewhere else," Grace told them. "I've still got some calls to make."

Jenn and Grace's shared cube was the heart of the office, where students hung out, ad hoc conferences happened, and problems got solved. The two tried out ideas and plans on each other and talked daily about students and the program and what they wanted to make happen. Grace was the more comforting and maternal; Jenn was more focused on what students needed to do. Their styles were different, but students saw in both of them the same deep interest and commitment to help.

Grace gathered her lists and her phone and stationed herself at a small table near the elevator, where she greeted students and reminded them to pick up their name tags. She checked names off her list and fielded more last-minute SOSs for rides. Seniors turned left down the hall to the Senior Academy room; underclassmen headed right, to the community room.

Older students knew the drill: cell phone off, name tag on, dump your backpack on the shelf by the door. Pick up your binder from the rack and sit down. Some freshmen got the drill right away; for others it took months of repetition and reminding for the routine to stick. Grace and Jenn stationed a tutor to remind them downstairs in the lobby, another here in the hall, and another at the door of the community room.

Chris Yanov strode into the room, still in a suit and tie from his afternoon meeting with a foundation. He reached his hand out. "Good to see you, Marlon. Thanks for coming early and helping out. We appreciate that."

Marlon proffered a limp hand and looked away.

Yanov printed down the left side of the whiteboard:

October 7th

316th Congress

Lesson: "What's Your Message?"

He'd posted the date, the Congress number, the lesson topic, and the schedule on the whiteboard for every Reality Changers meeting since May 2001. The schedule was the same every week. Anyone could have printed it, but Yanov insisted on doing it himself.

6–6:30 Hot Words

6:30–7 Dinner

7–7:30 Lesson

7:30–7:45 Congress

7:45–8:45 Study Time

8:45–9:00 Regroup and Dismissal

Yanov believed in structure. Tell students what was happening and what was expected of them. Keep it simple, keep it predictable. Repetition builds structure.

Every student's binder held a copy of the Reality Changers Constitution, written by the first cohort of students in 2001. It read:

Article I. All members must maintain a 3.0 GPA or above. All members who desire to attend the UCSD Academic Connections program to receive college credit must maintain a 3.5 GPA or above. Only the best of the best will go.

Article II. All members must attend the weekly RC program and turn in all progress reports and final grades.

Article III. All members must have no involvement with alcohol, drugs, gangs, or sex. These are all problems that teens bring upon themselves. Who needs more problems? We have way too many other things to be concerned about.

Article IV. All members must pass a drug test given randomly at least once a year.

Article V. All members must show up with an open mind, work hard, and tell the truth.

Article VI. All members must participate with active membership in at least one school activity, such as a club or a sport.

Article VII. All members must be role models in their community, including being leaders for preteens, for 25 hours per year. All members must contribute 25 hours of service to the Reality Changers program as well.

The constitution is a practical guide for academic success and personal growth. The first five articles prescribe behaviors that support achievement and are consistent with Angela Duckworth's focus on self-control and grit. Showing up, as Woody Allen reminds us, is 80 percent of life. Working hard and staying away from trouble significantly increase students' prospects for doing well in school. A structure of accountability, with clear rewards and consequences, helps students stay committed to their goals.

Articles VI and VII take aim at the achievement gap between students from lower socioeconomic strata and those from affluent families. Sociologist Sean Reardon has documented the significant widening, over the last fifty years, of the gap between what affluent parents and poor parents spend to promote their children's cognitive development. Affluent parents are able to invest substantially more money and more time in promoting their children's development: lessons; tutoring; cultural enrichment; travel; books, computers, and other learning materials; and exposure to novel experiences outside the home.[3] Poor students experience a much narrower range of enrichment activities and novel situations. Reality Changers' requirement that students participate in at least one school activity or play a sport promotes students' exposure to a wider universe of peers, adults, and experiences. Their involvement also increases students' sense of belonging, both to their organization or team and to their school, which most have not previously felt.

Reality Changers staff found community service opportunities, such as helping with a drive to collect clothing for families whose houses burned in a wildfire, working in a soup kitchen that served homeless people, and assisting with a 10K race to benefit a local hospital. Staff arranged transportation and accompanied groups of students to these projects. Students went to parts of San Diego they'd never seen, worked with people from across the socioeconomic spectrum, and functioned as helpers and givers. Service hours for Reality Changers increased their sense of belonging to the program. Experiences like these could not fully close the opportunity gaps between them and their affluent peers, but they enriched students and widened their understanding of the world.

Students drifted into the room in twos and threes, talking and laughing. Girls sat with girls, boys with boys; that was how they liked it. Tutors sat in the back rows. Students were to be in their chairs by six o'clock, cell phones off, binders open, ready to listen and take notes. By 6:05, thirty-one of the thirty-seven Tuesday-night binders were out of the racks and in their owners' hands.

Yanov welcomed the students, especially the new ones. Everything about him telegraphed business. His voice was strong, and he gave clear commands. He taught the "Hot Words" section and the lesson, introduced speakers, kept order, and directed traffic. He'd always admired game show hosts' ability to engage their audience and make contestants' dreams come true. Reality Changers helped students realize their dreams, but the program was a long haul and a lot of hard work. Yanov affected the hosts' hyperbolic style in part to keep his students interested. The meeting sometimes felt and sounded like a pep rally. "And no-o-w, *all the way from Golden Hill*, we have Juan Gomez, who's going to tell us his answer. Let's give Juan a bi-i-g hand!"

Younger students especially liked his style: things didn't bog down or get dull, and they got to applaud and cheer a lot.

Yanov kept the tone relentlessly upbeat. Drugs and alcohol, gangs, violence, and sex, prohibited in the constitution, were never mentioned at meetings. There was no talk about the risks of these behaviors, no urging students to avoid them. From his reading of Malcolm Klein, Yanov believed that talking about something gave it validation and importance. Activities he wanted to discourage shouldn't get airtime. But it's harder to teach coping skills if the conditions that require coping aren't acknowledged. The absence of any talk about these all-too-present realities in students' lives raised the question of how Reality Changers could help them deal with these stresses.

Yanov introduced Jesse Sanchez, a senior: he'd be teaching Hot Words this year. Jesse came to the Senior Academy on Thursday nights, and he was flattered that Yanov had asked him to do Hot Words on Tuesdays. He had a ready smile, and he was quick to say Reality Changers was the best thing that had ever happened to him. He spoke with a convert's zeal, exhorting, encouraging, pacing the rows of chairs.

"Okay, guys, tonight we're going to write a personal mission statement. Take out a piece of paper from your binder and draw a vertical line down the middle of your paper. At the top, in the left column, write 'I Have.' Under that, you're gonna write ten nouns that describe your qualities, your strong points. In the right column, write 'I Can,' and there you're gonna write ten verbs that describe how you interact with people."

Some more explaining, some examples, and most of the students got it. Five minutes to write. The chatter in the room increased. "Okay, everybody," Jesse exhorted, "work on your own stuff. Focusfocusfocus."

Hot Words was the hardest work of the night. It was English skills: vocabulary and usage and writing practice, and as the year progressed, public speaking. In Hot Words you had to stand up and read what you wrote or say what you thought. That kind of self-disclosure, even just two declarative sentences, was for most students excruciating. Hot Words revealed all they didn't know about English, how much they had to learn. How far they still had to go.

"Who wants to read?" Jesse asked. Silence. He paced the front of the room. No volunteers. "Let's go around the room. Luis, you start. Three qualities. Stand up."

Guys on both sides of Luis elbowed him. Girls whispered and giggled. Luis slowly unfolded himself from his chair and stood up. He was tall and slender, and his pants hung uncertainly on his hips. He looked around with a sheepish grin, then stared down at his notebook as though it had landed in his hand that very second. He inhaled slowly, started to speak, then dissolved into giggles.

Jesse stared at him, his arms folded.

Luis took another deep breath. "Determination, energy, humor."

"That's good, Luis. Let's give Luis a hand!" Students clapped. No criticism, no evaluation. It was enough that Luis had agreed to stand up, that he had revealed to the group a bit of how he saw himself.

The teaching at Reality Changers was earnest and hortatory, long on encouragement, short on finesse and follow-up. Yanov offered parables and stories to convey the values he aimed to teach, as well as exercises from English textbooks for lessons in writing and organization. Volunteer tutors drew on their knowledge and life experience. The intentions were always good, the offerings were uneven. Yanov didn't provide evaluations or feedback for tutors; and until Jenn designed a workshop for them, there was no attempt to improve their skills. Exposing students to the lessons and having relationships with their tutors, Yanov felt, was the chief benefit.

A few late arrivals took seats in the back, and Jesse walked through the lesson again for them. He moved around the room, praising, cajoling, insisting. Group applause for each person who spoke. Praise that they did the assignment and stood up and spoke about themselves.

"Having a goal. Poetic skills."

"Soccer skills. People skills. Observing skills."

Marlon Silva slouched in his chair, arms folded, binder closed. The minute hand on the wall clock hung between 5 and 6.

"Art skills. Storytelling skills. Jesús. Confidence."

"A way to make people smile. Honesty. Patience."

"Okay, these are good, very good. Now guys, look at your qualities. Can you tie them to the verbs in the right-hand column, make a statement about how you interact with people? Who can do that?"

They stared blank-faced back at him. The aroma of *pollo arrosto en salsa roja* wafted down the hall from the break room.

Jesse knew his limits, and theirs. "Okay, time's almost up. Keep what you've written in your notebooks. We'll work on them some more next week. Who's gonna say grace?"

He called on Ivett, a sophomore who hadn't spoken a word. She scrunched low in her seat and looked around for someone to deliver her from this ordeal. Jesse looked straight at her. She sighed and stood up. "Okay. Bow your heads, remove all headgear." A dozen or more baseball caps came off. "Lord, thank you for this meeting, and for our food, and help us all study hard tonight and do well in school."

When Reality Changers was based at the iglesia and major support came from the Presbytery of San Diego, the program couldn't avoid having a faith component. Prayers and Bible lessons were an easy fit for most students; religion was a familiar part of their home life and their community. Yanov had been raised in the Presbyterian Church, but his own religious convictions were fading. At Reality Changers he used prayers as one more opportunity for students to speak in front of their peers, and as a tool to help them stay focused throughout the three-hour session. The religious content drew from mainstream Christian values of helping others, doing good works, maintaining good character over material gain, and emphasizing self-discipline and self-control.

For the first seven years the Reality Changers website and all its publications used the phrase "Building first-generation college students who follow God's word." This year Reality Changers was separating itself from the Presbytery and incorporating as an independent 501c3 nonprofit organization. By summer, the descriptor "who follow God's word" was phased out of the website and program materials.

Students poured out of the community room and down the hall to the break room for dinner. The break room was at the east end of the building, and its large windows looked out onto the freeway and the tops of trees, all the way out to the mountains, fifty miles away to the east, a view that helped them dream.

Two pairs of parents stood behind a table, serving baked chicken, *refritos,* corn tortillas with *queso fresco,* shredded lettuce, and a hot, fruity salsa verde. Students talked and teased and flirted, but the talk stayed respectful: no profanity, no sexual references. That mattered, especially to the girls; Reality Changers was a safer, more comfortable place than school or their neighborhoods.

Thirty minutes later they were back in the community room. In the lesson, Yanov either spoke himself or invited a guest speaker who would inspire and challenge them. He was proud of the roster of people who'd spoken at the lesson over the years: city councilmembers who represented Golden Hill and City Heights and other districts where students lived, the chief of police, the superintendent of San Diego Unified School District, and the president of every four-year college and university in San Diego County. His own lessons and his guests' focused on the program's core values of service and scholarship, and on the attitudes and skills that would help them become successful students. The highly social and public style of the meeting provided many opportunities for those attitudes and behaviors to be modeled and extoled. The ideas were simple and portable. Look adults in the eye, shake hands, and introduce yourself. Be an example to your family and your friends. Don't go to bed until you've finished all your homework. Push yourself harder; you'll surprise yourself with what you can do. Don't give up.

On the whiteboard Yanov wrote, "Win-Win." He explained that a situation could have different resolutions: win-lose, lose-lose, or win-win. A soccer game was win-lose; that was how it was set up. Wars were lose-lose: even if one side looked like the winner, both sides lost a lot. The best kinds of solutions were win-win, where everybody gave something, and everybody got at least part of what they wanted.

"Think about win-win solutions in your life: with your parents, with your brothers and sisters. At school. With your friends. You set a model by your actions. Help the people you're with to work out a solution where everybody gets something. That's win-win.

"You'll win, too, because you don't rise to the top unless you're bringing people with you. Our theme this year is: 'What's Your Message?' Think about what *your* message is. Does it give the people you're with a chance to win too?"

The lesson ended at seven thirty, and students dispersed to their study groups. The groups of six to eight students met in workrooms, offices, the break room, at a table set up in a hallway—wherever they could find a space. Chris and Jenn and Grace had worked for a week to compose the groups, balancing new students with more seasoned ones, ambivalent ones with students fully on board with the program. The goal was a ratio of one tutor for every student, a student paired with the same tutor for a semester, ideally for a year. The lead tutor needed to be experienced and able to maintain a firm hand.

Study group started with Congress. In Marlon's group, Bianca, a sophomore and cocaptain of her school's varsity soccer team, was tonight's Congress leader. She stood up, four foot eleven inches in her hoodie and soccer shorts, and shushed the talkers. She read the Reality Changers Declaration of Purpose:

- We are Reality Changers, Agentes de Cambio. We are agents of POSITIVE change in the world that surrounds us. We get good grades because we are going to college.

- We are polite, courageous, and above all, honest. If we are not, please tell us so and we will correct our behavior the first time that we are told. We seek to always inspire others with our words because we desire to be positive influences at all times. We don't pull people down, but instead, we lift each other up.

- We hold ourselves accountable to God, our family, our group, and ourselves. Others may choose to accept reality. God willing, we choose to transform it.

- We show up, work hard, and tell the truth. We are Reality Changers, Agentes de Cambio.

She turned to Alma, sitting next to her and shook her hand. "What were your highs and lows this week, and what is your prayer request?"

"My high was that me and my best friend are in the same math class. My low was that I have to get up earlier now that school's started. My prayer request is that everyone study well tonight."

"Thank you." Bianca turned to José, next to Alma, and shook his hand. "What were your highs and lows this week, and what is your prayer request?"

"My high was I saw *The Incredible Hulk*. My low was that I had a lot of homework. My prayer request is that I get a good grade on my history test."

She engaged every student, every tutor. Congress took less than fifteen minutes, declaration of purpose included. It didn't look like much was going on, especially when the group was new: highs, lows, and prayer requests were brief and could sound glib.

In fact, Congress was one of Reality Changers' most effective tools. The job of leader rotated each week; even the most squirrelly freshman, when it was his turn, had to stand up, shake hands with the other members of the group, and ask them about themselves. Hearing each others' highs and lows and prayer requests helped students get to know each other, and it knit the group closer together. Within a few weeks, lows and prayer requests became more self-disclosing. Students spoke of an uncle in the hospital, a mom whose shift had changed and who now didn't get home until ten at night. The loss of an apartment. A car giving out. A cousin arrested. Tutors learned the stresses their students faced, and students learned that the tutors they idealized also suffered disappointments and losses and had fears. In training sessions for new tutors, Jenn stressed the importance of Congress. She told them, "Congress is the thing that makes Reality Changers different from all other tutoring programs. We aren't here just to raise our grades. We're a family."

Marlon's group met in the break room, and Grace was lead tutor. They were seven freshmen and sophomores, heavier on ambivalents and cutups than Grace would have wished. The room wasn't a good space for studying: the vending machines, leftover fruit punch from dinner, and even the windows were irresistible distractions. She was too often called away for the crisis du jour and would come back to find students ignoring their tutors, talking, banging on the vending machines.

Marlon's tutor, Nate, joined the group tonight and introduced himself to Marlon and José. "I'm a junior at UC San Diego, and I'm majoring in biology. This is my second year tutoring. Where do you guys go to school?"

José said, "Mission Bay."

Marlon didn't answer.

"What do you guys want to work on tonight?"

José opened his algebra book and showed Nate his assignment. Marlon said, "I don't have any homework." He put his head down on the table and pretended to sleep.

Nate worked with José on his homework and ignored Marlon. Marlon kept his head on the table, but he stole peeks at Nate and José.

At eight forty-five, tutors called time. Kids gathered their books and walked back to the community room. Robert hailed Marlon. "How'd it go?" Marlon shrugged.

"All right, everybody," Yanov called out. "This week, think about what your message is. What does it tell other people about you? And whatever happens this week at home, at school, with your friends, think about how you can make it win-win.

"Denise, give us a prayer to send us off."

"God, we pray that everyone has a good week and does good in school. Amen."

The meeting was over. The din of thirty-one voices rose in the room as students returned their binders to the rack, reclaimed their backpacks, and turned on their phones.

Yanov pulled on a reflective vest and picked up a walkie-talkie and two flashlights, one with a green filter, one with a red filter, for directing traffic. Outside in the drop-off area, a line of parents' cars waited. A car would pull up, and Yanov would lean down to the window and greet the parent, then call on his walkie-talkie to ask Jenn inside to send the student out. His interchange with parents was often as brief as "Cómo está," and "Bien." But parents saw him each week, and if they reported that things were not bien, he'd ask them to stay after the pickup so they could talk. Some nights he was there for another hour or more.

Tonight all was bien. Robert and Marlon headed out to their mom's truck. By 9:25 the 316th Congress had ended, the last student had been picked up, and Reality Changers' year was a month under way.

8 Breaking Faith, Breaking Free

Mi tiempo se acabado.

Chris Yanov

Reality Changers had been running just a year when Pastor Simpson told Yanov he'd be leaving the iglesia. Simpson had started the mission at the iglesia in the late eighties; now he was leaving the ministry to become a school psychologist. Yanov had called Simpson his copilot. He'd met regularly with the pastor and relied on him as an older, cooler head, someone he could bounce his ideas off. Simpson had had his back. He'd encouraged him about Reality Changers since it was a phrase on a napkin.

For the next four years, the iglesia ran without a pastor. Yanov reported to the board of the Presbytery, the regional administration of the Presbyterian Church, and the Session, the elected governing body of church members. He missed Simpson and their conversations; but he was building Reality Changers, and it suited him to have a fair amount of running room.

He banked his *Wheel of Fortune* earnings and cut back on substitute teaching. He subbed only at Kroc, where principal Bobbi Samilson and the teachers knew him well and treated him as a valued colleague. Three nights a week he went to classes at the University of San Diego for peace and justice studies and to pursue a second master's, in international relations; on Tuesday nights he ran the Reality Changers meeting.

During the day he raised money for his fledgling program and looked for volunteers. At college volunteer fairs, he told the stories of Reality Changers students and recruited dozens of undergraduates to come and tutor. At service clubs like Rotary and Lions, and at foundations and corporations, he talked about how Reality Changers' students were changing the harsh realities of their lives. Sunday mornings he and a few students would visit a Presbyterian church, where he talked about the program and students told their stories. Contributions flowed in and volunteers came in droves.

Yanov said, "I always wanted to be the person who could say the amazing words that everybody remembered, and inspire them to action." He was a compelling speaker, and part of his appeal was his gritty authenticity. He'd lived his convictions in the streets and in the city's bleakest schools, and now at Reality Changers he offered hope to kids who hadn't seen much of it. He understood that the most effective fund-raising speaks to people's values and provides them an opportunity to feel a part of the work they're writing their checks for. He carried a powerful message to his middle- and upper-class listeners: Reality Changers' engine of hope helped disadvantaged youth transform their lives, and they, his listeners, had the power to drive that transformation. As donors, they could see the direct effects of their gifts. As volunteers, they could help students themselves. His message resonated with church members, foundation officers, and corporate donors, who saw in Reality Changers a means to realize their own hopes of helping youth succeed.

Reality Changers had grown to more than eighty students. It was the largest, most visible program at the iglesia, and its operating budget was more than twice that of the church's. In Golden Hill and beyond, the iglesia was known as the church where Reality Changers met. Families came to check out the program and then joined the church. Several members of the Session, the church's elected board, had sons and daughters in the program.

When Yanov graduated with master's degrees in peace and justice studies and international relations, the *Wheel of Fortune* money was nearly gone. Yanov told the Presbytery board that building the program and fund-raising had become a full-time job; he couldn't do it any longer as a volunteer project. The board proposed that Reality Changers become a mission of the Presbytery. They would pay Yanov a salary, and he could continue to use the space at the iglesia. The Presbytery would also provide important back office functions like liability insurance and help with tax filing. Becoming a mission greatly enhanced Yanov's standing with the thirty-one Presbyterian churches in San Diego County: when he appealed to a congregation for funds, he spoke as one of their own. His salary from the Presbytery was thirty-five thousand dollars, a substantial raise over part-time subbing and financial aid.

Yanov was comfortable with Christian ethics as a guide for his life, but by the time he started college he'd distanced himself from Presbyterian theology. Though he called the iglesia his social and spiritual home, he never joined the church. When I asked him why he didn't, he quoted Paul's first letter to the Corinthians: "Let there be no divisions among you." He took Paul's injunction to mean that denominational distinctions were a distraction, and that joining a particular congregation wasn't necessary or even helpful for his work. He knew that his decision didn't sit well with some church members, but he believed that even though he wasn't a member he could still be part of the iglesia and build Reality Changers there.

At program meetings Yanov kept the religious content ecumenical, so that students of any religious background could feel at ease. He liked to say that a hard-core Muslim imam could walk in and not be discomfited by the prayers.

The hypothetical imam might have been comfortable with Reality Changers' ecumenical stance, but Pastor Efren Ordoñez was not. The iglesia's new pastor arrived in 2007 from Tijuana, where he'd grown up and gone to seminary. Golden Hill is less than eighteen miles from Tijuana, but the cultural distance is a chasm. In Mexican Presbyterian churches, the pastor is the sole authority. He makes all decisions for the church and the Session defers to him.

Ordoñez arrived to find a program under his church's roof that was better known than the church itself, with an annual budget twice as large. Reality Changers didn't teach Presbyterian doctrine, and its twenty-something white-boy director, who wore a goatee and dressed in baggy jeans and hoodies, didn't even belong to the church. Pastor Ordoñez called Yanov in for a talk. He reminded him that Reality Changers was a

Presbyterian mission, and it needed a strong dose of Presbyterian theology. He wanted to preach a weekly lesson and meet regularly with the parents. Yanov said no thanks. Yanov wanted to hang a banner, "Home of Reality Changers," over the side door where students entered on meeting nights. The pastor said no. He told Yanov he needed to join the church. Yanov balked.

Pastor Ordoñez wasn't the only complication. Reality Changers now served more than eighty students, some in the original meeting room at the iglesia and a second group at the Solana Beach Presbyterian Church, twenty miles away in the northern part of the county. Only a handful of the program's students now came from the iglesia. Yanov's waiting list had enough students on it to start a second group at the iglesia, but he wasn't sure that the Session would agree to a second night. As the program grew, tensions between its mission and the iglesia's became harder to ignore. Reality Changers wasn't as good a fit as when it started. Yanov knew that at some point he'd have to move, but he wasn't yet ready to leave the church community that had been his home since he was a college freshman.

The showdown came in the summer, at the monthly Session meeting. Yanov attended all the Session meetings, and when he arrived that night he found Reality Changers was the first item on the agenda. Meetings were conducted in Spanish. Pastor Ordoñez called the meeting to order and told Yanov to wait outside while the Session discussed their concerns about Reality Changers. The eight Session members looked at each other, at Yanov, and at the pastor. No one spoke. Yanov walked out and sat on a folding chair in the hall, a petitioner in his own community. Forty minutes passed. The door opened and Pastor Ordoñez beckoned him to come back in.

The pastor said the Session wanted Reality Changers to pay rent.

Reality Changers had given fifty thousand dollars in scholarships to students from families in the church. That wasn't enough?

The Session members looked at each other and looked down at the table. They talked about responsibility and collaboration.

The pastor said the Session wanted Yanov to take more responsibility in the church.

What did they mean by more responsibility?

They couldn't say.

Yanov asked, "Does anyone know what day is trash-pickup day for the church?"

No one knew.

"It's Thursday. Ten o'clock Tuesday night, after I've cleaned up the room where Reality Changers meets and set all the chairs back in place, I go around the building and collect the trash from the church offices and all the rooms and dump it out in the barrels. Then I haul the barrels out to the street. Trash pickup's not until Thursday, but nobody takes the trash out on Wednesday nights. It sits around for weeks. Nobody asked me to do trash. I started doing it when I started the program five years ago. Nobody had to know I did it. Now, what other responsibilities would you like me to take on?"

The room was quiet.

The meeting ran another two hours. They couldn't tell him what they wanted, except for more collaboration, and they couldn't say what that meant. They complained about kids putting their feet on the couches and dirty dishes left in the kitchen. Maybe, they said, he didn't have to pay rent.

Yanov walked out onto B Street and headed for home. Pastor Ordoñez was a serious inconvenience, but he was just doing what he believed a pastor should do and Yanov could live with that. What hurt him was the Session members' backing the pastor. Every one of those Session members knew him and knew Reality Changers. They'd watched it grow, put their own kids in it, seen what it could do. Now this.

At the next month's meeting, the Session told Yanov that the pastor should speak at Reality Changers' weekly meetings. They asked Yanov for an inventory of everything at the church that belonged to Reality Changers. He agreed to both stipulations.

Yanov said he had enough students to start another group, and he asked for the use of the meeting room for a second weeknight. He also asked that the church groups who used the meeting room on Sundays clean it up when they were finished, and he asked again to hang a banner, on meeting nights, that said "Home of Reality Changers." The Session voted. Pastor Ordoñez had laid his groundwork. Even the Session members who had kids in the program, who knew firsthand the work that Reality Changers was doing, lined up behind him. They turned down all three of his requests. Yanov said he would like the meeting minutes to document the fact that in the spirit of collaboration he had agreed to both of the Session's requirements, and that the Session had denied all three of his requests.

Some things were not spoken of in those two Session meetings. That Yanov wanted to use the church's space but he didn't want their new pastor to talk to his students. That he talked about loving the iglesia and how important it was to him to be part of its *familia*, but he never joined the church. That most students in Reality Changers were not members of the iglesia, and that there were sons and daughters of church members who couldn't be part of it because they didn't have a 3.0 grade point average. That, as Emerson wrote, we do not quite forgive a giver, and this white college boy was the one who was helping their children. It's impossible to know to what degree feelings like these shaped the Session's decisions. But feelings that are not spoken have no opportunity to be resolved, and they may have contributed to the Session's feeling that the gulf between Reality Changers' mission and their church's had widened so much that the two no longer fit under the same roof.

For Yanov it looked different. The only community of his adult life, one that was home and *familia* and the rock on which he'd built his life's work, had let him know that there was no longer a place for him. Walking home alone, he thought to himself, *mi tiempo se acabado*. My time has come.

The next day he started looking for a new space.

9 A Great Small Organization

There was that law of life, so cruel and so just, that one must grow, or pay more for staying the same.

Norman Mailer

Yanov stood on the roof of the parking structure behind the Workforce Partnership Building in late October 2008. A Santa Ana wind baked the air dry and drove the temperature on the roof into the nineties. To the west, he could see San Diego Bay and the Pacific; looking east, the Laguna Mountains rising six thousand feet. He loved the roof and the view; up here everything felt possible. He wore a black suit, pants with sharp creases, a white shirt, and red tie. His press conference started in half an hour.

Robert Silva and junior Eduardo Corona clipped an eight-foot-long Reality Changers banner onto the east wall, where Yanov would stand when he spoke. He'd be looking west, directly into the sun. The heat was fierce, and without sunglasses the glare was nearly blinding, but he'd put up with it. The banner and the mountains and the deep blue of the sky were a made-for-TV-news backdrop. The press conference was to announce a $250,000 grant to Reality Changers from the California Wellness Foundation, the biggest donation the program had ever received. He'd invited every TV and radio station, every print and online news outlet, in San Diego County to this press conference. Julio Marcial, the program director for the foundation, who'd made the grant happen, drove down from Los Angeles for the announcement.

Marcial stood by the banner, talking with Robert. Marcial grew up in Pacoima, a Hispanic neighborhood in Los Angeles, in public housing. His mother cleaned houses and his father was a gardener. He always assumed that he'd go to work with his father. Then his high school counselor told him he should apply to college. He was admitted to UCLA and Berkeley. He wasn't sure where Berkeley was, but he knew how to get to UCLA on the bus. He went to UCLA. Marcial got Reality Changers. He knew firsthand the kinds of limitations its students faced, and he liked a lot of things about the program: its long-term, four-to-five-year commitment to its students; the Presbytery's involvement; and the alliance with UCSD's Academic Connections. He liked its broad base of financial support and its use of volunteers to engage people in the community and make every dollar go further. He called Reality Changers a coral reef, a complex ecosystem.

For Reality Changers, the Wellness Foundation grant was a game changer. Yanov had carried the program on his shoulders for seven years: recruited students, supported and counseled them, run the weekly meetings, recruited volunteers, raised money, met with parents. Reality Changers' phone number was his home number; and more late nights than he could remember, he'd picked up the phone or answered a knock on his apartment door to find a student with a problem. The rent past due. An older brother arrested. The family's only car repossessed. He'd made Reality Changers his full-time, seven-days-a-week job.

The grant enabled him to hire staff and grow the program to one hundred students. Grace and Jenn had both tutored for Reality Changers, and the previous year they had worked as interns, learning every aspect of the program. They were smart and energetic and full of ideas, and they connected well with students. When they came on as salaried staff in July, he drew up an organizational table that assigned major responsibilities to each of them. Grace would be in charge of running the program and improving it. Jenn was tasked with building a core of 125 volunteer tutors, writing an operations manual, and planning for future growth. There were always more needs than he could meet, more to do than he could do, even in a seven-day work week. He was eager to hand off assignments to them so he could put his energies into what did best and loved most: fundraising and working with the orneriest, hardest-to-engage students.

Yanov believed that having Grace and Jenn aboard would make things easier for him, and he wanted to help them do their best work. Two months into the school year, things weren't panning out the way he'd intended. Grace and Jenn were a tight team. Working in their shared space, they each kept up with what the other was doing, talked over their ideas, cheered their successes, and supported each other when things didn't go well. They wanted this same kind of close connection with Yanov as well: they'd hoped that he would provide mentoring and support as they learned their jobs, would try out his ideas on them, and would ask for their input and keep them informed about plans and changes.

Yanov had never supervised anyone, never helped an employee learn a new job. He'd invented his own job as he'd grown Reality Changers. Training people didn't interest him. He and Grace and Jen all had too much to do; talking every day about what was going on felt like a waste of their scarcest resource, their time. He couldn't see that talking with Grace and Jenn, helping them learn their jobs, was an essential investment, one that would enrich the program and help them become the self-sufficient employees he wanted.

Later, he would frame his lapses as arising from his inexperience in allocating resources. When he was the sole staff, all the decisions about where to put efforts and money were his. Now his new employees wanted a say, not just about what he gave to them but also about the whole program. They always had questions about why he did what he did. They brought up things he hadn't thought about, especially about how Reality Changers worked for girls. When the new yearbook came out, they asked him: Why weren't any of the girls' stories featured in it? Or in the mailers? Then there was the new logo, the graduate with the diploma: girls made up fully half the program, so why did the logo on all the program materials show only a boy? When he went to talk with funders, he often took a boy; why didn't he take a girl too?

He explained that the most dramatic transformations—students walking away from drugs and gangs, raising their grade point averages from zero point something to 3.5—were what sold the program to donors. The program was full of boys with stories like this. The girls' transformations were equally impressive, but the challenges they faced were different. For girls, the major threat to their college hopes was getting pregnant, and joining Reality Changers nearly guaranteed that they would not. As of 2014, Reality Changers had served more than twelve hundred students, and only six, three boys and three girls, had been involved in a pregnancy. A pregnancy rate of 0.5 percent is an impressive achievement, and the year that Grace and Jenn were prodding him it was even lower; but he told them he felt he couldn't introduce a girl to donors by praising her for not getting pregnant.

Jenn and Grace sniffed. The girls earned more scholarships. Why did he spend so much time with the baddest boys and so little with the students who were doing what was expected of them?

That question again. Where to put scarce resources.

Their questions made him want to talk less, not more. Sometimes it was easier not to deal them in. He'd asked Grace to be Reality Changers' liaison with Academic Connections at UCSD, but when he got an email about a meeting with the Academic Connections staff, he went by himself without telling her. She was hurt and furious; she felt unvalued and undermined. He was baffled that a little detail like this would matter so much. His view was simple and myopic: "If I see something that needs to be done and I can do it, I go ahead and do it."

He didn't get that they needed him to recognize their good work. Jenn designed a workshop—to teach tutoring skills and provide guidelines for relating to students—for the new tutors she was bringing on. The workshop would help them be more effective and more likely to stay with the program, she explained to Yanov. He didn't praise her for her initiative, didn't ask her how the workshop went or whether it made a difference in tutors' effectiveness. She hoped for mentoring; she felt she got indifference.

The more disappointed and unhappy Grace and Jenn grew, the less he talked to them. The less he talked to them, the more disappointed and unhappy they grew. All three shared a deep commitment to the program; all three had good intentions. The less they talked, the more the gap between them widened, and the easier it was to see less-than-noble motives in the others' actions. Grace and Jenn saw Yanov as controlling, unwilling to relinquish any authority in the program he'd built. He saw them as unreasonable, critical, and demanding. Staff meetings—they insisted on staff meetings!—deteriorated into their angry interrogations and his angry protestations. He didn't know that staff meetings work better when the leader sets an agenda and a time limit.

Later he said, "I'd never worked for anybody, and I had no idea how to implement a support system for myself or for them. I knew I needed training in management. But compared to the daily student crises I was trying to solve that year, learning to be a better manager was a lower priority."

Daily he bumped into a fact of life for organizations: as a program grows in size and complexity, the old ways of operating no longer work so well, and the organization and its people must develop new ways. The move to the City Heights space, the Wellness Foundation grant, and scaling up to one hundred students all happened within six months. Ready or not, these changes propelled Reality Changers into a new developmental phase, with new needs. To serve one hundred students, the program needed a leader who could delegate and step back, welcome his staff's ideas, and build a supportive culture. That set of tasks was significantly different from what Yanov had undertaken as he built the program. Much of that year, he didn't understand what he needed to do; and when he did know, he didn't want to do it.

He worked late most nights. On meeting nights, once the meeting finished, he drove students home. It was after ten o'clock when he let himself into his apartment, and then he was restless. He watched TV until midnight but couldn't settle himself. He went to bed and lay in the dark, unable to sleep for hours. He played the day back and thought about everything that didn't work at the new building. He blamed his misery on the space: even though he had access to common areas and offices where the tutoring groups could meet, it was shared space, not his space. At the iglesia the couches were shabby and stained, but the kids had piled onto them and felt at home. In the big meeting room here, the chairs were straight-backed, hard plastic. Building management wouldn't let him hang program photos in there—the pictures of graduates with scholarship checks, of kids doing community service—and the citation from the U.S. Congress, all stuff that reminded students that they were part of something important. How would they know what they could do if they didn't see those reminders?

He wanted Reality Changers to have a building of its own. At the iglesia he'd been the Anglo son embraced by the Mexican American family, and the founder of Reality Changers; but the building wasn't his, and ultimately he couldn't ensure the program's future there. At the Workforce Partnership Building he was nobody special, just another tenant with a list of needs and complaints. A building that belonged to Reality Changers would fix so much of what was wrong. No more problems with building management, no more accommodating other people's agendas. It might even soothe the pain of losing the community at the iglesia that he had called his spiritual home for twelve years, and the pain of the relationships he left behind. He spent hours walking and driving around Golden Hill and City Heights, looking at buildings. Nothing affordable looked good; nothing that looked good was affordable. He was walking after midnight, searching for what he'd lost.

He'd always invited guests to Reality Changers. Speakers for the lesson, private philanthropists, foundation executives, and groups from corporations and churches and the Lions and Optimists and Rotary came to the iglesia to watch the program in action. "It's how we get our support," he said. "Bring in visitors every week, show them the program; then I talk with them about what we're trying to accomplish." Grants and donations flowed from these visits.

This fall he wasn't inviting speakers or donors. He didn't know when the building management would schedule something else for the community room and he'd have to crowd the meeting into the much smaller break room. If he invited visitors, what could he show them?

In fact there was plenty to show. Students were working as hard as they had every previous year, their ambitions were as lofty and their prospects as good, their stories as inspiring and as wrenching. Yanov had a corner office, Jenn and Grace had large open cubicles and their own computers and plenty of work space. Grace and Jenn were fine-tuning every piece of the program, and although he didn't say it to them, their work was making things run more smoothly.

Up on the roof the heat was rising. No reporters had shown up. Not a TV truck, not even a microphone.

Yanov didn't like where the banner was hung. "Take it off the wall."

"Grace said to put it there," Robert said.

Yanov gestured to the podium. "That's where I'll be standing. I want you guys next to me, holding it up."

They shrugged and started unclipping the banner.

He'd called the press conference for four o'clock so students could get there after school. A crowd of students in Reality Changers' cobalt blue T-shirts made a great visual for TV. By four thirty, Grace and two tutors and one more student were there. No reporters, no microphones, no TV cameras. The four students held the banner and squinted into the afternoon sun. Yanov walked to the podium and, flanked by Julio Marcial and the students holding the banner, launched into his Reality Changers stump speech for the benefit of his audience of nine. He delivered his challenge ("It isn't right that most Reality Changers students know more people who've been shot on the street than are on the road to college") as though he were talking to a packed auditorium and a full press gallery. He finished his speech, accepted a blowup of the check from Marcial, and everyone clapped.

"My idea of a good day is giving two fund-raising talks to big givers, then working at night with the roughest, hardest-to-tame guys in the program," he told Marcial as they walked back to the building. "I'm comfortable in a suit and tie and in jeans and a sweatshirt. Nothing in between."

This year Reality Changers needed a lot of in-between. Looking back on the year, Yanov would say, "We were a great small organization. [We moved to City Heights,] and that year we were a poor large one."

Yanov was also facing another kind of challenge. He turned thirty this year, and parts of his life he hadn't paid attention to were catching up with him. For seven years Reality Changers had filled his days and nights, and he fed it his weekends as well. It repaid him with a deep sense of purpose and the knowledge that he was making a vital difference in students' lives. Students craved the sunshine of his approval and offered him their idealization. Volunteers and interns looked to him as mentor and model. Parents heaped their gratitude on him. Donors admired him for the difficult work he did and the hope he brought to students and to them as well. The work demanded so much and gave him so much that it was easy to pay less attention to other aspects of his life, especially to relationships.

His girlfriend of several years had broken up with him; the amount of time he spent with Reality Changers was an issue. He played on a softball team, but after games he wouldn't join his teammates for a beer, because he didn't drink and he felt that hanging out at a bar was a waste of time. He said, "I don't like being in a situation where I don't have a role. Without a defined role, I struggle."

At Reality Changers he wore his roles gracefully: skillful host, connecting easily with everyone from barrio kids to city council members and CEOs; founder and chief visionary growing the program; articulate, persuasive fund-raiser. Away from work, away from the roles he'd created for himself, he didn't know what to do with himself.

When Reality Changers left the iglesia, Yanov also moved it out of his apartment. The two four-drawer file cabinets in his apartment that held all the program's files went to the City Heights space. The place where they had stood was empty, the carpet still flattened. Those file cabinets had guaranteed that he never had to think about how to fill his time; there was always something that needed doing. Now when he came home at night, the flattened carpet reminded him of how large a portion of his life was Reality Changers. How little else there was. He'd stopped giving students his home phone number and gave them the office number instead. "I used to get twenty to thirty voicemails a day at home," he said. "Now I get maybe one."

After the press conference he rode the elevator back to the third floor. Directly across from the elevators, Jenn was setting up the table where students signed in and picked up their name tags. Yanov scowled. "What's this doing here?"

"Remember, in staff meeting I said it would work better having it right where they get off the elevator, instead of down the hall?"

"It's not gonna work here. It's too close to the elevator."

"We need to try it, Chris. See how it works."

"Move it back." He turned and stalked down the hall.

10 Undocumented

History says, Don't hope
On this side of the grave,
But then, once in a lifetime
The longed-for tidal wave
Of justice can rise up
And hope and history rhyme.

Seamus Heaney, *The Cure at Troy: A Version of Sophocles'*
Philoctetes

The San Diego Junior Lifeguards' bus rolled north out of San Diego on I-5. The Guard's top swimmers were heading for the Junior Lifeguard Nationals in Huntington Beach, near Los Angeles. Swimming and lifesaving are serious business in Southern California, and Junior Guards are a summer institution in every beach city. Lots of kids join, but the ones who stay on through high school are the competitive swimmers and runners. Daniel started in Junior Guards in middle school. Now he taught lifesaving skills in the program and mentored the younger kids.

Daniel sat with Ed, his partner in the rescue relay, a race in which one partner grabs a lifesaving buoy and fins from the sand, sprints into the surf and swims 250 meters to rescue a swimmer, brings him to shore, and hands off fins and buoy to his partner, who does the same. Daniel and Ed had trained together all summer, swimming, rowing, running wind sprints on the beach, and weight training. They'd improved their endurance and lowered their times. They were excited and they were ready. Ed talked about which ones would be the teams to beat and made extravagant predictions about their performance. While Ed chattered, Daniel sat glum and silent.

"Border Patrol checkpoint up ahead," Coach McAllester called back. "Hope it doesn't take too long."

Daniel clutched his elbows.

Eighty miles from the Mexican border, the San Clemente Station of the U.S. Border Patrol squats on northbound I-5 in Orange County. A framework like a bridge superstructure, hung with overhead signs and floodlights, straddles the road. Six lanes of traffic slow to a crawl as *la migra*, Border Patrol agents, stand in every lane, studying the cars that roll past them, peering in the windows, looking for drugs and illegals. If they don't like what they see, they jerk a thumb, signaling the driver of the car or bus to pull over. They could make everybody get out. Open the luggage bay. Go through everybody's bags. Demand IDs. Daniel knew about people pulled out, put in handcuffs, and bused to the border.

They could spot him right away. His dark face. His only ID a Mexican consulate card. Pull him out in front of his teammates. Put him on the detainee bus. No Junior Nationals. No senior year. No college.

Coach McAllester didn't know Daniel was undocumented. Nobody at Junior Guards knew. He was one of their strongest swimmers, and the program director liked him a lot. He'd already told Daniel that when he graduated from high school he would recommend him for the San Diego Lifeguard Academy. That meant a guaranteed job with good pay every summer. Daniel didn't tell him that he couldn't take the job. Wouldn't even apply. He didn't have a Social Security number.

In grade school and middle school, he didn't think much about being undocumented. Now he thought about it all the time. He couldn't get a driver's license. He'd be eighteen in a month and he wouldn't be able to vote. He'd never held any kind of regular job, because he didn't have a Social Security number. Never been on a plane; they checked IDs. He and his family hardly ever traveled out of San Diego. The checkpoints.

He'd start his senior year this fall. Next June he'd graduate from high school and, with any luck, go to college. He wanted to go to the Naval Academy. No chance. Citizens only. His life should be opening up. He could already feel his future closing down.

He felt like an American. He'd never been back to Mexico since he came to the United States at eight. He loved this country. He wanted to live here and work here the rest of his life.

He hated the lies and evasions. Friends asked why he didn't have a driver's license. Why he didn't get a summer job. How come he didn't want to go to UC. He watched every word he said. One slip could bring the *migra* to their front door and put him and his sister and their parents on a bus back to Veracruz.

Alejandro Ortiz, one of Reality Changers' first students, was undocumented. He graduated from Yale the previous year with a double major in political science and biochemistry. Now he was back home, living with his parents. He couldn't get a real job. He was like a leopard in a cage. "I'm an Ivy League graduate," he'd told Daniel. "I watched my classmates go for great jobs in New York, and I'm living in my old bedroom. I have to ask my dad for money for a haircut."

Alejandro was applying to graduate school in biomedical engineering. School was the one thing you could do if you were undocumented. If you could find a scholarship. What would Alejandro do when he couldn't go to school anymore?

What would he do?

A few miles from the San Clemente checkpoint stands the University of California at Irvine, where sociologist Roberto Gonzales interviewed undocumented youth and wrote about their plight. His recent book, *Lives in Limbo*, is a searching and authoritative picture of the 2.1 million undocumented young people, whom he calls "the most disenfranchised group in America."[1] They came to the United States as babies and small children, they've grown up here, and they feel themselves to be Americans. Yet if they don't have a parent or an adult sibling who's a citizen, they have no chance of becoming citizens in the only country they know as home.

When they're in grade school and middle school, most undocumented students who know about their status do as Daniel did: they just ignore it. Some don't know they're undocumented; parents don't always tell their children. Public school offers a protective canopy, a space where they are included and can share with their native-born classmates the sense of rightful belonging. School systems follow *Plyler v. Doe*, the 1982 Supreme Court decision that held that all children, no matter their immigration status, are entitled to a free public education. Schools don't ask about citizenship status, and if they know a student is undocumented, they don't tell. Throughout high school, undocumented students study and learn and dream futures for themselves along with everyone else.

Plyler v. Doe arose from the Texas legislature's decision in the late 1970s that it would no longer reimburse school districts for the cost of educating children who were not legal residents. The state's school districts could either refuse to enroll undocumented children, or they could offer them a place in the classroom and charge their parents tuition. Several challenges to the law were consolidated as *Plyler v. Doe,* and the case was heard in the U.S. District Court in Houston. The judge ruled that a free public education was a right of all state residents. The state of Texas appealed to the Supreme Court. In 1982, in a five-to-four decision, the U.S. Supreme Court held that all children in the United States, no matter their immigration status, are guaranteed the right to a free public education. In the majority opinion, Justice William Brennan wrote,

> Public education has a pivotal role in maintaining the fabric of our society and in sustaining our political and cultural heritage; the deprivation of education takes an inestimable toll on the social, economic, intellectual and psychological well-being, and poses an obstacle to individual achievement.
>
> It is difficult to understand precisely what the state hopes to achieve by promoting the creation and perpetuation of a subclass of illiterates within our boundaries, surely adding to the problems and costs of unemployment, welfare, and crime. It is thus clear that whatever savings might be achieved by denying these children an education, they are wholly insubstantial in light of the costs involved to these children, the state, and the nation.[2]

A big green highway sign read: "Customs and Border Patrol 2 miles. Prepare to slow down." Daniel sunk his head between his knees. He should never have agreed to come. He should have begged off. He didn't want to beg off. He wanted to go to the Nationals. Today it could all end.

Traffic was backing up. The bus slowed to a crawl and joined a bolus of cars that crept toward the checkpoint. The checkpoint offices were a cluster of one-story cinderblock buildings painted the color of sand. A parking lot close to the road was filled with Border Patrol vehicles: officers in olive-green uniforms and black lace-up boots lounged against an SUV, smoking. Under the superstructure, officers stood in the glaring sunlight. Daniel's heart pounded. His skin was clammy. He was going to throw up.

The officers were young guys in mirrored sunglasses and baseball caps that said "U.S. Border Patrol." Some of them were Latino. The Junior Lifeguards' bus pulled even with the guy in their lane. He looked hot and bored. He wasn't stopping cars. Not even looking. Just waving everyone through. Daniel slumped in his seat and stared at the floor. He wanted to get a closer look at the Border Patrol guy but he didn't dare.

The driver downshifted and pushed the bus back up to speed. Daniel lay against the seat, limp. In this traffic, they had another hour to get to Huntington Beach. He'd need every minute to pull himself together.

Life has become a little easier for undocumented youth since Daniel sweated through the San Clemente checkpoint. In 2012, President Obama's executive order created the Deferred Action for Childhood Arrivals program, which enables undocumented youth thirty-one years or younger, who were brought by their parents to the United States as children, to register with the U.S. Citizenship and Immigration Services. Registration confers legal status for two years, permitting the person to be in the country and to obtain authorization to work. It has provided many immigrant children—including many Reality Changers students—with valuable breathing room. But before this federal program was implemented, Daniel's experience was typical for undocumented youth.

They were safe at school; but as they approached the ordinary milestones of adolescence, they learned, painfully, that the game wasn't the same for them. When they and their friends turned sixteen, their friends got driver's licenses; but undocumented students didn't, because they couldn't show proof of legal residence. Their ID was a Mexican consulate card, which was good for getting into an R-rated movie when they were seventeen, but it wouldn't help them get across the border. When their friends drove down to Tijuana to party, they didn't go, because without a visa or a green card they might not be allowed back into the United States. They couldn't get a job, part time or full time, because they didn't have a Social Security number.

Sixty-five thousand undocumented youth graduate from high school each year, and before the Deferred Action for Childhood Arrivals program their futures fell off a cliff. They could not legally drive, vote, work, or serve in the military. Alabama and South Carolina explicitly prohibited their enrolling at any public postsecondary educational institution. Thirty-three states still charge them out-of-state tuition, creating a financial barrier almost as high as an outright prohibition. Fourteen states, including California, now allow them, if they meet residency requirements, to claim in-state tuition and receive state scholarship funds. When Daniel and his peers at Reality Changers were applying to college, no matter how distinguished a student's high school achievement, no matter how bright her academic promise, if she was undocumented no state would grant her state-funded scholarship aid. Lacking access to low-cost higher education, fewer than 5 percent of undocumented students went on to college. The rest ended up in low-paying jobs in the underground economy. In time they married and started families. They constituted a pool of talent, ability, and love for their adopted country that federal immigration policy elected to waste.

A year after Jonny Villafuerte threw rocks at the iglesia windows, he joined Reality Changers. When Daniel was a senior in high school, Jonny was a senior at Point Loma Nazarene University in San Diego, majoring in psychology. As a volunteer at Reality Changers now, Jonny was dean of students, charged with motivating and supporting the most ambivalent kids. Chris and the program had changed his life.

He would graduate in May. He wanted to become a high school counselor and help kids like himself. Jonny Villafuerte was exactly what every urban school system was looking for: a fluently bilingual young man with the street cred and work experience to work effectively with Hispanic students. San Diego State had a good master's program in school counseling. He'd heard that it was a lot of work—but he could handle that. The part he couldn't handle was paying for it; he wasn't eligible for any federal or state financial aid. Even if he could pay for school, he'd never get hired, because he didn't have a Social Security number.

He'd lived in San Diego since he was three and he thought of himself as American, but he was born in Tijuana and his parents crossed to the United States without papers. If he were a citizen he'd be writing his grad school application right now. Without it, who was he kidding? This time next year he'd probably be peeling avocados in some restaurant kitchen.

His girlfriend, Anna, was a citizen; and she'd offered to marry him. If they got married, he'd have a good shot at a green card. He desperately wanted that card, and to become a citizen, but not that way. Marriage was sacred; it wasn't something you played around with.

He didn't like to think about his future; there was too much he couldn't control. When people asked what he would do, he shrugged and said that his faith was strong. God had showed him the way this far; he would see what God had planned for him. When he said those things he sounded passive, as though he didn't care what happened. He cared intensely. He thought about it every day. Being undocumented was the central fact of his life; it controlled everything else. But he couldn't change the facts, and sometimes it was easier to leave it to God than to think about how powerless he was.

Conversations with the undocumented students always ended up at this place. Karina would talk only so much about what she wanted to do after college. Then she dropped her eyes, her voice barely audible. "You're just living this normal life, and you don't realize; and then you do, and you see that you're not like everyone else."

She spoke of her mother, who believes that God is watching over them, and that whatever happens is his will. Her mother would say, "We've waited so long. We can just keep waiting."

Daniel said that being undocumented affects everything in his life. "I'd really like to have a girlfriend, but then I think: How can I burden her with my situation?" He said, "If I became the same as everybody else, I'd be inspired to look into things I've always wanted to do." For a moment his face lit up. "I could be a city lifeguard in the summer. I'd apply to the Naval Academy. I really want to travel. I'd study abroad. I'd have a girlfriend."

The costs of being undocumented have been enormous for these young immigrants, in expectations lowered, hopes dimmed, and aspirations squelched by their situation and by a self-imposed, self-protective passivity. Growing up knowing that they could be summarily removed from the country, losing friends, severing family ties, undoing all that they've accomplished, creates what anthropologist Nicolas De Genova has called "an enforced orientation to the present."[3]

The Deferred Action for Childhood Arrivals program has meant that Daniel and Karina and Jonny no longer live in fear of deportation and can work legally, but it has not changed a central fact of their lives and those of all undocumented immigrants: the pervasive awareness that all they have is temporary, conditional.

In *Lives in Limbo,* Gonzales amplifies this idea: "The possibility of apprehension and deportation creates uncertainty that leads many undocumented individuals to understand their own futures as revocable. They learn to live with the knowledge that all they have can be taken away in an instant. This enforced orientation to the present inhibits many undocumented immigrants from committing to long-term plans because they experience their assets—including jobs, friends, and material possessions—as temporary. Each event that forces them to confront their legal limitations and each threat of apprehension and deportation reminds them of the stark reality that at any moment, their lives could change."[4]

Gonzales presents a compelling economic argument for a path to citizenship. If they could come out of the shadows, many undocumented youth would serve in the military; even more would seek scholarships and pursue higher education. As legal residents and ultimately citizens, they would earn more money, pay more taxes, purchase more goods, and contribute more to their communities. A 1999 Rand study found that educating immigrants to their full potential would cost state governments more per immigrant for about five years after high school. After that, the states' investment would pay off in a lifetime of substantial increases in taxes paid on higher earnings, along with significantly lower expenditures on public health and social services.[5]

Every year, beginning in 2001, Senator Richard Durbin of Illinois had introduced the Development, Relief, and Education for Alien Minors, or DREAM Act, which would create a path to permanent resident status for undocumented minors graduating from high school. If they demonstrated good moral character—that is, no felony arrests—and served honorably in the military or graduated from a two-year or four-year college, the DREAM Act would allow them to apply for permanent resident status (the coveted green card) and then work toward full citizenship.

The DREAM Act could have opened doors for Alejandro and Jonny, Karina and Daniel, doors they already saw closing. Eight years in a row it had died on the Senate floor. Now, in 2008, Barack Obama was running for president, and he'd vowed to sign the DREAM Act into law. They couldn't vote for the man they believed could save them. They could only watch and hope and stay out of the way of the *migra*.

Daniel and Karina would write their college essays this year. Yanov kept telling them that a strong essay would build the foundation for their future. They would write their best, but they knew that until the DREAM Act was law, they were building their futures on sand.

11 Three-Day

I didn't know San Diego was so beautiful.

Robert Silva

Robert shivered in his hoodie. He wished he'd brought his winter jacket. It was an hour before sunrise, and the sky was the dull aluminum color of the pot that his mother used for cooking beans. Hector, Grace's husband, maneuvered the car in the long line on Jimmy Durante Boulevard that was backed up half a mile from the Del Mar Fairgrounds north of San Diego. They had plenty of time to get into the fairgrounds; the opening ceremony didn't start until six thirty. The wait was making Robert crazy; he wanted to jump out of the car and run past all the cars and up to the check-in table. It was the Friday before Thanksgiving, the day he'd been working toward since July. Back then, when he heard the radio spot about the Susan G. Komen Three-Day, he felt like the speaker was talking just to him. Sixty miles in three days, right here in San Diego, a huge fund-raiser for breast cancer research.

Streaks of orange and pink unfurled across the sky by the time Hector let Robert and Grace off at the gate; they made their way to registration and then to the stadium, where the ceremony would be. They walked into a sea of pink hats, pink scarves, pink boas, pink T-shirts, pink pants— more than four thousand walkers laughing, drinking coffee, talking, the PA system pumping "Staying Alive" and "I Will Survive." People carried poles with tall pink banners announcing whom they were walking for: "Wife," "Mother," "Sister," "Daughter," "Friend." Speakers from the Susan Komen organization and breast cancer survivors congratulated them for their commitment and told them that today they were not just marchers but a community; today they started an amazing journey. Strangers danced together and hugged and cried. Four thousand walkers coalesced into a weaving column six across that coiled around the infield, streamed out of the fairgrounds, and turned south onto the Pacific Coast Highway. People introduced themselves to the walkers around them and asked, Who are you walking for? Grace had made pink satin sashes for herself and Robert that said "Angel Walkers." Robert told everyone who asked about his mother and baby Angel. Grace had lived through the story with him since February, and still, every time he told it her tears came.

He was a junior then, the first year he'd really worked at school. By February he'd begun to believe that he really could go to college. Then his mother was diagnosed with stage 4 breast cancer, and her doctor said that even with treatment her chances of living a year were 30 percent.

"I wanted to be there for him," Grace said. "I was so worried that his mother wouldn't make it, and he needed to have someone there for him. I decided that I'd step in whenever I had to, to keep him on course. He'd come so far. He couldn't lose it now."

Even after his father threw him out of the house and he started his senior year while living in a garage, he kept his focus. Taking care of Angel and his mother mattered more than anything.

He brought Grace two registration forms for the walk. Registration was $90 for each of them. They sat on her desk at home for a week. When she sat down to do the bills, there they were, the pink band across the top. She went through the bills and added up what she and Hector owed this month. Nothing to spare. She breathed out a long breath, then picked up a pen and wrote a check for $180.

The Three-Day kept Robert going through the fall. The days he felt like he couldn't walk uphill one more time, when dinner was tortillas and a single slice of baloney, when he missed his mom and Angel so much he cried in his bed, he focused on the walk. He used to be so closed. Now he wore his pink ribbon pin all the time, and he'd explain to everyone he met why he was wearing it. Every day at school he talked to kids and teachers about what had happened to his mother and why he was doing the Three-Day in November.

Every walker needed to raise twenty-two hundred dollars in pledges. Robert couldn't imagine raising that much money, but he'd never had a goal that mattered so much. At school he started a Key Club, the high school service club sponsored by Kiwanis. He was founder, president, and chief visionary, and he persuaded the club to do Coins for Cancer, a service project to raise contributions for his walk. Members glued pink crepe paper onto milk cartons, and every week, every day, Monday through Friday, he led club members wearing pink ribbon pins and carrying the cartons into the lunchroom to ask students for change. Mostly they got pennies and nickels. By the week of the walk, they'd collected more than seven hundred dollars.

Grace told her family that for her birthday and early Christmas presents, all she wanted was pledges for the Three-Day. She gave a Halloween party and asked all of her guests for contributions. When she and Robert checked in at the fairgrounds, they had their forty-four hundred dollars in pledges.

A few weeks before the walk, his Uncle Santiago lost his job and there was even less to eat. Robert heard a knock at the door. His grandmother opened the door, then closed it. She jerked her head toward the door. "Tu padre."

Robert walked outside. He leaned against the garage, arms folded across his chest.

"Hello, Robert," his father said. "You look thin."

Coming here, he knew, wasn't easy for his father. Too bad. He wasn't going to be the bigger man today. This time it was his father's job.

"I'm not eating much, and I'm walking four miles a day."

"Your mom wants you back. Your sister and brother want you back."

Robert looked down at his shoes. If he looked at his father, he'd cry.

"Ball's in your court, Robert. You can come home if you want to."

He came home for his mother. The kitchen was a mess, and the vacuum was broken. He fixed the vacuum, washed the cars, and cleaned the kitchen. He jumped all over Marlon. He'd joined Reality Changers only because Robert told him he had to, and with Robert not at home Marlon screwed off. Some weeks he didn't go, and when he went he fooled around and made trouble with a couple of other freshman dudes. Marlon went to Lincoln High, and now that Robert was back they walked to school together in the morning. As soon as he was out of his brother's sight, Marlon would ditch. When Robert found out, he was furious. How could Marlon be as dumb as he'd been?

The walkers wound south through Del Mar, a glossy beach town that rises gently from sea level at the fairgrounds to fifty-foot sandstone cliffs that overlook the ocean. The sun peeked out from thick gray clouds. The walkers talked and sang and wondered when they'd get to Crown Point, the spit of land on Mission Bay, twenty miles away, where they'd camp for the night.

Below Del Mar the coast road dropped and the view opened up. Below them lay Torrey Pines State Beach, where waves rolled onto the beach in wide, shallow crescents, foam scalloping their edges like extravagant lace. The sky was pale, the ocean a deeper blue, and they met at the horizon in a vapory blur. The road ran for a mile between the beach and a lagoon where snowy egrets paused in their fishing and stood one-legged, watching the procession. At the far end of the beach the road started uphill again, a steep, long climb. The line thinned out, the slower walkers lagging. Grace's legs hurt. She and Hector had walked a lot in the last two months to help her get in shape, but it wasn't enough; this morning she felt as though she had sandbags tied to her ankles. Lots of walkers passed her. It was only ten o'clock on the first day, and here she was, sagging.

Robert walked backward uphill in front of her. "Grace," he exhorted, "come on!" He sprinted up the hill, then back to her. He moonwalked in front of her, laughing and cajoling. He plucked her backpack off her shoulders and draped it on top of his. He ran uphill with two backpacks, carrying the "Mother" banner. For three years Grace had been his tutor and mentor, telling him he could do it, helping him believe. This weekend, his job was to help Grace do the walk. He'd carry her the twenty miles each day if he had to. His other job was to keep talking to people. Every time he talked with someone, he felt like he was helping his mom and Angel.

They followed the Coast Highway up onto the mesa, past UC San Diego's campus and downhill into La Jolla on streets that wound along the shoreline. Waves crashed against the rocks just below them, and sea lions basked on a crescent of beach. The clouds drifted away, and the sun on the water made it the color of turquoise. Robert turned to Grace and said, "I didn't know San Diego was so beautiful." He'd lived all his life in San Diego, and he'd hardly seen its coastline. He'd never walked its downtown or hung out in Balboa Park, the city's iconic park that is home to its museums and the zoo and the great plantings of palms.

The sun had set and it was dark and cold by the time they made it to the field of hot pink tents at Crown Point. Grace was ready to collapse in the tent, but Robert insisted she get up and come with him to dinner. He talked to everyone around them while they waited in line for dinner and while they ate. After she'd eaten, Grace felt better and went with him to hear more survivors speak.

Saturday, the second day, they walked south through Pacific Beach, and when they stopped for lunch, Hector and Robert's mother and Angel and Debbi Leto and twenty Reality Changers students were waiting for them. Debbi brought enough pizza for everyone. The walk back to Crown Point to spend the night didn't seem so long.

On Sunday they walked south again, into downtown San Diego. Knots of people stood on the sidewalk, family members and friends of the walkers who cheered them on. Some stores were draped in pink bunting, and signs said, "Go Walkers" and "You're amazing." Another long hill from downtown up into Balboa Park for lunch, and another rally with speakers and music.

On Sunday Robert remembered that seven days from now was the deadline for Cal State applications. Every other Reality Changers senior was at the City Heights offices pounding on his essay. Here he was, on the Three-Day, camping next to the bay and walking to Balboa Park. That was cool. He was doing things he couldn't have imagined a year ago.

He'd barely started his essays. Chris would tear them apart. Let him. He'd never get into a UC campus anyway, not with his grades. Any Cal State campus would work for him. Stuff like starting the Key Club and walking the Three-Day was what mattered to him, and where he learned the most. He said to Grace that he was better at getting experiences than getting grades.

When Grace woke up on Sunday the sandbags on her ankles weighed three times as much. She couldn't walk another twenty miles. She'd do it.

They were doing what they'd set out to do, living out Robert's dream that they'd worked on for months.

At the end of the day, on the walk back to Crown Point, they looked at each other, amazed. We did it. We really did it. Robert draped his arm over Grace's shoulder. He wished this walk would never end.

12 Essay Crunch

Achieving my goal of college is now as close as the ceiling is to my head.

Karina Vasquez

On the bus ride downtown I saw gang members on every corner, and I knew I could have been one of them, falling into drugs and violence, maybe ending up in jail. I was heading to an athletic store to buy shoes. The night before, a bunch of guys from a gang beat me up and stole my sneakers. A week earlier they'd asked me to join their gang. I wanted to focus on school and improve my grades. That decision cost me a bloody nose and my old shoes.

Fernando Carrillo sprawled in a chair at the back of the Senior Academy room while Yanov read his essay. His chin rested on his chest, and his smile sagged below a wisp of mustache. He was starting goalkeeper on his school's varsity soccer team, and in goal he was fast, aggressive, confident. Writing was a different game: it was hard labor, and the words came slowly. It was nine thirty on Saturday night, and this was his fifth rewrite. He'd been here since three in the afternoon. Seven other seniors hunched over computers. All of them had been here the day before, too. The air in the room was humid, and warmer than the hall, from the heat of so many bodies. The application deadlines for both the UC and the Cal State campuses was midnight a week from tonight, the Sunday after Thanksgiving.

A month before the application deadline, Yanov had kicked the college essay project into high gear. He opened the Senior Academy room on Saturday and Sunday afternoons and didn't shut down until the last senior was finished, sometimes well after midnight. The room became a secular chapel devoted to this ordeal of his devising. Tonight his jeans hung loose and his sweatshirt hood drooped down his back like a monk's. He hadn't shaved for three days, and he hadn't paid much attention to eating.

All fall he'd hammered away at the seniors, telling them how important their application essays were. How critical they were to admission to the schools they wanted, to launching the futures they dreamed of. How punishingly difficult it was to produce a good essay. How hard they'd have to work, how much harder it would be than anything they'd ever done. He talked of late nights and countless drafts.

The buildup was calculated. He believed that working in the company of their peers under deadline pressure loosened students up and helped them produce their best work. For the seniors, the setup was irresistible: Out late at night, working alongside their friends on a high-stakes mission, their futures in the balance. Hanging out with Yanov, who believed in them and demanded more of them than they thought they could do. It was a pain the way he kept marking up their drafts and pushing for more, but an adult who set the bar high and pushed you until you found more inside than you knew you had was potent stuff.

The improvement they saw from draft to draft helped them believe they really could do this and could get into college. Late nights and sleep deprivation weren't downsides; they were part of the attraction. It was essay as crucible. Enduring Yanov's edits and writing repeated drafts until they secured his blessing was the seniors' rite of passage.

Yanov was right about the importance of their essays. Many of the seniors' transcripts were not strong. They weren't readers. Their resumes weren't larded with internships and special courses and travel, the cultural capital that a life of privilege affords. A different set of experiences shaped the lives of Reality Changers' students. Many of them shouldered substantial responsibilities, caring for younger siblings, cooking, and managing the household while their parents worked. Most held part-time jobs. Daily they negotiated two cultures and two languages. They set higher academic and personal goals for themselves than the kids they knew, and stuck to them in the face of their peers' incomprehension and scorn. They kept their balance in the face of family members' drug use, deportations, pregnancies, and prison terms, and, always, the grinding uphill climb with too few resources.

Yanov understood that his students' life experiences were their personal capital, indicators of their grit and determination. Your stories are powerful, he told them, and they're what you have. Application essays were their chance to tell those stories and reveal their strengths and accomplishments, and they needed to tell their stories as skillfully as they could. Before they started, the seniors had no clue how hard they'd have to work to produce an essay that met Yanov's standards. Without his prodding, most would have written a draft or two and called it a day. Yanov's treating their essays so seriously got their attention. If he cared so much about their essays, they'd better care too. The weekend sessions provided the structure they needed to stay with the task, draft after draft. They understood the stakes: get into college or look at a career in fast food or lawn maintenance or telemarketing.

The Senior Academy tutors helped them with a lot of the work that applications entailed: asking for recommendations and following up to be sure they got them, looking for financial aid, meeting submission deadlines, and generally keeping the complex, unfamiliar process on track. They helped the seniors with essays on regular meeting nights, but the weekend and late-night sessions they were happy to leave to Yanov. Those sessions were his invention and his arena.

He helped students figure out what they wanted to write about. He read their drafts and pushed for specifics. What do you want your reader to see? Have you shown your reader why this matters? He gave them line edits, meticulous sentence-by-sentence reviews of word choice and punctuation, grammar and usage. He handed back papers covered with his comments in red ink, with a clear set of tasks for the next draft. For as many drafts as it took.

> On the bus ride home, a guy I'd seen in the neighborhood approached me. Instead of a threat, he had a smile, and he made me an extraordinary offer: "Would you like to join Reality Changers?"

Yanov looked up at Fernando. "You're getting there. This is better."

The first time I came, I was astounded by all the students who studied so hard. When the semester ended, I'd made a huge improvement. My GPA went from 1.5 to 3.75. I paid attention in class, asked questions, and stayed after school for tutoring.

. . . If I had joined a gang, I wouldn't be here writing this essay. I'm no longer on the verge of joining a gang, but instead I'm on the verge of going to college.

·   ·   ·   ·   ·

Barack Obama won the presidency, to very little notice among the seniors. This fall, all that mattered to them, all they could think about, was getting into college. Most were applying to the UCs and the Cal States. The UCs, the University of California campuses, are the state's major research campuses: Berkeley, San Diego, Irvine, Los Angeles, Riverside, Santa Barbara, Merced, Davis, Santa Cruz, and San Francisco. Seniors in California high schools must rank in the top 9 percent of their class to be considered for admission. The California State University campuses are the state's higher education workhorses, twenty-three campuses concentrating on undergraduate education. Seniors must be in the top third of their class to apply. Both systems use a single application for all their campuses.

Kimberly Palafox applied to St. John's University in New York, but that was a long shot. The Cal States looked more possible. She liked Cal State San Marcos, in northern San Diego County. The campus, just eighteen years old, served a large Latino student population and a lot of transfer students from community colleges. She wrote about the barriers she'd faced just to get as far as applying to college.

"Soft bigotry of low expectations" described my French 5–6 class. When my teacher was encouraging many of her students to take her Advanced Placement French class the following year, she didn't even look in my direction. A whole year in her class and she didn't think I was capable of succeeding at the next level. I was crushed. Still, I raised my hand and said I was willing to take her class next year. She gave me a strong, stern look that indicated her discomfort, suggesting that I shouldn't even try and that I was just a waste of her time. She asked me if I understood the difficulty of the class, in the most discouraging tone that I'd ever heard. Now I felt worse than invisible, feeling doubted and incapable, but I took the class to test my limits and to prove her wrong. Sure enough I surprised that teacher and the other students by earning a B in the class.

Saturday night, the weekend after Thanksgiving. Karina Vasquez finished up Chris's edits from the previous day. Everything else on her UC application was done. She needed Chris to look at it one more time and then she'd submit it.

Sometimes I ask myself why I have to share a single 10′ × 10′ bedroom with my two brothers and my parents. When I climb onto my bunk bed, mindful of the ceiling that is a mere twenty-four inches from my head, I realize that although my personal space is so small, I have had many accomplishments that can make up for the space that I lack. On the wall hangs my latest scholarship check from Reality Changers, for UC San Diego's Academic Connections. For the past three summers I have earned college credit taking Performing Identities, Dimensions of Psychology, and Photography and Ethnography.

I've placed other academic awards and family portraits around that scholarship check. The awards remind me of all the hours I've spent completing assignments and studying for those excruciating AP exams, while the portraits symbolize my strong ties with my parents, brothers, and grandparents.

Karina's family belonged to the Iglesia Presbiteriana, and when she started eighth grade, her mother asked Yanov to let her join. He said bring him her first-semester report card; she needed to show a 3.5 average to join. In January, Karina brought him a card full of A's. Her father drove her to the meeting every Tuesday, but he never asked her anything about what she did. He could have come in, but he waited outside in the car in the cold, then drove her home in silence. His aloofness hurt; he must think she wasn't good enough to go to college. On the nights of the monthly parents' meetings, he drove her mother to the iglesia. She went to the meeting, and he waited in the car. Her mother told her that on the way home he asked about everything Yanov said in the meeting. In her senior year, Karina figured out that her father was scared for her. He'd left school after the eighth grade. Going to college, especially going away from home, was so far from his experience. He couldn't protect her. Couldn't even ask her about what she was doing.

Her family had gone back to Mexico only once, in the summer of 2001, when she was ten. She met *los abuelos, los tios y las tias,* and *los primos,* the grandparents, the uncles and aunts and cousins that her parents had always talked about. They stayed with her grandmother in Durango, and at dinners on Sunday they ate *gallina borracha* and nut cakes, and she met more cousins than she knew she had. When it was time to go home, her mother cried and her father grew even quieter than usual. At the crossing in Tijuana, her parents said to act natural, just answer the *migra's* questions. The U.S. officer leaned in the truck window and asked her what her address was. Where did she go to school? She knew that saying the right thing to this man who looked like a soldier was important. She had to give the right answers or they couldn't go back to their house. Her little brother cried and wouldn't talk to the officer. He shrugged and waved them through.

After the attacks that September, the border hardened. Many more *migra,* with rifles now. More questions, and now they asked for passports. Karina's family didn't dare cross again; they might not get home. She kept in touch with her cousins, first by email, then on Facebook and via instant messaging, but it wasn't the same. Her father's mother was sick a long time, and he couldn't go to visit her. She died, and he couldn't go to her funeral.

> My strong bonds with my family will give me the strength that I will need, and my achievements in high school have helped me build a foundation for success in college. Soon I will not greet my father with a kiss at night, or help my mother fix the stove, but once I arrive to my college dorm I will have more personal space, which will allow me to expand my thoughts, amplify my goals, and develop new aspirations. Achieving my goal of college is now as close as the ceiling is to my head.

Yanov glanced over the paper. He looked up and smiled, and he jerked his thumb straight up. "Ready to go?"

She nodded.

"Want me to call it?"

She nodded again and ran back to her computer.

"Drum roll!"

Heads snapped up. Everyone looked at Chris.

"Karina's going to submit!"

Students turned toward her, cheering and waving. She clicked on the "submit" button, and they drummed their hands on their desks and stomped their feet in a thumping, accelerating tattoo that rose in volume and washed over the room, rattling the windows and booming out into the night.

·   ·   ·   ·   ·

Sunday night after Thanksgiving. The submission deadline a few hours away. The night before, the students had made a big push, six seniors working until two thirty in the morning. Yanov was sagging. Tonight just a few seniors were here, working in Jenn and Grace's area. Tonight was the cleanup: he would get them to fix the loose ends on their drafts and would make sure everyone submitted. Yanov worked in his office, and every half hour or so he picked up a red pen and walked out to see how things were going.

Robert Silva walked in, the first time he'd come since the Three-Day. "Hey, Chris, can you look at my essay?"

"What you got?"

"Third draft."

"You saw how long Fernando's been working on his. He's on his twelfth rewrite."

"When's the deadline for the Cal States?"

Yanov rolled his eyes. "Midnight tonight."

Two hours later, Robert was hunched over a borrowed laptop, sweating as he worked through Yanov's edits. Beside him, Jesse was working on an essay for Stanford, whose form he called "the longest application in the history of applications."

Fernando brought Yanov his UC essay for a final check and heard what he longed to hear. "Looks good. You're ready to go."

Fernando walked back and stood on his chair. "Okay, guys, drum roll!"

Robert and Jesse thumped their desks and stamped their feet. Fernando grinned. At ten o'clock, Robert was the last to call it a night. "That's what I got, Chris. I just want to submit it and go home."

Outside, a thick fog enfolded the buildings. Fog rolled in waves across University Avenue, muffling the freeway traffic. The street lamps cast a sepia glow in the fog, and the wide street was as empty as a time before cars. There are weathers that promote dreaming and the blooming of possibility. A first snowfall will do it, and so will fog like this. Admissions committees would make their decisions; but for tonight, Reality Changers' seniors could live in hope and possibility and the prospect of admission wherever their hearts desired.

13 Santiago Milagro and the Four-Year Plan

Just promise me this. Promise me you aren't going to change me.

Santiago Milagro

Yanov laid out the Hot Words assignment: Write a short essay, two paragraphs minimum, about who holds the power in your family. Not just who has the obvious power but who has the less obvious kind, too. Students groaned and opened their notebooks. The black rectangles of the windows reflected them hunched over their papers, bodies heavy with fatigue. Most of them had gotten up before six this morning, and it would be ten o'clock when they got home tonight. In the kitchen down the hall from where they were studying, parents were warming a huge pot of chicken with mole, the velvety dark sauce redolent of chocolate and smoked chilies, whose aroma drifted down the hall into the meeting room.

Just two paragraphs. Then they could go to dinner.

Santiago Milagro, a freshman, pulled up his hood and closed his notebook. He folded his arms across his chest, stuck out his legs and yawned, eyes shut, mouth wide open, full sound effects. Every syllable of his body language announced that he would not be doing a thing tonight, and fuck you for asking.

It was typical Santiago, stonewalling to pull Yanov to him. Yanov watched the show and, presently, walked over and stood by his chair. "What's going on, Santiago?"

"This is such a dumb assignment."

He started to elaborate, but Yanov was looking past his head toward the door, where three board members from a local foundation were walking in. He'd invited them to observe the program tonight. He motioned to Jorge, one of Reality Changers' first alumni, who was tutoring. "Jorge. Santiago needs to do his Hot Words. He's a four-year plan."

The *four-year plan* was Yanov's term for ambivalent students who might need as long as four years to commit to the program. On the way to greet his visitors he saw Carlos, who shot video for the program, and he put him on the Santiago detail too. Jorge settled into a chair on one side of Santiago, Carlos on the other. Neither one had a clue how to get him to do his assignment.

Jorge didn't get this kid. In eighth grade he'd been desperate to join Reality Changers, best thing that ever happened to him. Santiago had the opportunity handed to him, and he was pissing it away. "Put something down, Santiago. Put anything down. If you'd started writing five minutes ago you'd be done now."

Santiago slouched lower in his chair. Yanov had walked out on him. Left him with these fools. He wasn't writing anything for them. He shoved his fists into his sweatshirt pockets.

Carlos watched him and shrugged. He leaned over Santiago's head and said to Jorge, "I saw the dumbest movie last night. I don't know why I kept watching."

Jorge listened while Carlos told him the plot. Then he told Carlos about his class on immigration. "We interview people who've crossed. Today I talked to this guy who'd tried seven times before he made it. Seven times. Once he almost died of hypothermia in the back country."

Santiago looked around. Yanov was gone, the fools were talking to each other, and kids were already coming back from dinner. The rich aroma of *mole* hung in the air. If he didn't get down there soon, there'd be no food left. He opened his notebook and, in a few minutes, filled the page. He ripped it out, dropped it in Jorge's lap, and stalked out of the room.

•   •   •   •   •

This was Santiago's second year in Reality Changers. He'd joined the previous year, in the eighth grade, on the first day of school. Joining wasn't his idea. He'd slept late that morning and fooled around at home, and before he left for school he chugged two wine coolers. When he got to Wilson Middle School, he didn't feel like going to class, so he hung out in the parking lot. That's where Yanov found him. Yanov was checking attendance that day, every classroom, every period. Milagro was already marked absent for the first five periods. At the start of sixth period, Yanov smelled the miasma of alcohol before he saw Santiago slumped on a bench.

Yanov had subbed in a couple of Santiago's classes the previous year and he'd taken note of the chunky boy with hair like black steel wool who skipped so much that kids called him the Ditcher. With his perpetual scowl and a genius for provoking teachers, he was Yanov's favorite kind of challenge: could he get this guy believing he had a future before he sent himself down the tubes? He'd built Reality Changers by engaging feisty, hungry, ambivalent kids. Turning a guy like Santiago was the work that mattered most to him. It was what he knew how to do.

"Where you been, Santiago?"

"Home."

"You're supposed to be at school."

"Didn't feel like it."

"You been drinking?"

"Yeah."

"I'll make you a deal. I can walk you down to the principal's office and get you expelled on the first day of school. Or you can join my program."

Yanov preferred to recruit by praise and inspiration, by pickup games and sharing pizzas. Yet with high-risk guys like Santiago, whom he saw as his greatest prizes, he had no illusions. Without serious arm-twisting he'd never get them into the building. Once they were there, the students and the program would wrap their arms around them and hold them. But if he didn't muscle them through the door, the good stuff wouldn't have a chance to work.

Santiago had come to Reality Changers less than half the time the first year. He sank into the iglesia's sagging couches, round face peering out from his hood. He didn't unzip his hoodie and he didn't talk. Still, he showed up for school more than he had. Kids stopped calling him Ditcher. Something was working, but Yanov knew that it wouldn't be fast, and that there would be a lot of sideways and backward.

When Santiago noticed he was doing well, it rattled him, and he blew it up. He kept himself perpetually in the principal's crosshairs at Wilson, always about to be suspended.

Once the previous year during lunch at Wilson, Santiago told Yanov that he'd keep coming to Reality Changers on one condition. "Chris. Just promise me this," he'd said. "Promise me you aren't going to change me."

Yanov heard this from a lot of students. For the boys especially, committing to Reality Changers was a radical change. It meant stepping away from a persona—tough guy, contemptuous of school, breaks rules whenever he feels like it—that gave them standing with their peers. Victor Rios writes that for many poor and disadvantaged boys, this persona is a way to preserve their dignity in skirmishes with police and teachers whose message is that they are bad and will end up in juvie or prison. Boys claim the ascribed badness as theirs and become what their accusers predicted. The costs to them are enormous, in punishments and lost opportunities, but the boys reckon the gains in dignity and a sense of control as worth it.[1] At Reality Changers no one insulted them or predicted bad outcomes; here their bad-boy identities just got in their way. The shift in message and atmosphere was disorienting. Worse, joining Reality Changers and working hard at school could cost them friendships, even get them beaten up. They needed months, and some of them needed years, to move away from that persona.

There were other complications. Aiming for college could put them at odds with their parents' expectations that, after high school, they would go to work and contribute to the family. Initiatives that are the norm for many students—volunteering for projects, seeking out a teacher for help— some parents saw as presumptuous. At home their children were expected to be quiet, self-effacing, and deferential to adults. Looking directly at an adult, offering a hand to shake, or introducing yourself would be rude.

Reality Changers didn't try to change students, Yanov told him, but it did ask them to dig deeper into themselves. He hoped Santiago could hold on to that.

Before the end of eighth grade, Santiago's mother pulled him out of school and took him and his little sister back to Mexico, to the tiny village of Rincón de Tlapita, where she grew up, where half the people were his relatives and everybody knew him. At the end of the summer his mother and sister stayed in Rincón. Santiago made the two-day bus trip back to San Diego alone, and he now lived with his aunt, his mother's sister, and her husband. His aunt and uncle fed him and gave him a place to live, but they both worked two jobs, and they didn't notice much of what he did. He was lonely, and he longed for his mother and sister and "mi pueblo." He was all of fourteen.

With considerable urging from Yanov, he found his way back to Reality Changers. He was a freshman at Patrick Henry High School now, and he'd grown six inches over the summer. He cultivated a scraggly mustache and bristly sideburns that crawled down his cheeks all the way to his jawline. He went to school most days, and he worked on his assignments. First grading period he made two A's and four F's. He told Yanov he was going to bring all his grades up to A's. Yanov's goal for the year was simply to keep him coming to meetings. Any Tuesday night that he didn't walk out, Yanov counted as a success. Enough of those nights might stack up into something Santiago could claim as his own, something he could build on. He was in the same study group as Marlon Silva, and every week the two of them found a way to disrupt the group.

Trying to connect with him was like hugging a cholla cactus. Jonny, the dean of students, had the softest, least threatening style of any adult in the program. Santiago dismissed him as a wuss. Bob, the lead tutor for his tutoring group, was a retired teacher and a seasoned tutor who managed his students with a mix of firmness and encouragement. Santiago treated him with frozen contempt. Around girls and women he was wooden. He wouldn't talk at all to Grace or Jenn or any of the female tutors. Wouldn't even look at them. Yanov was the only person he talked to.

He'd lost everyone who mattered—his father so long ago he could barely remember him. Now his mother and his sister. He hadn't heard from them, not a letter or a phone call since he'd come back to *el norte*. Getting close to anybody at Reality Changers besides Chris was too hard; he couldn't bear the longing, couldn't risk another loss.

Every Saturday morning he called Yanov. A lot of the younger boys did. Yanov would pick them up in his truck and shoot baskets or go for a run, then go get a pizza. It was a lot of time to put in with the kids, he said, but that was where the relationships got solidified, the trust built. Yanov had a small house in Ensenada, in Baja California, where he went to rest and think. This year he was driving down every other weekend, and students had stopped calling. All except for Santiago. Every Saturday when Yanov was in town, the phone rang and there was Santiago's husky baritone, at once demanding and pleading. "Hey Chris. What you doing?"

.   .   .   .   .

Students filed back into the community room for the lesson, and Yanov talked about one of his favorite themes: perseverance and sticking to your goals. When the lesson was over, students headed off for Congress and study time, and Yanov sat down to talk with his visitors from the foundation.

Santiago stood by the doorway at the other end of the big room. He opened his binder and leafed noisily through the empty pages. He took off his backpack and rummaged in its contents, pulling things out until he found a pen. He held his backpack by one strap and swung it in circles.

Yanov looked up. "Santiago. You're supposed to be in your study group."

"I gotta ask you something."

"Later. I'm talking to these people."

"I gotta ask you *now*." He looked at Yanov as though he wanted to inhale him.

Yanov excused himself and walked the length of the room. "What's up?"

"I gotta know: is there a meeting next Tuesday?"

"Every Tuesday, Santiago. Every Tuesday. Come on, let's walk down to your group."

Students like Santiago were part of the balancing act that Yanov built into the program from the beginning. The four-year-plan guys were prickly, ambivalent, and painfully slow to commit. Even when they did commit, they were the hardest students to work with; they continually tested their own decision and the staff's tolerance. For Yanov, keeping a guy like Santiago—surly, brittle, easy to lose—coming to the program was at the heart of what he wanted Reality Changers to do. He was willing to put up with their provocations, to flex the rules, to do what it took to keep them coming. He was exquisitely attuned to what each of them needed. Usually it was some variant of what Santiago was pulling for tonight, a demonstration of his caring.

The staff and volunteers, and the students who played by the rules, could accommodate some of their stuff, but only so much. It was part of the daily calculus of Reality Changers, how to balance Yanov's and Grace's and Jenn's efforts between the students who were most motivated and the ones chronically at risk of leaving. The decisions hadn't been any easier before he had staff, but then he hadn't needed to justify them to anyone else. This year Jenn and Grace watched him flex the rules for Santiago and Marlon and others, and they didn't always get why he did what he did. They wanted clear rules and expectations, rewards and consequences applied evenly. Yanov was good at meeting the needs of his four-year-plan guys, and not nearly so good at helping his new staff understand why ornery, disruptive guys like Santiago should get extra helpings of his time.

He finished up with his visitors and walked them to the elevator.

Yanov and I had agreed we'd talk after his visitors left, but he never made it back to his office. I waited for a while; and when he didn't show up, I walked down the hall to look in on the Senior Academy. Just beyond the Senior Academy room, there was Santiago, sitting on the floor in the hall. He'd unzipped his hoodie and his dark head was bent over a book. He was reading out loud from *The Adventures of Huckleberry Finn.*

"The Widow Douglas she took me for her son, and allowed she would sivilize me; but it was rough living in the house all the time . . ." He stumbled over words, and he repeated sentences and exhaled with dramatic exasperation, but he kept going. Beside him on the floor, Yanov sat and listened.

14 Walking on Water

I feel like I'm swimming laps all day.

Daniel Merced

Between Christmas and New Years, the nights were cold but the days were warm and bright, T-shirt-and-shorts weather. School was out, and Reality Changers took the week off as well. Students slept late and played video games, and they hung out with their friends at malls and the movies and parties. They traveled with their families to visit relatives in LA or Anaheim or Stockton. If everyone in the family had papers, they might go to Mexico to see cousins and grandparents there.

Jesse and Kim and Karina and Daniel's winter break wasn't like that. The four of them were working on the Common App, the joint application form accepted by most private colleges. The Common App deadline was midnight on December 31. Yanov opened the office late each afternoon and stayed until the last student was finished. The night after Christmas, they were there until two in the morning. Kim and Karina pulled their shining dark hair into utilitarian ponytails, and Jesse and Daniel and Chris hadn't shaved since Christmas Day. The dark windows reflected their scruffy looks back at them, and the shadowless fluorescent light gave everyone a washed-out tan the color of cardboard.

They bunched themselves in Jenn and Grace's workspace, eating frozen Costco burritos that Yanov microwaved and brought them at their computers, so hot on the outside they burned their tongues, yet still frozen at the center. They typed and ate and dripped salsa on their jeans and their keyboards, deshabille and fatigue their badges of honor. It was a weeklong, high-level exercise in grit, and if you didn't want to be here, you wouldn't get it.

"We're nerds," Kim said with a grin.

She'd get into Cal State San Marcos for sure, but she spent her week working on the Common App because she wanted to go to college in New York. She was the oldest of four girls, and she'd grown up as an auxiliary mother, cooking and housecleaning and looking after her sisters. "If I lived in Mexico," she said, "I wouldn't even be in school. I'm a girl, and giving me an education would be wasted." Reality Changers had helped her imagine more possibilities for herself and a life beyond her family, beyond San Diego. In her essay for the Common App, she was writing about learning kickboxing.

Yanov handed back her draft, drenched in red ink. "That's a start," he told her. "Now make me feel the fatigue and pain you feel in the ring."

The stakes were especially high for Daniel and Karina, who weren't eligible for a Cal Grant or Pell Grant. Daniel had already applied to twenty schools, the maximum allowed on the Common App. This week he was writing individual applications for another fourteen colleges. It felt like swimming laps. Loyola Marymount. Churn down the lane, touch the wall. Flip turn, kick off.

St. John's. Churn, touch, flip.

Duke. Kick and turn.

Northwestern. Keep cranking.

Get into one of these places, or live at home and ride the bus to San Diego City College.

In Yanov's office, there were stacks of files on the floor, plaques that sat where he dumped them on a bookshelf when he moved in during summer. Another bookcase held group photos of kids at Academic Connections, a few books, and lots of binders. A monitor, a keyboard, and a landline phone sat on the desktop. That was all. No pictures of family or a girlfriend or a dog or a favorite place. No Post-its, no doodles or clippings. Nothing on the walls. No jacket or baseball cap forgotten on the coatrack in the corner, no takeout leftovers or spare pair of sneakers—nothing marked the space as his. His office was neat, and as impersonal as the big meeting room he complained about. After eight months, it looked as if he'd arrived yesterday and didn't plan to stay.

This year was his *annus horribilis*, the hardest since he started the program. The school year was nearly half over, and he still felt stuck. He couldn't settle into the new space. He could point to a lot of things he didn't like, but he couldn't name what bothered him. All he knew was that nothing felt right. Little things made him mad. He forgot to eat or didn't feel like eating. He'd lost weight. His clothes hung loose. He had to push himself to get through the day, then at night he couldn't sleep.

He was grieving: he missed the iglesia. It was his *familia* and home and the place where he'd started Reality Changers..

Tonight, with just the four seniors working, he had too much wait time between edits. He couldn't focus on his own work, couldn't think. Couldn't tolerate sitting in his office. But when he stepped out it was worse. Right next to his office, boxes were piled in a cubicle, still there from the move, crammed in like some obscene squat and threatening to spill into the walkway. All the stuff he never unpacked or found a place for—because the hole in his heart from the iglesia made him not want to try, because this place didn't feel right and he didn't want to think he'd be staying. More than thirty cartons full of binders and T-shirts and old yearbooks; photos of graduating seniors accepting blowups of scholarship checks; and Frisbees and Nerf footballs and lanyards and Styrofoam coolers. Programs from every year's Scholarship Banquet, photos of guest speakers surrounded by the kids at the iglesia, albums with pictures from the first three years, and Reality Changers signs and banners and posters and calendars. Beanbag chairs, banged-up file cabinets, and a folding table with a big stain on the top.

He called the cubicle the junk pile, and he winced every time he walked past it. The pile was a sloppy, daily reminder of all that he'd lost. Here on the southwest corner of the third floor of the Workforce Partnership Building, all he had was rented square feet. No culture. No *familia*. No rock to build his program on.

The third night, Kim stood up and called for a drumroll. Jesse, Karina, and Daniel stomped and cheered as she pressed "send" and launched her Common App. She thanked them, thanked Chris, then pulled on her jacket and left. Down to three, and nothing to edit for a while. Yanov stood in the doorway and glared at the junk pile. He wrapped his arms around the highest box on the stack and lowered it to the floor. He walked into his office, came back with a box cutter, and slashed the tape.

A peppery, fruity aroma wafted out.

Here was the seating chart from the 2005 scholarship banquet, splashed with somebody's mom's salsa, still pungent. Here was the banquet program, with the photo of the fourteen graduates, their first big class. Suzie Lozano won a Gates Millennium Scholarship that year, one of eight in California. She got the news just before the banquet, too late to get it into the program. The Gates Foundation paid for her tuition, room, board, and books and gave her a stipend for living expenses for four years at UC San Diego. They would do the same for a master's and doctorate if she wanted them. Suzie, who'd worked as a waitress six nights a week during her junior year after her mom got laid off, her tips the family's only income.

Here was Miguel Cerón, grinning like a little kid, holding the blowup of his scholarship check from Harvard. Here was Jonny, who'd thrown rocks at the iglesia windows; in May he'd graduate from Point Loma Nazarene. And Jorge. Even with a girlfriend and a baby daughter, Jorge kept his grades up throughout his senior year and made it to UC San Diego. Nine of these guys would be graduating from college this spring. Their class put Reality Changers on the map.

Yanov sat on the floor, every whiff of old salsa bringing back memories of that amazing spring. It was close to freezing outside, but with this box he had the month of May.

Daniel was standing behind him. Could Chris look at his Dartmouth essay?

> My team from physics class participated in the Walk on Water competition. I helped design and build an intricate pair of shoes that would enable us to walk across a swimming pool without getting wet. . . . This competition, along with being on my school's swim team, are only two of the reasons that I feel like I'm swimming laps all day.

Good start, Chris told him. You've got something; now tell me the reasons. Give me the details.

Chris hefted the box and carried it around the corner to the workroom, where the building held a copier and floor-to-ceiling cabinets, provided for the floor's tenants. He opened a few cabinets. Empty. Fine. He'd claim them for Reality Changers. Scholarship photos and memorabilia in the first cabinet. Reality Changers' T-shirts and visors in the next. Pens and markers and staplers, file folders and binders, in the next. He opened four more boxes and claimed three more cabinets before the seniors hung it up for the night. For the first time since they'd moved in here, he could see over the top of the junk pile. Should have done this months ago.

The next night, he started in again. Here were all the college pennants he'd hung at the iglesia, one for every college where a Reality Changers graduate went to school. How could he have left them in here for so long? Building management wouldn't let him pin them to the walls, but if he attached them all to a piece of line, it wouldn't be hard to hang the line up every week. Make the meeting room look like it belonged to Reality Changers. All those freshman and sophomore boys who showed up an hour before the meeting and goofed around at Jenn and Grace's cubicle: attaching the pennants to a line, and hanging it up before each meeting, would give them something to do.

What else could he put up in the community room? How about a giant Reality Changers banner? Those guys could put it up and take it down every meeting. This was Reality Changers' home. It wasn't perfect, but he was here. Might as well move in and start improving the place. What could he do about those god-awful plastic chairs?

Every box he unpacked reminded him of what he had, and the more he remembered what he had, the more ideas bubbled up, ways to claim the space for RC.

At ten o'clock, Jesse stood up and climbed onto his chair. His hair was greasy and he'd been wearing the same sweatshirt and jeans for three days and he didn't smell very good. "That's it, guys. I'm brain dead. Stanford and Harvard are gonna have to take what I send them. I'm gonna get some sleep. Tomorrow night my family eats twelve grapes at midnight for the new year, and I've got to be awake for that."

Yanov and Karina and Daniel pounded their desks and cheered for him as he headed for the door. He turned, gave them a grin, and waved. Half an hour later, Karina uncurled her back and stood up.

"Okay," she said, looking at Yanov and Daniel. "I've just submitted my Common App. Hope somebody likes it." They drummed and whooped for her as she gathered up her papers and stuffed them in her backpack.

After she walked out, Yanov and Daniel looked at each other. Daniel was wearing the same bright pink T-shirt and torn jeans that he'd worn since the day after Christmas. Yanov's lucky UCSD sweatshirt was spattered with refritos. Neither of them could follow a train of thought for more than two sentences. Yanov said, "Let's call it a night. Go home, sleep in. Tomorrow's New Years Eve; we'll start in the afternoon and get you out of here in time to party."

The next afternoon Daniel settled himself in front of the screen again. Harvey Mudd College. Down the lane, touch the wall. Haverford. Kick, turn, go. Swarthmore. Touch the wall, kick off. Final lap: polish the water essay.

> I am one of 57 Hispanic students on the school bus that travels from a tough part of town to a much better neighborhood. At school I am seen as a rare specimen, a mutation within the outsider population who does not drive a fancy car to school. I have good grades. I have taken Advanced Placement classes, and I have passed six AP exams. I've been on the school honor roll and, combined with my performance in swimming, the San Diego Union-Tribune named me to their All-Academic Team.

Yanov sat on the floor of the copier room with the last boxes. Sixteen seniors had graduated last June, every one of them starting a four-year college. He'd moved the program from Golden Hill to City Heights and gotten the Wellness Foundation grant. They'd admitted more eighth and ninth graders this fall than they ever could have fit into the program at the iglesia. Jenn and Grace had come on board; and even if it wasn't easy, having them meant he could spend more time working with the toughest kids and talking to funders. He'd plowed through the paperwork to become a 501c3 organization, freestanding, separate from the Presbytery. In January—next week!—he'd have his first meeting with his own board. Another new hire, a PR and communications person, would start next month. The economy was in the tank, but end-of-year donations to Reality Changers were at a record high, more than $130,000.

Maybe he did have some things to celebrate.

At nine o'clock Daniel's mother called. The family was going to a party in Eastlake. Would Daniel be finished in time to come?

Soon.

She called again at ten. Daniel handed his phone to Chris. She invited him to the party.

> For a long time I felt alone on those laps across the pool and across the city, until I found Reality Changers. This program helps inner-city teens like me become first-generation college students. It has introduced me to other low-income students who have learned to not just survive in the deep end, but to break through the crashing waves and strive for higher education. Through Reality Changers I have earned a $3,500 scholarship to UC San Diego's Academic Connections. I took A Critical Approach to Social Issues, in which we discussed many problems that affect my life—prejudice, poverty, and social inequality—through which I have maintained my balance and refused to fall to the bottom . . . almost as if I have learned to walk on water.

At 11:20 Daniel pushed the submit button. He and Yanov pounded the desktop and stomped and yelled. Then they dashed out to Yanov's truck and drove out to Eastlake to welcome in the new year.

15 Reset

Reset (computing): to clear any pending errors or events and bring a system to normal condition or initial state.

The first week of January, the first Reality Changers' meeting of the new year. School was back in session, and by late afternoon, as students made their way to the meeting, the sky was already dark and the air was cold. Winter break was history; there was nothing ahead but exams. Spring was so far away it felt like a myth. They could barely remember why they should put down their game consoles and their phones and head out into the dusk to go to Reality Changers. They shivered and pulled their hoodies close.

The school year is a long march, and right after winter break students can feel they're lost in a frozen swamp. Yanov saw it every year, how hard it was, especially for younger students, to get back on course in January. To show up for meetings and community service, to keep grinding out homework, when the payoffs seemed so far away as to be invisible. Every student in the program had a serious measure of grit; none of them would be there if they didn't. But on bleak winter afternoons, especially for younger students, perseverance and passion could falter. Reflecting on grit, psychologist Angela Duckworth writes, "The achievement of difficult goals entails not only talent but also the sustained and focused application of talent over time."[1] Reality Changers had a critical role to play in the hard work of sustaining and focusing, and in January the program needed to step up: Reset students' expectations. Keep goals in focus, and the pay-offs in sight. Support their efforts, no matter how uneven.

RC had to be a vital presence for them, the place where they could see they weren't alone. Where they could connect with other kids who worked hard, where going to college was everybody's goal. A holding environment that shored them up when their resolve crumbled, and that helped them recharge their passion and perseverance. Yanov's task always, but especially throughout the winter months, was to make Reality Changers a place they'd want to come.

A sandwich board with the silhouette of a young man in gown and mortarboard holding a rolled diploma greeted them at the building entrance. The board, with a clutch of blue and white balloons bobbing on ribbons above it, announced, "Reality Changers Tonight!"

In the lobby three student greeters stood by the elevators beside another sandwich board that announced, "Reality Changers Tonight, Third Floor."

"Hey, great to see you."

"Happy New Year! It's gonna be a good one."

"Yo, girlfriend, *bienvenidos*."

The greeters spoke to every arriving student and shook each one's hand. On the third floor the elevator doors opened onto a space transformed. A brand new banner, four feet high and stretching the length of the lobby, proclaimed, "Reality Changers, Home of First-Generation College Students." More greeters shook students' hands, walked them to a table and handed them their name tags. It felt like coming to a party.

President-elect Barack Obama, in life-size cardboard, extended his right hand and welcomed them into the meeting room. A huge banner—the guy with the diploma now larger than life—hung from the ceiling to the floor and stretched across the room like a stage curtain. It cut off the back third of the room and created a smaller, cozier space. Pennants hung along the walls: UC San Diego, Dartmouth, San Diego State, UC Santa Barbara, Cal State San Marcos, Cal State LA, Cal State Long Beach, Cal State Northridge, Harvard, University of Virginia, Beloit, University of Michigan, Berkeley, Northwestern, Duke, UCLA, and every other college that Reality Changers graduates attended.

The plastic chairs were gone. In their place, six large faux-suede couches formed a U facing the whiteboard. The floor in the middle was covered by an orange area rug with yellow and red Aztec motifs. Two more couches sat behind the U.

Students piled onto the squashy couches and sprawled on the rug. Delicious odors wafted down the hall from the break room, where parents were heating huge pots of posole. There were corn tortillas, radishes and limes and shredded cabbage. Tonight felt like Reality Changers back at the iglesia. For the first time, the bland, uninspired meeting room felt like home.

Yanov strode into the room at the stroke of six. "How d'ya like it?"

"This is *so* cool!"

"Not gonna miss those chairs."

Students clapped and whistled.

"Welcome to the new Reality Changers of 2009. It's a new year, and we've got a lot to do." His glance moved slowly around the room, as his last sentence sank in.

"It's January, and it's crackdown time. I'm the crack and you're going down. Exams are coming up fast. Some of you have been slacking off." The room was dead quiet.

He paced in front of the whiteboard. "People haven't been showing up every week." Students stared down at their notebooks. "A lot of you need to get your grades up. What you've been doing won't cut it for Academic Connections. You need to be here every week, working with your tutors. If you're not, come summer, you'll be watching your friends go off for three weeks at UCSD while you're sitting at home watching reruns."

In *Schooling for Resilience*, their study of single-sex schools for Latino and Black boys, sociologists Edward Fergus, Pedro Noguera, and Margary Martin found that "behavioral engagement, the extent to which students exhibit behaviors associated with high performance, such as turning in their homework, participating in class discussions, punctuality and good attendance, was the single most important predictor of student grades."[2] Yanov didn't make an explicit connection between students' engagement at Reality Changers and their school performance, but students got it. The behaviors that RC taught and expected of them were the behaviors that fostered high achievement at school. If you were screwing up at RC, you were probably doing the same at school.

Tonight Yanov was reset, full of his old energy, doubling down on his mix of tough coachspeak, magnified threats, and high expectations. As he'd cleared out the junk pile, he'd cleared out a lot of his own junk from the past year.

He wanted to do more than remind students of program expectations. He wanted to help them learn to reset themselves, remember why they were here, and recommit to their goals. To strengthen their own internal perseverance and passion generators. In Hot Words he told them, "Imagine you know an eighth grader whose brother's been murdered in a gang fight. You're going to write a letter, telling her why she should join Reality Changers. You've got fifteen minutes. Tell her what coming here could do for her."

When time was up he called on Theresa Palafox, Kim's sister, a junior. "Stand up and read what you've got." She rolled her eyes but she stood. At Reality Changers you had to read your stuff aloud. You might never get to like it, but you learned to do it.

"Reality Changers," she read, "is not like your ordinary group gathering, but more like a family." Abel, another junior, wrote, "Everyone here is great, and we help each other keep going. When somebody does good, it helps everybody." José, a freshman, read, "It's like Olive Garden: 'when you're here, you're family.'"

The students headed off to dinner, and Yanov set up the next reminder of Reality Changers' expectations. He pushed a small, wheeled table down the hall and positioned it directly across from the restrooms. He laid out individually wrapped plastic cups with covers, in rows across the tabletop. He wedged both restroom doors wide open. Half an hour later, as kids walked back from dinner, Yanov and the table stood in their path.

Drug test.

Yanov was matter-of-fact and serious. He tested twice a year, every student, no advance notice. One girl at a time in the girls' bathroom; one boy at a time in the boys' bathroom. Testing was embarrassing—nobody liked peeing in a cup and then handing the cup over to Chris—but it was part of the routine. As he handed each student a specimen cup, Yanov asked, "Is there anything you want to tell me?" Most just took the cup. A few drew him aside and confessed: "I said curse words to the old guy who lives next door and yells at me." "I beat on up my little brother." "I was disrespectful to my mother."

Tonight no one confessed to using. But it had happened in the past. Yanov would tell the penitent that he could skip this test but would be on probation. His attendance, his grades, and his commitment to the program would be watched very closely, and there would be another test, a last chance, sometime soon. In eight years nobody who took the test had ever tested positive.

.   .   .   .   .

Back in December, as seniors submitted their college applications, the tutors saw a sea change wash through the Senior Academy. The seniors, relieved of the pressure of applications, turned their attention to Facebook. Phones were prohibited at Reality Changers, but they brought them anyway and texted from their laps. They gathered at others' desks, talking about the Lakers' prospects, about the new *Grand Theft Auto* or *Dancing with the Stars* and where they'd be going over Christmas. Debbi Leto and her tutors saw this happen every year, the relaxing and lifting of mood, and before Christmas they didn't push back. They told the seniors what a big job writing their applications had been and praised them for the way they'd stepped up.

In January the seniors came back to a different message: the school year was less than half over, and they had serious work to do. From now to graduation, their job was to apply for the scholarships and grants and loans they needed to support their dreams. Finding money required as much work as their applications and was every bit as important. Sure, they'd get some financial help from their colleges; but count on it, what their colleges would give them wouldn't cover the full package. Housing. Meals. Books and materials. Travel. Money for burgers and movies and clothes and whatever. Especially this year, as the recession deepened, state funds and college endowments were feeling the pinch. Already some Cal State campuses were saying they couldn't deliver the scholarship dollars they'd said they could the previous fall. The seniors needed to come up with a whole lot of money.

Martha Berner understood, far more than the seniors, how much they needed every scholarship dollar they could find. Forehead furrowed and dark-brown hair graying at the temples, she wore an air of perpetual concern. She grew up Martha Chavez in National City, a small city that sits between San Diego and the U.S.-Mexican border. Her parents always spoke English at home, she said, because "they'd seen too many kids start kindergarten without English, and most of those kids had a hard time in school." In high school she told her counselors she wanted to go to college. It still stung that her counselors and teachers hadn't taken her seriously. She was a Hispanic girl; she'd just get married. She got a BA in social science at San Diego State and then a master's degree in education, and she taught elementary school for thirty-two years. At Reality Changers she wanted to ensure that every senior had the help with college that she wished she'd had.

She stalked the Internet like a bounty hunter. Each week she dragged in her finds and handed the seniors a new list of scholarships. Deadlines were different for every scholarship, she told them. They needed to be here every week to get the new list and keep on top of deadlines. She found scholarships for students who wanted to study economics. For students who were part Native American. For students who lived in North Park, a neighborhood in San Diego. Who wanted to attend Humboldt State. Or Purdue. Scholarships from California math teachers. From Masons and Elks and Soroptimists, from societies of civil engineers and from credit unions and accountants. Each scholarship had its own application to complete, usually one requiring an essay, and its own deadline.

Martha made two lists, one of scholarships that were open only to U.S. citizens and the other of scholarships that didn't make that restriction. She delivered the appropriate list to each senior and asked each one what he or she had applied for since the previous week. Martha's soft voice and insistent questions made it impossible to put her off. A senior who followed every lead on Martha's lists would be busy five nights a week and every weekend.

They had to get going on FAFSA, Debbi said. The Free Application for Federal Student Aid was the six-page financial disclosure form that every college, public or private, used in order to determine financial aid. It was byzantine in its complexity, less user-friendly than a federal tax return. It was due in a month. Walt, who'd been a guidance counselor since before the seniors were born, was the FAFSA expert. He waved the application in the air. They could find it online; here was the URL. The form was packed with questions like: "Did your parents file an income tax return last year?" and "What was your parents' adjusted gross income for last year?"

Walt started with the section about taxes. He explained the difference between a 1040 and 1040EZ, then walked the students through the questions on the form and, for each question, told them where in their parents' 1040s they could find the answer. He might as well have been speaking Urdu.

Fernando slumped in his chair. He muttered, "I never heard of a 1040. I don't get it."

Karina sat very quiet. Most of the other seniors didn't know she was undocumented, and she didn't want to say anything. What if something she put on the form got reported to the *migra?*

Robert's father didn't tell anybody any of his business, especially about money. Especially now that things were so bad between him and Robert's mother. How was Robert going to get a tax return out of him?

Jesse didn't know whether his mother filed returns.

It wasn't just that the FAFSA form was long and complicated, or that Martha's lists meant filling out more applications than any human would want to contemplate. It was also this new message from their tutors that unsettled the seniors. Last fall, it was all about their applications and so much praise and so many congratulations when they got them in. Now Debbi and Walt and Allie and Martha were talking a whole different game. The seniors had worked all through high school just to have a shot at their dreams. Now the news from their tutors was that they had to find the money to fund their dreams. The tutors would help them and give them advice, but the seniors had to start thinking about money like adults. Most weren't yet eighteen.

Their parents wanted to help, but they didn't know how things worked here. They hadn't gone to college; some hadn't gone past eighth grade, and that was back in Mexico. Figuring out the FAFSA and calculating how much money they'd need and how much they'd have to earn in the summer and while they were at school, and making the plan work all through next year and the year after that, and after that—all of this would be up to them.

Kim Palafox got it. She came home from her job at Chick-fil-A at ten o'clock on a Saturday night. The house was dark and her parents were asleep. There was an envelope for her from St. John's. She waited until one in the morning, when Theresa came home, to open it, just the two of them in the quiet house. The letter welcomed her to St. John's University Class of 2013. Theresa whooped and hugged her, and they danced around the room and texted Grace. Kim woke her mother. Her mother said, "That's good, *mija.*" No questions. No hug. Not even a smile. She didn't wake her father.

St. John's was her first-choice school and she'd gotten in. Tuition, room, and board were twenty-five thousand dollars a year. They offered her ninety-five hundred dollars annually in financial aid. With air fares to New York and other expenses, she'd have to come up with twenty thousand dollars a year for four years. There was no way her parents could do that, no way she could do it. She'd have to see where else she got in. She carried the letter from St. John's in her purse the rest of her senior year.

The seniors took in their tutors' message about money as best they could, unevenly, with lapses and detours. They downloaded scholarship applications. Except when they didn't. They talked to their parents. Or they forgot to talk to them; or they couldn't and asked Yanov to talk to them. Debbi would remind them to bring in information and they'd forget. Painfully, slowly, they slogged through the FAFSA.

Nothing—not endless scholarship applications, not even the FAFSA—could undo their growing knowledge that they were on their way. The year had turned. It was 2009, and they were the class of 2009. Needing a ton of money couldn't stop them. They were going to college.

16 The Guy Inside

After I started Reality Changers, there was a little, and a
little more, and then an explosion.

Jorge Narvaez

In eighth grade, Jorge Narvaez was a tough guy. One day at Kroc he got
into it with another guy, and they agreed that they'd settle it after school.
News about fights traveled fast at Kroc, and at lunch "this annoying white
guy came up to me in the courtyard and talked about how fighting was a
bad idea. He said, 'Promise me you won't go.' That was hard."

Jorge didn't fight that day. He wondered about the white guy who cared
enough about him to mess in his business. He learned that the guy was a
sub and his name was Yanov.

In those days Jorge thought often about his father, a handsome man
who smiled and played his guitar and sang to his mother. His father also
drank a lot and smoked crack, and there were awful nights when he was
high and beat Jorge's mother with his fists. One morning when Jorge was
seven, after his father left for work his mother pulled out the woven plastic
shopping bags that she took to the market. She filled one bag with dishes
and cooking pots, and he stuffed his and his little brother Eric's clothes
and a few toys into another. She filled a third bag with her own clothes and
hustled the boys out of the apartment. They rode the trolley to San Ysidro,
at the international border, and walked across into Mexico. His mother
was crying. They rode the bus to Guadalajara, where her family lived. The

houses were smaller there and closer together. Everything there felt more closed and confined than in the United States.

When Jorge was ten, his mother met Gustavo. Soon they got married, and they and Jorge and Eric came back to the States. Gustavo had a green card, and Eric had been born in the United States, but Jorge and his mother had no papers. Back in San Diego, the streets were wider and clean, the buildings went up much higher, and he felt like he had more room to breathe. At first he was hopeful. His future wouldn't have to be fast food or landscaping; he could go to school and get a good job.

In their tiny apartment, the TV was always on, there was a lot of yelling, and no one had any space of his or her own. His mother and Gustavo fought a lot, and Jorge fought with Eric. They lost that apartment, and for a few months they moved from one relative's place to another. His mother wanted him to do well in school, but she couldn't read English and couldn't help him. She worked cleaning houses and came home exhausted and collapsed on the couch. She and Gustavo both worked hard, and still there was never enough money. By the time Yanov talked to him in the courtyard at Kroc, Jorge's hopes were curdling. He saw the life he wanted slipping out of reach.

Yanov told Jorge about Reality Changers and invited him to join. It was the best offer he'd ever had. Yanov even picked him up and drove him to the meeting. The night at the iglesia when Jonny and his crew threw rocks at the windows, Jorge was inside studying. He couldn't understand why the guys outside wouldn't do what they needed in order to join RC. "Reality Changers was the best thing that ever happened to me. It was survival. That simple."

He couldn't wait to get to meetings. Reality Changers felt like a family, one that worked. Chris was the father he wished he had, and Chris's confidence that he could make it was the scaffolding on which Jorge could build his dreams. When he joined, he didn't know how he'd keep a 3.0 grade point average; the next year, in ninth grade, he made a 3.5, joined the Biology Club, ran track, and found a new girlfriend.

His 3.5 earned him a scholarship to Academic Connections. The first day, he walked into his dorm room and looked around:

Bed.

Desk.

Chair.

Shelves.

Closet.

All his. Nobody else in the room. First time in his life he'd had a room of his own. He shut the door and sat on the bed, breathing hard. "You're not gonna let this go," he told himself. For three weeks he studied marine ecosystems, spending days on the beach gathering invertebrates and learning how to classify them. He began again to dream a future for himself. Maybe oceanography. Or law school.

School helped him stay focused. The more stuff he did at school, the more together and stable he felt. He was elected vice president of the Associated Student Body. He deejayed at school dances. He joined the Model United Nations program. He kept running track. He made A's and B's.

Things got a little better for his mom and Gustavo, and the family moved to an apartment that had a garage with a storage area in the back. Jorge claimed the storage space as his. He brought a table and a lamp from the house and put it in the storage space so he could study there. Then he moved his mattress out there, too. When he and his girlfriend, Nancy, needed a place to be alone, he brought her there.

In the spring of his junior year Nancy told him she was pregnant. He was happy and excited. And scared. "I'd continued the chain." His grandfather had fathered his first child when he was fourteen, and Jorge was born when both his parents were still in their teens. He'd always told himself that he'd be the man to break the chain. Do his life differently. Now this.

He told Chris. Chris's face grew very serious. He said that Jorge had violated the rules of Reality Changers, the rules he'd helped write. He'd have to resign.

At the next meeting, Yanov, grim-faced, said Jorge had something to say. Jorge walked to the front of the room and faced the students sprawled on the couches. Tears stung his cheeks. It was a couple of minutes before he could speak. Yanov stood a few feet away, fists shoved in his pockets. He was resigning, Jorge told them. He'd gotten his girlfriend pregnant.

The room went dead quiet. Chris really meant what he said about the rules.

Some kids cried, and for weeks everyone was mad at Chris. Yanov hated making Jorge resign. He'd come so far, and he still needed the structure and support that Reality Changers provided. But Chris had to show the other students that their actions had consequences, that the program rules were serious business.

Jorge was scared. Reality Changers had kept him on track. He knew he couldn't stay on track by himself. He'd never get to college now. Yanov promised him he'd spend three hours a week with him and help him work on college. Most weeks he kept his promise.

Nancy was the youngest of seven girls. Her six older sisters and their husbands bore down on Jorge. Forget school, they said. He was going to be a father; he needed to get a job. Jorge wanted to support Nancy and their child, and he also wanted to hold on to the new life he was building. The day after school was out, he started work at a construction site; all day he hauled cinder blocks in a wheelbarrow. He'd made better than a 3.5 GPA for the school year, and Yanov had said that, even though he'd had to resign, Reality Changers would send him to Academic Connections. He took three weeks off for Academic Connections, and the day after it ended he was back pushing the wheelbarrow.

Senior year he started his UC application online. In November, a week before the deadline, he hadn't started on his essays. Yanov spent Thanksgiving Day with his family in Camarillo, and the next morning he drove back to San Diego, picked up Jorge, and brought him to his apartment. Over the next thirty-six hours, Jorge ground out his essays. He wrote, Chris edited, he revised. Over and over. Three hours out for sleeping. Both of them were surprised at how much his essays improved over all the drafts. Jorge's ordeal that weekend became the template and model for the Reality Changers essay crunch.

The UC system charged fifty dollars for every campus a student applied to, and Jorge applied to six. Yanov wrote a check to the regents for three hundred dollars. Because he was undocumented, Jorge couldn't apply for state or federal assistance, and he couldn't see how he'd ever pay for college. His mother reminded him that in 1987, when he was less than a year old, his father had registered him during the amnesty for undocumented immigrants. That registration gave him a Social Security number and made him eligible to apply for a green card, the proof of permanent-resident status. With a green card, he would be eligible for financial aid. Jorge found an immigration lawyer to file the permanent-resident application for him. Immigration and Customs Enforcement assessed a penalty of a thousand dollars because he'd been in the country illegally. Yanov figured that paying that penalty would be cheaper than Reality Changers' paying for four years of college. He wrote Jorge a check for a thousand dollars.

Alexa Narvaez was born in December of Jorge's senior year in high school, a baby girl, beautiful and healthy. Nancy's sisters cranked up the pressure. He was a father now. He should marry Nancy, quit high school, and go to work. He stood his ground. Monday through Friday, he and Nancy got up at four in the morning and made thirty *tortas,* sandwiches on thick Mexican rolls, for him to sell at school. By second period he'd have sixty dollars, enough for a few days' diapers for Alexa and ingredients for the next day's *tortas.*

Berkeley, UCLA, and UC San Diego offered him admission. In May his permanent-resident status came through, making him eligible for a Pell Grant and Cal Grant. In September, Jorge and Nancy and Alexa moved into an apartment in UCSD's family housing, and he started classes at UCSD.

Jorge's face was slender, and he had wavy brown hair cropped short and intense hazel eyes. He was wiry and compact, with a restless energy; even sitting he seemed to vibrate. At UCSD he didn't have enough hours in the day for all the projects he wanted to join, all the demonstrations he wanted to be part of, and all the time he wanted to spend with Nancy and Alexa. He felt stressed all the time and suffered extremely painful cluster head-aches. His first two years, he ended up every quarter on academic proba-tion. He and Yanov stayed in close touch, and Yanov's steadying influence was his rudder. Reflecting on how much his life had changed because of Chris and Reality Changers, he laid his hands on the tabletop, fingers close together. He spread his fingers a little, then more. "After I started Reality Changers, there was a little, and a little more, and then an explo-sion." His hands opened wide and held the air.

By his third year he was more settled, able to concentrate on academics. He was especially interested in immigration studies and photography. Nancy was pregnant again, and that summer he worked two jobs so that she could quit her job and take it easy for her last trimester. Eliana Narvaez was born that fall. Jorge was surer in his commitment to Nancy, and he adored both his daughters. Nancy's sisters saw how hard he worked, and how he helped out with the girls. They didn't understand why college mattered so much to him, but they eased up.

He came back to Reality Changers to tutor. It wasn't easy. New tensions bubbled up for him with Chris. He wasn't a frantic seventeen-year-old any longer: he had three-plus years of college under his belt; he knew what he could do and what he could offer the program. He wanted more responsibility at Reality Changers. Most of all, he wanted Chris to recognize how much he'd grown. It still stung that Chris had made him resign in front of everybody, and it hurt that Chris still treated him like he was in high school. He said, "Chris keeps everybody dependent on him. He needs to listen to other people."

Yanov said, "Jorge always has good intentions, but he's scattered. I ask him to get some T-shirts from the storeroom, and I have to spend twenty minutes cleaning up the mess he makes." They were like a father and son whose relationship changes as the son grows up. The old bonds of affection and gratitude were still strong, but each was disappointed. Each felt that the other didn't see him clearly, didn't appreciate all that he'd done.

Jorge's hopes soared the night the old guys came. José Aponte and Joe Cordero read about Reality Changers in a story I'd written for the *Reader*, San Diego's major alternative paper. They came see what Yanov was doing, and how they could help. Cordero was Mexican; Aponte, Puerto Rican. They'd come of age in the sixties, when there weren't any programs for Hispanic kids and nobody talked about valuing diversity. Each of them had toughed it out through college, then risen in his job. Aponte was director of the San Diego County Library System, and Cordero was head of human resources for the city of San Diego.

Yanov invited them to speak during the lesson. Each talked about his own uphill climb, about teachers' skepticism, experiences of blatant prejudice, and how they kept themselves going. They were candid and authentic; students listened in rapt silence.

Jorge had tears in his eyes. These guys were the fathers he wished he had. They were old enough to be Chris's father. It would be so great if Chris brought these guys aboard. They could talk to him. Maybe Chris would listen to them the way Jorge wished he'd listen to him

Students went off to their study groups, and Yanov asked Aponte and

Cordero what they thought. They were impressed with the program, and they were full of ideas about how they could contribute. "We're brokers," Cordero said. "We know everyone in the community. We can connect you with local Hispanic alumni from any college you want."

"The county library system has a position titled Student Worker," Aponte said. "I could provide jobs for RC students. I could park a bookmobile behind the building every week." Cordero added, "We could put together an advisory board of influential Hispanics, especially some women. The girls here need to see women who can be models for them. We know those women. We'd meet quarterly: you tell us what you need; we can help you get it."

They named a Hispanic judge who'd grown up poor in South Bay and graduated from Harvard and Harvard Law School. They also knew a vice president of the gas and electric company. "You're doing great work here, but we think we could help you improve."

This white boy had the organization and he had the kids. The two visitors had lived through so much, and now they were in positions where they could give back. They wanted Yanov to invite them in. Cordero said, "José and I consult on diversity. We charge $250 an hour. We'll help you for free."

Aponte said, "You can use a mentor. We're glad to be that mentor."

Yanov heard them out politely and thanked them for coming. He didn't take them up on any of their offers. Didn't ask for another meeting. He'd met a lot of guys like these, from an older generation of Hispanic leaders. He appreciated their coming, and their ideas were good, but he didn't have the time or the infrastructure to implement them. Bringing these guys aboard, even as consultants, would anchor the program in the Hispanic community. Even though almost all of Reality Changers' students were Hispanic, the program was in City Heights now, among immigrants from so many countries. He wanted the community to see Reality Changers as open to students of all ethnicities and cultures.

Jorge caught up with Chris at the end of the evening. "What'd you think, Chris? You gonna work with them?"

"No, I don't think so." He didn't tell Jorge anything more, didn't explain why.

Jorge went home defeated. Chris wasn't going to change.

Jorge left the next week for Yucatán to work with his professor on research on immigration. While he was there, he thought about where he wanted to be in ten years, and where he wanted himself and his family to be. It was hard for him and Nancy right now; they loved their daughters, but taking care of two little girls took so much time and energy. But when it was just the two of them, things were good between them. While traveling in the Yucatán, he bought Nancy a beautiful dress made in the traditional style. When he got home he gave her a diamond and asked her to marry him. He called his father in Texas. His father was a jeweler, and Jorge asked him to set the stone for him. They'd get married in the summer.

17　Rocks on Her Legs

You're going to college if we have to rob a bank.

Rosario Lozano

Suzie Lozano, a member of Reality Changers' first graduating class, was applying to graduate school in information science. For a question on the application about why she wanted to study this subject, she wrote about the six-month fellowship she'd done at a research institute in Thailand. She'd worked on a study of the Mien, a marginalized tribe in rural Thailand, and in her application she drew a parallel with her own experience.

> When I first moved to the United States from Mexico at age ten, I lived in a Spanish-speaking community that shared my heritage, language, and culture. Although my community's isolation was not as profound as the Mien's, I was separated from mainstream American culture in some important ways. My lack of competence in English and deficits in cultural understanding undermined my ability to pursue my education. I lacked access to information about college and SATs, and I didn't know any adults who could help me improve or even tell me when I was doing something wrong. The Mien faced more severe disadvantages than I did, but I know what it means to lack education and political voice.

Suzie's father left soon after they moved back to the United States. With a sixth-grade education and almost no English, her mother had a hard time getting work. For years Suzie and her brother and sister had no birthday presents. Nothing at Christmas. When she went into a store with her mother, Suzie knew not to even look at cereal or candy or toys; there was no money for those things.

On the first day of school, her mother had to work, and it was up to Suzie to walk with her little brother to their new school. At the school, her little brother started crying. "He held on to my leg and begged me not to leave him. I wanted to cry too. I'd been in the U.S. two years, and I felt like a complete outsider."

She picked up enough English to understand what her teachers were saying, but she couldn't speak or write very well. Other kids' English was good, and they talked about TV shows and stores and video games she'd never heard of. There was so much to learn. She was placed in ESL classes and stayed there through eighth grade.

She couldn't let what she didn't know stop her. She joined Advancing Via Individual Determination (AVID), an in-school program that helps disadvantaged students learn academic skills and supports them in college prep courses. Her middle-school AVID teacher was the first person who helped her believe that going to college was a real possibility.

AVID offered meetings for parents about college, and her mother brought Suzie and her older sister. She was determined that her children would go to college. They learned about community colleges and four-year universities and SATs, and about what courses to take in high school. At the branch library, Suzie found computers with an Internet connection, and librarians who would help her find answers to her questions.

In high school she got a job at Papa Doc's, a barbecue joint, two evening shifts a week, three to eleven thirty. In the guidance office, while Mrs. Pincher, her counselor, filled out her work permit, Suzie studied the fliers on bulletin boards. One was about scholarships. She asked her counselor, "Can kids really get money to help them go to college?" Mrs. Pincher said, "The majority of students from this school don't go to four-year college. If you go to community college, money won't be a problem." She stood up and handed Suzie the permit. The conversation was over.

The way Mrs. Pincher talked to her felt awful, like she wasn't worth a counselor's time. She couldn't let other people's judgments stop her. Later she went back to the guidance office and talked to another counselor,

Mr. Thompson, who told her she could do anything she wanted to. She started doing her own research about scholarships.

She found her way to a Prepare for College course offered by Cal-SOAP, the California Student Opportunity and Access Program, and the program sent her to Academic Connections that summer. In her Ethnic Studies course the instructor assigned a lot of reading, articles in sociology and anthropology and ethnography. The readings were really hard, and her English comprehension and writing skills still weren't at the level she needed. She read the articles over and over until they made sense, determined to do well in the class and participate in discussions. She looked at the kids in her class; most of them had read so many more books and they knew that their parents could pay for college. Next to them, she said, "I felt like I had rocks tied on my legs."

Jorge Narvaez, a guy she knew from middle school, was also in her Academic Connections class. He told her about Reality Changers, and on the last day of Academic Connections she rode down in the dorm elevator with Jorge and a guy who was helping him move out: Chris Yanov. Before the elevator doors opened on the ground floor, she'd told Yanov that she wanted to join Reality Changers. In the fall of her junior year, RC was still a very small program at a very small church, but the juniors were its largest class, fourteen strong. Jorge was part of it, and so was Jonny Villafuerte.

At school she still felt the rocks on her legs sometimes, but at RC she was with thirteen other students like her, who were all working for the same goals. "Reality Changers gave me motivation. It surrounded me with good people. The message was always that I could do it. I could take college prep courses and I could go to college. It surrounded me with positive voices. I began to believe in myself."

Then her mother lost her job cleaning offices, and what Suzie earned in salary and tips from Papa Doc's was the only money coming in for the family of four. She bumped her workdays up to five nights a week, with only Sundays and Tuesdays off. She worked until eleven thirty on weeknights and until two on Fridays and Saturdays. She did homework until she fell asleep, got up and rode the bus to school and did it all over again. She was always tired. She was small and slight and the trays were heavy, and when she came home her arms and legs ached. Tuesday was the easiest night of her week. Reality Changers' meeting finished at nine thirty and she was home by ten, lots of time to finish her homework and still get a night's sleep. "In the spring I went back to Mrs. Pincher to ask her to sign for me to take Advanced Placement history. She refused. AP classes were hard, she said, and places in the class were for students who could handle the work. I said I could do the work, and that my history teacher had encouraged me to take his AP class. She knew I'd been in ESL classes, and she wouldn't sign the form."

Mrs. Pincher's refusal was devastating. All year at Reality Changers, Chris and her tutors had told her that she was smart and could certainly go to college, and she'd begun to believe them. But here was her guidance counselor, who was supposed to know all about college, telling her she couldn't cut it in a high school AP course. That she shouldn't even have a chance to try. Could Mrs. Pincher be right and Reality Changers be wrong about her?

> I earned a scholarship from Reality Changers to Academic Connections that summer, and I took Politics and Ethics. I studied really hard; I wanted to prove I could do it. In the fall, I went back to talk to my counselor again about AP history. I told her about Academic Connections. She said, "You shouldn't waste your time with AP classes. Unfortunately, people like you don't get into four-year colleges. You should aim for something more realistic, like junior college."

People like you.

> I felt disappointed, vulnerable, and angry. My best source of information was telling me to stop trying.

> By then I wasn't taking no.

> I talked to Mr. Thompson, another guidance counselor, who was also my PE teacher and track coach. He was outraged. He helped me research who could be in AP classes, and he went with me to talk to Mrs. Pincher. If I was willing to be challenged, he argued, I should have a chance. I took AP history and made an A. The more I did well at school, the more I came to believe what Reality Changers saw in me.

> Growing up poor, in an unfamiliar culture, I learned painfully that access to information is critical and too often limited. I also came to understand the importance of having an advocate. Advocates like Mr. Thompson have made all the difference in my life and my academic success. Now I want to be that advocate for disadvantaged groups. I want to learn how to adequately

present information, how to provide all users the access to information that should be their right.

During Suzie's senior year, Debbi Leto and the other tutors talked to the seniors as though their going to college were a given. They'd have to work harder this year than they ever had, but they could do it. Suzie believed her. She'd get in somewhere, she felt sure. She'd always worked hard; now she lost count of the application essays she wrote, and lost count of the drafts Chris made her rewrite. By the time she sent off her UC application, she could see that she'd become a better writer.

Every week she spent hours combing the Internet for scholarships. She was admitted to UC San Diego, but in May she hadn't heard back on some of her scholarship applications, and she was scared that she wouldn't have the money to start college in the fall. "No te preocupa," her mother said. "Tu vas a ir a la universidad aunque tengamos que robar un banco." Don't worry. You're going to college if we have to rob a bank.

The letter came from the Bill and Melinda Gates Foundation. She was named a Gates Millennium Scholar, one of eight in all of California. The scholarships were for Hispanics and African Americans, American Indians, Alaska natives, and Pacific Islanders who showed high academic achievement and leadership. The Gates Foundation would pay her full tuition, room, board, books, and living expenses for four years of undergraduate school. A full ride. The same full ride for a master's degree and a doctorate, if she wanted. She read the letter again. She read it five times, then she brought it to Reality Changers for Chris to read. He said it was for real, and she began to believe it.

"Getting the Gates was like flipping a page," she said. All her life, money had been a huge worry and a barrier to her hopes. Now everything was paid for. Everything was possible. UC San Diego was really her place now. Not just three weeks in the summer; she'd be there for four years. She could take as many classes as she could handle, and she could work with professors on their research. She could apply for fellowships to travel and study. Her freshman year, she took a heavy course load and didn't try to do anything else. She needed the whole year just to get used to the change in her reality.

Having enough money was an amazement, but being named a Gates Scholar did something even more important. It was proof to her and to everyone else, both in her high school and at UCSD, that she belonged in college. She could do the reading and write the papers and make the grades. All through college she worked especially hard to show the Gates Foundation that she was worthy of their confidence.

The Gates even paid for travel, which allowed her to take the fellowship in Chang Mai, Thailand. And attend UCDC, the university's program in Washington, DC, where she interned during her junior year as a researcher for the House Education Committee and did research in the Library of Congress. And it enabled her to accept another fellowship, this one in Brazil. By the time she graduated in political science, the rocks had fallen away from her legs. A year later, she entered the master's program at the University of Michigan's School of Information Science.

18 Stars and Projects and Everyone Else

No movement is as coherent and integrated as it seems from afar, and no movement is as incoherent and as fractured as it seems up close.

Troy Duster PhD, Professor Emeritus of Sociology, University of California, Berkeley

Jesse Sanchez couldn't believe his luck. In a week he'd fly to Washington and go with Chris to President Obama's inauguration. The new president, a man of color. Of all the students at Reality Changers, Chris had picked him to go. Chris told him not to tell anyone, and Jesse hadn't, except his mom. Chris treated him like someone who was going places. So much had happened since he joined Reality Changers. He'd gone to Academic Connections and, later the same summer, to the Chicano Latino Youth Leadership Program. His teachers had encouraged him to apply to private colleges, and Chris had told him the same thing. Now he was waiting to hear from Harvard and Columbia and Stanford. Everything had started with Chris's confidence in him, with Chris's encouraging him to raise his sights, to dream bigger. Reality Changers and Chris's help were the best things that had ever happened to him.

Jenn walked into the cubicle she shared with Grace, dropped her backpack on the floor and sat down hard. Grace looked up. Jenn spun her chair to face her. "Jesse's mom was helping out yesterday, and you know what she told me? She said Jesse's going to the inauguration. With Chris. Chris invited him. Can you believe that?"

Grace rolled her eyes. "I can believe it."

"Does he have any idea how this'll look to the other kids?"

"Or to us. We work here, and we find out secondhand."

Grace and Jenn asked Yanov for a meeting. They walked into his office grim-faced and shut the door. "We hear you're taking Jesse to DC. What's up with that? We're the program staff. Why didn't you tell us?"

"It just came up. Congresswoman Susan Davis's San Diego office said that if Obama won they'd have some tickets to the inauguration. First come, first served. I was the first person at her office the morning after the election, the first on the signup sheet. I asked for one ticket, for myself. It wasn't going to be an RC thing at all. Then right after New Year's, her office called me and said they could give me the ticket only if I would take a student. I said okay."

"Why didn't you tell us?"

"You were both on vacation that week, remember?"

"We've been back over a week."

Yanov slumped in his chair. He was going flat out—meeting with big donors; buying the new furniture and building the upbeat mood; establishing RC as a 501c3, separate from the Presbytery; holding his first board meeting; still running the Tuesday meeting; and keeping up with Santiago and a couple of others—but in Jenn's and Grace's eyes he couldn't do anything right.

He'd never intended to take a student. He was a political junkie, and going to the inauguration was his treat to himself. He'd gone to George W. Bush's first inauguration, and now he wanted to see Obama's. He had zero interest in babysitting a high school student, but Congresswoman Davis had made a speech about Reality Changers on the House floor, and he had a congressional citation from her; if taking a student was what he had to do to get onto the Mall, he'd do it.

"How did you choose Jesse?"

"Jesse wants to be San Diego's first Latino mayor. He's the only student who's interested in politics. It'll be really interesting for him."

"The inauguration would be interesting for a lot of other students. Why weren't the rest of the kids offered a shot at this?"

Because this wasn't a Reality Changers trip. Because if he had to take a student to get his ticket, he wanted a mature kid, someone who could handle whatever came up. This wasn't going to be some luxury tour. It'd be freezing in DC, and they'd be eating cheap, sleeping cheap, taking the Metro, and walking a lot. Jesse could roll with that. It would be a lot easier if the trip could stay under the radar. He'd told Jesse he could tell his mom, but other than that, to keep it to himself.

"What about an essay contest or a speech contest? You do speech contests all the time. The trip could have been a prize for the winner."

This thing came on such short notice that there wasn't time to do a contest. Even if he'd had more time, he didn't have the energy. He was spread so thin. Inviting Jesse was the easiest solution.

After winter break he and Grace and Jenn had all been busy. He hadn't seen a time to stop and tell them. More to the point, he hadn't felt like telling them. They'd have a million questions. They needed to know *everything* about *everything. Every day.*

He got their million questions now.

"If you're going to do it, why not take a boy and a girl?"

"There was just one ticket."

"Did you think about how this would go down with the other students?"

"I didn't intend for them to know."

"What does that say?"

He heard them out, but he didn't back down. They could challenge him all they wanted, but he was the executive director. For Jenn and Grace the conversation felt like so many others. They'd tutored for three years, been staff for more than six months, and they carried big pieces of the program. But Chris still ran Reality Changers on his own. He didn't ask for their input. When they brought up their concerns, he stonewalled them: he either minimized the problems or said they didn't understand the whole picture. He kept so much to himself and cut them out of the loop. They called him Fort Chris.

·   ·   ·   ·   ·

Yanov picked stars, articulate, personable students whose stories of what they'd overcome and what they'd accomplished would resonate with donors and help with fund-raising. Jesse was made to order: his mother cleaned houses, his father left before he was born. He was handsome and well-spoken, a football player and a wrestler. He looked up to Yanov and was eager to please, always willing to help out. Yanov also picked tough-guy stars like Robert Silva and Eduardo Corona, lively, extroverted guys who'd gotten into trouble and then rebuilt their lives with the help of RC. So much the better if they looked a little gangsta; when Eduardo talked to donors, his shaved head and baggy jeans brought home to his listeners the distance he'd come.

He coached his stars on public speaking and helped them develop the facts of their life stories into compelling narratives. He reminded them how impressive their transformations were, and that telling their stories could really help Reality Changers. He asked his stars to take on additional responsibilities in the program, like leading a tutoring group or teaching the Hot Words section. He brought them along when he met with potential funders. His currency with the students was the precious gift of his interest.

Yanov also picked long shots—four-year-plan guys like Robert Silva and now Santiago—who were most at risk for quitting school or slipping back into gangs. These guys were at the heart of his quest, the reason he started Reality Changers. He'd gone to thirteen funerals for kids under eighteen, and he couldn't bear the thought of one more funeral, especially for a Reality Changers student. Of course, the long-shot guys needed extra helpings of his time. He was glad to give it. Bringing these guys to the program was where he and Reality Changers could have the greatest impact. Keeping them in the program meant keeping them alive. He was sure of it.

Grace and Jenn called these students his projects. When he needed help with his project guys, he expected his staff to pour the same kind of attention and caring on them that he did. He didn't tell them much about his thinking or make the case for why it was a good idea. He just expected them to jump in and help out. They pointed out that all of his stars and all of his projects were boys. This year that was true. But there were girls. In the very first class, the kids from Kroc, there was Perla Garcia. She was a seriously outsize personality, all brass and confidence, a terrific speaker. He'd taken her on plenty of talks. This year Cecilia Villegas, who'd come through the program and now went to Point Loma Nazarene, was site director for Thursday nights. He met with her every week to help her handle the job. It'd be fine with him to have more girls as stars.

He wasn't oblivious to the girls' needs. He'd intentionally hired Grace and Jenn so that the girls in the program would have strong young women as role models and advocates. He hoped that they would identify potential stars among the girls, more big personalities who could also become the face of the program. Jenn and Grace formed warm connections with the girls, but prospecting for stars wasn't their priority. He'd told them he wanted them to look for girls with high potential, but he hadn't asked them who they thought might fit, or talked with them about what to look for. He didn't know that saying something once wouldn't get the job done.

·   ·   ·   ·   ·

Gustavo was late. For the third week in a row he slid into the end of the line for dinner, forty-five minutes after the program had started, missing Hot Words altogether. He'd skipped a couple of meetings before Christmas break. Grace was worried; the big guy with a paunch had been excruciatingly slow to commit to Reality Changers, and even now, as a junior, he seemed always on the verge of slipping away. She sat down across from where he sat shoveling in *chorizo y papas*. She asked him what was going on. He shrugged and kept eating. How did he like Reality Changers this year? His shoulders sagged.

"It's changed. Not like it used to be. It's so lame."

"What do you mean?"

"Chris got no time for us anymore."

Grace nodded.

Yanov had always recruited students with his time and interest. Shot hoops with them, took them out for pizza, sometimes to a ball game. Until this year every student had had his phone number, and he'd told them they could call him when they had a problem. His modus operandi worked when the program was eight students, then twenty. Even last year, with more than sixty, he'd stretched himself and managed to be available to just about any student who wanted more of him. This year, with more than one hundred students, he couldn't provide that kind of availability. The discrepancy between what he lavished on his stars and projects and what everyone else got became painfully obvious. Jenn and Grace saw how it affected students, but Yanov didn't seem to notice.

In a program that expected so much of them, students needed to know that the playing field was level. It was level for the formal rewards: make a 3.5 grade point average, and you'd earn a scholarship to Academic Connections, no question. Keep your attendance at 90 percent or better, and you'd earn a week at Forest Home, a summer camp in the San Bernardino Mountains, automatic. But Yanov's interest and time, so precious and nourishing to adolescents, flowed mainly to his chosen stars and bad boys.

Guys like Gustavo, who'd known Yanov at Kroc, who'd hung out with him and gotten rides home and come to Reality Changers because of his interest in them, felt their loss. They said the family feeling was gone. Girls said it was great that at RC girls were treated with respect, but that it hurt that the stars always seemed to be boys. It wasn't fair, they said, but they wouldn't tell Yanov how they felt; they feared he'd see them as ungrateful.

A few tried to broach the subject. Some of the girls talked to Grace and Jenn, and some students talked to their tutors, but most students couldn't name their loss or speak about feeling less valued. Gustavo's complaint, "Chris got no time for us anymore," was as much as any of them could say. They didn't have the language to talk about what they felt; and even if they did, with no acknowledgement from the adults that there was a problem, and no formal process for talking about their discontents, they felt unable to speak. So they did the things that adolescents do when they feel unheard. Some blamed themselves, deciding it must be their own shortcomings that made them not chosen. Others went numb, cared less, and didn't try so hard, because what was the point? Some stayed away. Throughout the fall Grace and Jenn had felt a malaise growing. After word got out about Yanov and Jesse's trip, the malaise pervaded every meeting.

Fergus, Noguera, and Martin, who studied Black and Latino boys' school functioning, reported that whether students felt they were treated fairly was a critical determinant of how engaged they were in school. They wrote, "The degree to which students conform to the behavioral expectations of their school is predicted by their sense of fairness, safety, and belonging in the school setting."[1] Students felt that Reality Changers was a safe place, and they felt they belonged; but the fact that Yanov spent so much of the precious currency of his time and interest on the stars and the bad boys felt, to many students, distinctly unfair.

At meetings Yanov looked at students slumped on the couches, blank-faced and listless. He'd done so much to energize the meetings; now this. He was puzzled and irritated. He couldn't see the connection between his actions and their wordless protest. "Okay. Tonight we're going to write about how you handle conflict. It could be with your parents, or a teacher, or a friend, whoever."

Three girls in the back whispered and giggled.

"All right! Quiet everybody!" He glared. "Irina, you're going to have to write about this. Do you understand the assignment?"

Irina lowered her eyes and shook her head.

"José. Would you like to explain the assignment to Irina?"

José was talking to Marlon. He looked up. "Um, no."

"Then what are you guys doing, talking instead of listening?"

Jenn and Grace told him what students said to them, connecting the dots between the apathy in meetings and his investing so much time in his stars and projects. He dismissed it; students always had gripes.

He couldn't get Jenn and Grace to see how important the stars were for fund-raising. How urgent it was to hold the tough guys and the four-year-plan guys in the program.

They called him on his tone deafness.

He wouldn't listen.

Fort Chris.

Yanov saw and understood more than he let on to Grace and Jenn. He knew he wasn't providing them with the mentoring they needed. He saw every week that students who did all that the program asked of them felt neglected. All those needs were valid, and both Grace and Jenn, and the students, deserved a better response than he was providing. There wasn't enough of him to do everything. That question nagged at him: when there are never enough resources, how do you allocate them? Right now he had his hands full with fund-raising and keeping the high-risk students in the program.

Yanov's capacity to identify the most urgent tasks, pour his efforts into them, and plow past obstacles was one of his great strengths. He decided for himself what was most important and didn't invite discussion or hear out Grace and Jenn. He'd achieved impressive results working on his own; but now that he had employees, this approach was incurring serious costs. No surprise that his priorities felt to Grace and Jenn like fiats. The two of them raised a million questions with Yanov because they didn't feel like stakeholders; they felt like his gofers.

He'd tell them once why he did what he did, but if they didn't get it or didn't agree, he wouldn't try again to help them understand. He retreated to fortress mode: they might not like everything he did, but he'd carried Reality Changers this far. There were always students who were unhappy with the program, he reasoned, but they weren't complaining to him. The program was in a transition year, and there were some bumps, but the sky wasn't falling.

He was right; the sky didn't fall. He and Jesse went to Washington and saw the sights and watched the inauguration from the Mall, and every Reality Changers student knew about the trip. They didn't talk to Chris about the trip or about some kids getting more of his time. Most decided that Reality Changers was helping them a lot, and that the stuff that wasn't fair they'd just have to suck up. But Yanov's unwillingness to talk about the issues and listen to staff's and students' concerns ate away at Reality Changers' core asset, the feeling of family.

A month after his trip to Washington, Jenn and Grace were no longer talking to each other about Yanov stonewalling them. They were talking about how much longer they could work there.

19 Going the Distance with Eduardo

I didn't know anybody that graduated high school or did anything good with their life.

Eduardo Corona

The roar of the chopper's engine was so loud that Eduardo thought it was going to land on the school playground. This was getting way too serious. They'd just meant to have a little fun. He'd been out on patrol, the nightly walk around their territory that his gang required him to do, when he ran into Pedro and Aurelio. He'd joined Reality Changers just a couple of months earlier, in the fall of his freshman year, but he hadn't quit the gang. His older sister and brother both belonged; he couldn't just walk away. Tonight, he hadn't wanted to hang with Pedro and Aurelio, but it was winter break, and he hadn't seen them in a long time, and they had beer, big thirty-two-ounce bottles, in their backpacks.

They ended up over by Central Elementary, scoping the campus for tagging some other time. Eduardo was hoping that that was the end of it and he could go home. Then Aurelio found a window unlocked, and he boosted Eduardo up. It opened into a hall of classrooms, all the doors open. They ran from room to room, dumping stuff off shelves and grabbing up laptops and bags of chips. In the darkened science room, they shoved over desks and smashed a terrarium on the floor. Pedro found a fire extinguisher and started spraying the walls.

Eduardo heard voices and the crackle of a walkie-talkie. He peeked into the hall and saw the gleam of a flashlight, ran to the door where they'd come in, and bolted onto the playground. Cop cars pulled up all around the campus, red lights flashing, radios blaring. The helicopter's searchlight lit up the playground like the big Caltrans lights. No place to hide. Then the cops had the three of them on their stomachs on the blacktop, hands behind their heads, a million cops walking around.

His lawyer told him he was in trouble, but he didn't know how much until his hearing. His father was working construction out of state, but his mother was there in the courtroom, and Chris had come, too. He'd known Chris just three months, and here he was, showing up in court for him. Judge Frank Devanney read the charges and the police report out loud. He regarded Eduardo from the bench and said, "Young man, you're looking at six years in the California Youth Authority. What do you have to say for yourself?"

Eduardo couldn't speak. What they'd done was so dumb he didn't know what to say.

The night before his arraignment he'd talked to his father on the phone. His father told him, "Don't end up like your brother and sister." His sister was twenty. She had two kids, four and two years old, with different fathers, and she wasn't married. His brother was doing a lot of dumb stuff, breaking and entering, and everybody knew the cops were watching him.

His lawyer approached the bench and handed the judge a Reality Changers yearbook. Chris must have given it to her. The judge flipped through it and then gaveled a recess. He told Yanov to come to his chambers.

When court resumed, Judge Devanney said to Eduardo, "I'll give you one month to prove to me that you're the man in this yearbook and not the gangbanger that the cops arrested. If you're that kid, you'll be remanded to Juvenile Hall. If you're who this yearbook says you are, I'll put you on probation."

Eduardo was already in trouble at his high school. A rival gang ran the school, and he got jumped a lot; he couldn't not fight. The day he went back to school after his hearing, the assistant principal told him they knew what he'd done and he was no longer welcome. He would have to go to ALBA. Alternative Learning for Behavior and Attitude, the school for kids who were kicked out of regular school. The school was a cluster of trailers surrounded by an eight-foot fence, on the back lot of another high school. Guys from other gangs looked out the windows and spotted him as he walked into one of the trailers on his first day. They banged on the windows and yelled threats about what they were going to do to him. The principal did the best he could to protect him. A security guard escorted him from one class to the next and watched him during lunch. He wasn't allowed to use the restroom, because that was the place he was sure to be jumped. He was released half an hour early so he could get home before the other guys could get to him.

Guys from the other gangs talked trash to him between classes and threw pencils and food at him during class and at lunch. He smiled at them when they threw stuff, and the rest of the time he ignored them. He wasn't going to fight. He kept his attention on the teacher. Whatever those guys did, he only had to last a semester. Whatever they did to him was better than six years in the California Youth Authority.

His probation officer set his evening curfew at six. If he was seen out later, his probation would be revoked. If he was seen anytime in the company of gang members, any gang, his probation would be revoked. He came home from school and did his homework. In a month he had doubled his grade point average to 3.8.

The only place his probation officer allowed him to go after six was Reality Changers. He went on Thursdays, his regular night, and then, just to get out of the house, he started going on Tuesdays as well. He liked it at RC. There were guys there he knew from rival gangs, but they weren't in their gangs anymore, and they were talking about college. This was a new conversation for Eduardo. His older friends all sold drugs, and that's what he had thought he'd do, too, if he lived that long. He didn't know anyone who'd graduated from high school and done something good with his life.

His GPA that spring earned him a scholarship to Academic Connections. He'd grown up in City Heights, and he hadn't traveled much beyond it, so UCSD's campus, with its towering eucalyptus trees and grassy open spaces and huge buildings, was like another planet. He hadn't known there was anyplace like this in San Diego. It was exciting to be here, but it was also uncomfortable. Nobody except the other kids from Reality Changers looked like him. Almost everyone was white or Asian. He felt he didn't belong.

The first day he walked into his mechanical engineering class, the Asian guys and white guys stared at him. The instructor stared at him. His was the only brown face in the room, his head was shaved, and his jeans dragged on the floor. His arms and chest bulged under his white T-shirt. The question was all over their faces: what's this badass doing in our classroom?

He sat in the back of the room. He'd never seen math like the equations on the board. He listened to everything Mac, the instructor, said, and slowly the math began to make sense.

Their assignment the second week was to design and build a weight-bearing bridge that would span two tables set twenty inches apart. Their materials were copy paper, popsicle sticks, pencils, staples, and tape. They'd bring their bridges to class, and Mac would load on weight. Bridges would be judged on their weight—lighter was better—and on how much weight they could hold. They learned a lot of formulas and how to set up calculations. The other students all had fancy calculators with screens. He had a pencil. Mac loaned him a calculator.

The first day, he worked out a design in his head, one that would use only paper and tape. He rolled two pieces of paper into one tube and taped it. He made four more tubes the same way, and a deck to go over them so that the weight would be pushed down and outward. He turned it in that day. His design made sense to him, but all week he watched the other guys use staples and popsicle sticks and pencils. Their structures were more elaborate, their bridges heavier.

The day of the competition, Mac wheeled in a hand truck piled with encyclopedia volumes and dictionaries and fat textbooks. He added books to each bridge in turn, gently increasing the loads. One by one the bridges collapsed. The heaviest ones fell first. Mac kept loading books onto Eduardo's bridge. It weighed only 7.5 grams, and it held up under even more weight than Eduardo had calculated. It held the greatest load relative to its weight of any bridge in the class. Mac waded through the piles of books and the collapsed bridges and declared Eduardo's bridge the winner. He held Eduardo's arm up like a prizefighter's. The white guys and the Asian guys looked at each other and looked at him, and then they clapped.

"After that I knew I could do college," he said. "It was time for me to change." He told the gang he was done.

He wanted a fresh start. In the fall he transferred to Junípero Serra High School, which was out in the suburbs, with a student body that was mostly white. Mr. Ramirez spotted Eduardo the first day. Ramirez worked for the district office, and he knew who'd gone to court, who'd gone to ALBA. He shoved Eduardo into an office and got up in his face: "I know your brother. I know your sister. What gang you in?"

"I'm not in a gang."

"What are you going to do to this school?" He picked up Eduardo's transcript. "A 3.8. This isn't yours."

"It's mine."

Later in the semester Mr. Ramirez found him in the hall. He put out his hand. "I was wrong about you. I apologize. I heard about your bridge. Congratulations."

By the start of his senior year, in 2009, Eduardo was confident he could go to college, maybe even get into one of the UCs. Chris told him he should take AP courses; grades from those were weighted more heavily than others and could really bring up his GPA. He signed up for AP biology, AP government, and AP Spanish. Government and Spanish were interesting, and the teachers were cool. Biology was really hard. He didn't know a single other student in the class, and when he came around for help the teacher was always busy or wasn't there.

By October he was panicked.

"Chris! What you got me into? I've never seen homework like this biology. Every night, man, I'm up 'til 2 A.M."

"You're a smart guy. You can do it."

He couldn't tell Chris how bad it was. But he couldn't do the homework—he didn't even understand most of the words he was reading. After a while he quit trying. At the end of the first grading period, he made a D, but he didn't tell Chris or anyone else at Reality Changers.

In January, UC Riverside offered him admission. Maybe he'd get out of this mess alive.

First semester grades came out a few weeks later. He'd flunked AP biology.

The letter with the University of California seal arrived in April. It said his admission to UC Riverside was contingent on satisfactory completion of his senior year. Failing a course did not meet the criteria for satisfactory completion. This letter advised Eduardo that the offer of admission to the University of California Riverside was rescinded.

He slumped in Yanov's office, his face gray, tears coursing down his cheeks. "I've let everybody down. All you guys were helping me, and I blew it."

"Don't give up," Yanov said. "We're going to appeal this thing."

After Eduardo left, Yanov crushed sheets of paper into wads and hurled them at the wall. This was his fault. He'd blown it worse than Eduardo. He'd pushed him to take those AP courses, and then he hadn't kept tabs on him. Eduardo kept saying everything was fine. He should have checked with him every week, insisted on seeing his homework and his tests. If he hadn't had time to do that himself, he should have assigned someone else to do it.

He pushed kids too hard sometimes. He had to push them, or they'd never find out what they were capable of. Some kids stepped up. Others couldn't do it, and that was okay. The worst was when they couldn't do it and wouldn't say so or ask for help. He didn't always read them right.

Eduardo had come this far. Now he needed some help to get the rest of the way.

Yanov called Riverside's office of admissions. Grace made the two-hour drive to the campus and talked with an admissions officer, who said she'd bring Eduardo's case to the full admissions committee for review.

The admissions committee wrote him to say they had reviewed his appeal, and that he was a member of the incoming class. Reality Changers buys every senior a sweatshirt for the college they'll be going to. In the group photo taken that year, Eduardo wears his UCR sweatshirt and he's smiling a huge smile of relief. Cindy Marten, the principal of Central Elementary, the school he'd vandalized, heard about the way he'd turned his life around, and she came to RC to meet him. Things were breaking his way.

He went to his orientation weekend in June. His name wasn't on any of the lists. An admissions officer took him aside. He said that even though the committee had sent him that letter, they'd already given his place in the freshman class to someone else. He would need to leave campus. The letter that made it official arrived in July. After a careful review of his appeal, the admissions committee had agreed to support its original decision. He would not be admitted. They wished him well with his academic career.

No college.

Too late to apply anywhere else.

Sunk.

Eduardo wouldn't leave the house. He slept or watched TV or played video games. He couldn't face his RC friends, couldn't bear to hear them talk about when they'd be leaving, what they'd bring to college, what courses they'd take. They were leaving and here he was, stuck in City Heights. He'd blown his chance and lost his future, and now he'd never get out.

Yanov had never seen him so low. His moping was way worse than his tears. Yanov wasn't worried that Eduardo would go back to his gang. He worried that he'd sit at home for years, give up hope.

He had to make something happen.

Later that week he called Bernadette Nguyen, the principal of Woodrow Wilson Middle School. Wilson's campus was in the heart of City Heights, a few blocks from Reality Changers' building. Yanov and Nguyen had talked the previous year about starting a Reality Changers group for Wilson students. Starting one this year wasn't on his to-do list, but now he told her he was ready and he had the guy to do it, a Wilson alumnus.

"We're starting a new project," he told Eduardo. A section of eighth graders, all from Wilson."

"That's where I went."

"Right. The principal and I want to get together the eighth graders with the worst GPAs in their class and offer them a shot at Reality Changers. I want you to come to work for Reality Changers and be the site director for the Wilson group."

"No way, Chris. I didn't even get into college."

"You're the right man for the job. You know better than anyone what those kids are dealing with. Think about the difference you could make in their lives."

"I can't do it, Chris. How can I talk to them about going to college when I didn't even make it?"

Still, he started hanging around Reality Changers; it was better than staying at home. He agreed to come on staff part time to work with the incoming seniors on their applications.

Yanov insisted Eduardo come with him to meet with the forty Wilson eighth graders with the lowest GPAs. Ms. Nguyen told them they were invited to the meeting because of their interest in improving themselves. Yanov introduced Eduardo, who told them about Reality Changers, about students who'd been where they were while in eighth grade and now were going to college. RC would be starting a new section in January, just for students from Wilson. There were twelve places, and they'd go to the students who showed the greatest improvement in their GPAs between then and the end of the first semester.

If those Wilson dudes could help themselves, maybe he could do the same. Eduardo wrote his application for the spring semester at San Diego State, and he signed up for a biology course online. He was lifting at the gym when a San Diego State admissions officer called, inviting him to join the school's spring freshman class, with a full ride for tuition. He showered and ran over to Reality Changers and into Chris's office. He took a deep breath. "Chris. I'm starting at SDSU in February. If you still want me, I'd like to be site director for the Wilson kids."

"That'd be fine, Eduardo." After Eduardo left, Yanov high-fived the air.

Five girls and seven boys came for the first meeting of the Wilson cohort. They didn't talk to each other, just shuffled in and sat on the couches and stared at the floor. Yanov welcomed them and congratulated them on their hard work. Eyes stayed on the floor. He introduced Eduardo as their site director.

"Let's go around the room," Eduardo said to them, "and each one tell the group a little about ourselves. I'll go first. I'm Eduardo and I grew up in City Heights. I graduated from Wilson." He paced the front of the room, shaved head, baggy jeans, looking like a gangbanger, talking like an evangelist. "Back then, most people didn't think I'd live to be eighteen, I was so deep in the gang. Reality Changers saved my life. It showed me that I could do something different, and now I'm a freshman at SDSU."

They wouldn't look at him. Wouldn't even look at each other. Wouldn't introduce themselves. Still, he knew a lot of them. That guy had lost two brothers, both murdered by gangs. This one was on probation for stabbing a kid. There was Aurelio's little brother. Aurelio who was with him that night at Central Elementary, who was doing hard time now for burglary.

These guys' lives were like his life used to be.

This could work.

"Okay, let's get started. Open your notebooks. Write a paragraph about what you did to get yourself into Reality Changers. Nobody goes to dinner until they finish their paragraph." He loomed over them, arms folded across his chest, scowling.

A month later he couldn't shut them up. They came early, first to hang out with him, and soon to hang out with each other. They ate dinner together and they helped each other with their homework.

20 The Guy Outside

I'd come out of my AP class and meet my friends coming out of ESL classes.

Jonny Villafuerte

Jonny Villafuerte was a senior at Point Loma Nazarene University. Seven years earlier he had been a bald-headed punk throwing rocks at the iglesia windows. Now he was Reality Changers' Tuesday-night site director, and part of his job was helping students stay on track. He wanted to keep them believing that doing well in school and going to college was their path to a bright future.

For himself he wasn't so sure. He'd graduate in May, which was three months away. For four years he'd managed not to think about graduating, but now it was three months away, in his face every time he looked at a calendar. When he thought about graduating, he felt sick.

His father kept telling him to look for restaurant work, as a waiter, bus boy, whatever. Going to college had changed his life, but what was the point of all his work if he ended up a waiter? All his life his mother, Claudia, had told him about her and his father's coming to the United States and about her dreams for him. She talked about how important school was, how he needed to do well. He wanted to please her, but when he was young it was hard to sit in their small apartment and do his homework. Always he could hear his parents talking about *la migra* and people who got caught and what they would do if they were caught. He wanted to hang out with his friends, play soccer, and forget for a while about not having papers. Still he listened to his mother; he knew that his dreams started with his parents' dreams.

Claudia was slender and beautiful, with wide-set brown eyes and a high forehead. She spoke softly, but with a confidence earned from twenty years of making way her way in a culture so different from her own. In Mexico City her father was a bodyguard for the president of the Bank of Mexico. Claudia and her three brothers were expected to work hard in school, and it was understood that all of them would go to the university. She was fifteen when she met Ramiro. He'd come to Mexico City from Michoacán for medical care after a car crash; and after his injuries healed, he'd decided to stay in the capital and make a better future for himself. She'd never cared so much about a boy before.

In a few months she was pregnant. She and Ramiro were frightened. If her father found out he would kill him. Ramiro had an uncle in Tijuana. They could go there and then cross to the United States, where they could make a life for themselves and their baby.

Ramiro left first. He called her from his uncle's house to tell her which bus to take. Tijuana is 1,716 miles from Mexico City; her trip was three days of bouncing on rutted roads, hours between bathroom stops, the dust from the road sifting into her hair, her teeth, her clothes. She washed her face but never felt clean. She was six months pregnant, and the food from the vendors where the bus stopped—tacos dripping grease, beans that smelled bad—made her feel like she'd throw up.

In Tijuana, Ramiro's Uncle Tomás talked to them about crossing. They'd need a coyote to smuggle them across. The coyote charged three hundred U.S. dollars for each person, cash up front. Even with the coyote, crossing was very dangerous. If *la migra*, the U.S. Border Patrol, caught them, they'd go to jail in the United States and then be sent back to Mexico. They had no money. They'd have to stay in Tijuana until their baby was born and save money to pay the coyote.

Ramiro found work delivering bottled water. The bottles were heavy and the hours were long, and he came home exhausted. Claudia didn't know anyone in Tijuana, and she was lonely at Uncle Tomás's house. Before Jonny was born they found a place of their own, small and drafty, just a bedroom and kitchen. They had to go outside to reach a bathroom they shared with other tenants. No matter how much Claudia cleaned their apartment, the floors and table remained dirty from the dust that blew in through the cracks. The tap water ran yellow; nobody drank it.

Jonny was born, a vigorous, handsome baby. Claudia thought about home, where she'd had everything she wanted, and about her parents, who didn't even know they had a grandson. She and Ramiro had no health insurance, and sometimes they didn't have the money to buy diapers and formula. When Claudia's mother found them in Tijuana, she hugged Claudia and her new grandson, and they wept. She came back every few months with money and baby clothes and news of Claudia's brothers. Claudia's father didn't come; he was too hurt and disappointed, her mother said.

At every visit, her mother reminded her that she could come home and go back to school. They'd take care of Jonny while she finished high school and while she went to the university. Their offer didn't include Ramiro.

When Jonny was three, Claudia was pregnant again. They couldn't keep depending on her mother's handouts. They needed to cross. Ramiro crossed alone and made his way to San Diego, where his cousin lived, in a part of town called Colina del Oro, Golden Hill. Claudia liked the sound of the name. Ramiro stood with the other men on a street corner and got work painting houses, cleaning yards, and sometimes in construction. In six months he sent her three hundred U.S. dollars.

Finding a coyote was easy. Everybody knew somebody who knew a coyote. They hung around the bus station in Tijuana, looking for people coming from the interior. "You want to cross?" they'd ask. The man her neighbor knew said he could get her across. She closed up the apartment and gave her cooking pots and utensils to a woman in the building. Uncle Tomás brought her and Jonny to the coyote's house in a section of town near the beach. She gave him the three hundred dollars, and then they waited. Jonny was restless, and as the afternoon and evening dragged on, she worried whether she could keep him quiet. She didn't have any toys for him, not even a snack. She'd been told to bring nothing; even a backpack could look suspicious. She wore a simple dress and sandals.

Much later, another woman came with two little girls, and after midnight the coyote led them out from town, into the back country. The night was cold; Claudia shivered in her sundress. Everything was still. The moon was new, and the sky was overcast; they couldn't see anything. Claudia was very pregnant now, so big she was clumsy and always tired. They walked a long time in the darkness. If they had to run, the baby inside might be hurt. If they ran they could get separated—what if the coyote ran away with Jonny?

The coyote pointed down the hill to a wire fence. That was the border. They needed to crawl under the fence, then walk to the road beyond. On the other side of the fence three pickup trucks faced them, engines idling, headlights blazing. *La migra.* When the trucks left, they could cross. They crouched in the brush and waited. Claudia was cold and stiff. Jonny slept. The *migra* sat in their trucks.

In the east the sky began to lighten. The *migra*'s trucks were still there. They started the long walk back to town. Claudia found a room in a grimy hotel and laid Jonny on the bed. She called Ramiro in tears.

He came back that night. Crossing into Mexico was easy; but coming back, he could be caught, and that would be the end of all that he'd built in *el norte*. But he couldn't leave Claudia and Jonny there.

The next day he told the coyote to have the car waiting on the U.S. side, on the road from the beach. Ramiro and Claudia left the hotel in their summer clothes, Jonny in Ramiro's arms. They walked to the beach, then walked north, a young family on a holiday outing. They turned and walked away from the beach and into the chaparral, until they found the wire fence. They scrambled under it and into the United States.

They made their way toward the road, ducking into the brush every time a car approached. In half an hour they found the car parked on the shoulder, the coyote's driver waiting. They climbed in the back and slumped down in the seats. Claudia held Jonny and cried.

For a year they lived with Ramiro's cousin in Golden Hill. Ramiro found full-time work at a Mexican restaurant close enough to walk to. He bused tables and washed dishes, peeled avocadoes and onions, and in time he was promoted to cook. José—Jonny's brother, Joseph—was born, a U.S. citizen. They found an apartment of their own, close to Ramiro's cousin. Claudia took care of her boys and learned enough English to buy groceries and read the street signs and pay their bills.

There was always the worry about *la migra*, about being arrested and sent back to Mexico. But their sons were healthy, and their apartment had heat and a bathroom inside. The dust didn't blow in, the water ran clean, and the electricity stayed on all the time. They could buy all the food and clothes they needed and toys for Jonny and Joseph. For themselves, they bought a television and a bedroom suite.

They missed the look and the tastes of home, though. Claudia longed for her mother's *sopas* and posole. You could buy those things in stores here, but they didn't taste right. They missed their families too, especially at Christmas, on birthdays, and on *el dia de los muertos*, the Day of the Dead. On that day, families all over Mexico go to cemeteries, bringing food for their relatives who've died; there's feasting and music and dancing, and the party lasts all night. She was lonely in this country of paved streets and cold eyes.

She thought about how her life had changed. She'd been a schoolgirl, her father's darling, heading for the university. Now she was a mother living in a strange country with two small sons who depended on her. When Jonny started kindergarten, Claudia understood that they would be staying in America. She'd had to give up on her own education, but for her sons it could be different. They could go to school here and make good lives for themselves.

Jonny spoke only Spanish when she took him to kindergarten at Brooklyn Elementary School in Golden Hill. Every day he brought home papers in English, so she read the newspaper and switched the TV from *telenovelas* to American channels in order to work on her English. She learned enough to help Jonny with his homework. He was a smart boy; he could do his homework and still have time to hang out with his friends, draw, and play soccer.

After sixth grade Claudia told him he'd be going to Kroc instead of Roosevelt Middle School, where most of the kids from Golden Hill went. Roosevelt had a lot of gangs. They had honors classes at Kroc, she told him, and programs like AVID, and it wasn't "just all Mexicans." The Kroc teachers would ask more of him. Jonny wanted to stay with his friends, so he sulked and pled with his mother. She was immovable.

Jonny figured out how things worked at Kroc. "If you were a guy you had two choices: you were hard, or you were a nerd." Jonny was a soft-looking boy with a sweet smile and thick, black hair that spilled over his forehead. He spent hours drawing superheroes and lowriders and characters from

Grand Theft Auto. He could letter in a bulging script that looked like it was part of a gang tag. Kids loved his lettering, even paid him a few dollars to write their names on their jackets or backpacks.

At Kroc, the Lomas26 guys made it harder for him to stay a nerd. Lomas left kids alone in grade school, but now guys whom Jonny had known since first communion started leaning hard on him to join. If you didn't belong, you could get beat up just walking to the taco shop. Last summer he saw them bust a kid's head with baseball bats, the blood pouring out. He didn't want any part of that.

He hoped he could get by if he looked like them. He got his hair buzzed down to an eighth inch of black bristle, and he wore checks and plaids and baggy denims that dragged on the sidewalk. He ditched the backpack his mother had bought him, carrying just a binder. Backpacks were for nerds and white boys.

At school Mr. Yanov would walk over to the coral tree where Jonny hung out with the hard guys. He'd say hello to Jonny, ask him how he was doing. It felt good that Mr. Yanov was interested in him, but when he came over to the tree Jonny squirmed. He was trying to fit in with these guys, and the white-guy substitute talking to him did not help.

In the spring during eighth grade, Yanov told Jonny about the program he was starting for kids who wanted to go to college. It sounded like something for nerds: maintaining a 3.0, meeting every week at the iglesia. The Lomas26 guys would know in about two seconds that he was going to that program. He said he'd think about it. He thought, no way.

Lomas26 guys kept leaning on Jonny, at the bus stop, at school, at the barbershop. He knew he'd have to do something. Most nights he sat in the small bedroom he shared with his brother and talked on the phone with his close friends. Instead of joining Lomas, they'd start their own crew. Just guys they knew, who'd have each others' backs. Like *familia*. Five of them started their own crew, strictly tagging, which they also called bombing. No territory, no fights. They'd be FBK, Forever Bombing Kali (*Kali* was their spin on *California*). Jonny felt great. They weren't little kids anymore, and now, with their own crew, they could take care of themselves.

They boosted cans of spray paint from the ninety-nine-cent store and hung out in an alley near Jonny's house, talking about the tags they were going to do. They'd drink a beer if one of them had snatched a six-pack when the guy at the liquor store wasn't looking; and sometimes older guys bought them beer. One night they went over to the iglesia when Chris was sitting in there with the schoolboys; they'd teach him a lesson. They yelled and threw rocks until he came out and talked to them, but he wouldn't let them come in.

A year later Jonny was a freshman at James Madison High School and FBK had grown to twenty guys. They'd left tags from El Cajon out east to Chula Vista in South Bay; they'd bombed whole sides of some buildings down on Euclid Avenue. People knew their signs. FBK was getting a name.

Still, he worried about his future. He knew he needed to change. He thought about it every time his mother cried about his coming in late, which was pretty often now. She'd sit on the couch crying, and tell him how worried she was for him. His father yelled, and sometimes he'd get so mad that he locked Jonny out of the house. The lockouts Jonny shrugged off. His mother's crying stayed with him. He kept his eye on what Reality Changers was doing. He heard about their meetings, about the tutors who were college students and the way people treated each other with respect.

At crew meetings, guys drank a lot of beer now and sometimes tequila. Nothing else at meetings, but Jonny knew who was smoking weed, who was doing rock and coke. Some guys wanted to do more than tagging. Jonny couldn't risk getting arrested—his father had a green card now, but his mother had no papers and neither did he. He could be deported at anytime. He started working harder at school, went to an after-school tutoring program, and brought his grade point average up to 3.0. Just in case.

The summer after ninth grade his friend Julio said he was thinking about joining Reality Changers. He and Julio lived on the same block. If they both joined they could walk over to the iglesia together, which would be a good idea, because when the rest of FBK heard about them joining, there would be some serious hassle.

That September, Jonny and Julio walked past the alley where FBK hung out, and down B Street to the iglesia. Chris met them at the door and shook their hands. Fifteen kids, girls and guys, were sitting around the table. Every one of them stood up and shook their hands. Jonny wasn't used to that kind of welcome.

He didn't miss a meeting all year. He pushed his GPA up to a 4.0, and the next summer he went to Academic Connections and studied robotics. Those three weeks at UC San Diego sealed the deal. If this was what college was like, he was in. Back at Madison in the fall, he signed up for AP classes.

Things were complicated at Madison: guys from three different gangs went there, and they fought in the halls and the bathrooms. FBK was a tagging crew, not a gang, but that didn't make his life any easier. He needed his books at school now, especially for AP classes, but carrying a backpack would be like wearing a target on his back. He dug out his old backpack from Brooklyn Elementary and sprayed tags all over it. That prompted some guys go after him, but it also said, *Don't mess with me.* A lot of guys gave him some room. Other kids paid him to tag their backpacks.

He stayed in FBK. He still dressed like them in oversize hoodies and baggy jeans, still came to all the meetings, and he stayed friends with everyone. They were the guys he knew; he couldn't imagine his life without them. He helped design their tags and worked on the big ones, sometimes all night. Since he'd joined Reality Changers, he didn't use any drugs. Guys would offer him stuff, and he'd just say no thanks, he was being drug tested. A lot of guys were on probation, which meant random testing, so his saying that he was being tested made him seem more like one of them. "It was my free pass," he said. "I didn't want to use, and RC only tested twice a year, but they didn't know that."

Still, he could feel the distance opening up between himself and the rest of the crew. He felt it especially when he walked out of an AP class and caught up with his friends coming out of ESL classes.

He wanted to go to Point Loma Nazarene University in San Diego. He loved the campus, with its rolling lawns and ocean views, and the school's strong Christian culture. Point Loma admitted him, no questions asked about his immigration status. They also offered him some scholarship money, but not enough to cover his costs. That was a disappointment; he'd ride the bus to San Diego State. Two weeks before Point Loma's fall semester started, Yanov told him that an anonymous donor had stepped up to cover Jonny's tuition and room and board there.

FBK threw him a party for his eighteenth birthday. It was a big party, with beer and tequila and some other stuff, and lots of people. Guys from a rival gang showed up, and fights broke out and spilled into the street. Jonny heard police sirens and then a police helicopter overhead. He spent the night of his eighteenth birthday hiding out in a friend's apartment. He had to rethink his connection with the crew. He was going to college now; he couldn't do the crew stuff anymore. It helped that Point Loma was way across town from Golden Hill, and that he didn't have a car. When guys from the crew called, he said he couldn't get a ride.

College was harder than he'd ever imagined. He was shocked at how poorly prepared he was for the work: the amount of reading, and how much he was expected to write. He was living out his dream, but at the start of every semester he would ask himself whether he belonged in college. His mother was proud; his father didn't say anything; and he didn't know what he thought.

In May 2009 he'd graduate with a bachelor of arts degree in psychology. He'd get a job; what kind he didn't know. He'd have to see what God had in mind for him. He caught sight of himself in a store window: he'd worn the same hoodie for a week, his shoulders were hunched up around his ears, and he walked with a heavy, halting step. He looked like the guys who slept in the canyons and looked for work in the Home Depot parking lot.

21 Getting In

Por tus esfuerzos siento que mis sacrificios van a valer algo
grande y mis suenos van a ser realizados.

Julia Sanchez

Back in November and December, when the seniors sent off their applications, they felt like they were shoving everything that mattered in their lives into bottles and flinging them off the Ocean Beach pier. Forty feet down to the water, no controlling where the waves would take them: what would happen now? They'd worked so hard for so long, and now a bunch of people who'd never met them would decide what they could do.

Second semester started and the work kept coming. Nothing stopped just because everything they wanted was on the line. Read assignments, write papers, take tests, show up for practice. Their tutors kept reminding them that the game wasn't over. Colleges could admit you, but if you blew off your last semester and tanked your grades, they could take their offer back. The tutors sounded the way adults so often do, trying to scare them into being good. Except they knew it was true. The previous year Ana Garcia got into UC Davis, and then she blew off her last semester. Davis pulled her admission and her scholarship, and she scrambled all summer to find a college that would take her.

Now in February and March, the letters and the emails were coming. Fat envelope, thin envelope, no envelope. This week or next or the next. Sometimes the news came in email, in the form of a code to enter on the college's website. Hearts in their mouths, hearts pounding, every time they passed the mailbox or the computer.

Where can I go?

What am I worth?

Will I be able to build the life I've dreamed for myself?

What if I don't get in anywhere?

They saw signs and portents if the mail came early or if it came late, in how many emails landed in their in-boxes, whether they stepped on a crack in the sidewalk. Open the letter. Click on the email. The news about their futures spilled out.

The second week in March, the late afternoon light on University Avenue was as clear and sharp as in a Hopper painting. The mountains to the east were bathed in golden light and everything seemed possible. At Reality Changers, Robert and Daniel and Kim stepped off the elevator with their news.

Daniel, the swimmer, had acceptances from UC Santa Barbara and UC San Diego and Northeastern Arizona. Berkeley hadn't sent its acceptances yet. MIT rejected him, he told Jenn, because they hadn't received his SAT scores. He'd checked MIT on the form that asked where he wanted his scores sent, but MIT said the scores didn't get there. He shrugged. Jenn rolled her eyes. Parents who knew their way around colleges would have been on the phone in seconds, hunting down the scores, insisting on a reconsideration.

Kim put off writing to St. John's admissions department for as long as she could, then emailed to say she wouldn't be coming. She pulled up Cal State San Marcos's website and clicked on her Statement of Intent to Register, her SIR. San Marcos was nearly an hour's drive from her house, in North County, the sprawling suburban and rural area of San Diego County that lies north of the city and south of the Orange County line. Tuition plus all the fees amounted to about five thousand dollars a year, and she had a Cal Grant that offset part of that. She was still working at Chick-fil-A, and in the summer she'd go full time, as many hours as she could get. By August she could buy a car and still pay most of her fees. She wouldn't have to ask her father for much.

Robert Silva, who walked the Susan G. Komen Three-Day for his mother, didn't get into any of the UCs. No surprise. Cal State Fullerton turned him down. So did Northridge. He was disappointed, but he didn't have time to think about it much. Things were getting weird at home. His mother had filed for divorce, and his father had moved out, bought an RV, and parked it in front of the house; that was where his father was living. Robert ignored him as much as he could and kept himself focused on the tutoring program he was organizing for freshmen and sophomores at Lincoln High. The envelope that arrived from Cal State Los Angeles was thin, and he didn't open it for three days. The letter welcomed him to the class of 2013.

Cal State LA was good, he told himself. Julio Marcial, the program officer from the California Wellness Foundation who'd authorized RC's big grant, lived near the campus. Robert had connected with him when he first came to Reality Changers to observe the program, and they'd emailed all year. Julio saw Robert as a impulsive little brother who needed an older brother's guidance. For Robert, he was Uncle Julio who praised his community service and kept reminding him to keep his grades up. In LA he'd have someone looking after him. He said, "There are some kids who do their best in school. For me, as long as I'm in school and making progress, I'm good. I figure that I learn more from experiences than I do sitting in a classroom."

That week in the Senior Academy he stood up and said he was about to send his SIR. The Senior Academy tutors made a big deal of SIRs. Seniors stood up and announced they were going to hit "send," and everyone, students and tutors, gave them a drumroll.

Fernando Carrillo, who'd lost his shoes because he wouldn't join a gang, opened a letter from UC San Diego congratulating him on being a member of the freshman class. The next day he opened an urgent email from the admissions office saying the letter was a mistake. Someone in their admissions office clicked on "print" for the wrong list, and letters of acceptance went out to forty-seven thousand applicants they'd turned down. He went back to watching his mailbox. A letter from San Diego State came the next week. He waited a week. No one called or emailed to say it was a mistake. Tuesday night he called for a drumroll for his SIR.

Chris Estrada, an indifferent student and a strong soccer player, got a scholarship offer from Cal State Dominguez Hills and an invitation to try out for its soccer team, which had won the Division II national championship the previous year. He was also admitted to Point Loma Nazarene University. He had to choose. He loved soccer, and he liked a college that supported his faith. Faith mattered more. He sent his SIR to Point Loma.

Now it was the last week of March, when the most selective schools sent their notifications.

Jesse, whom Yanov had invited to Obama's inauguration, had acceptances from Columbia and Swarthmore and Duke. He wasn't sure where Swarthmore was. Ashley Solano, who had been a year ahead of him at RC, was a freshman at Duke. He'd talked with her at Christmas, and Duke sounded like a good place. Maybe he'd go there.

The afternoon the email came he was at home by himself. His brother was out with his friends and his mother was grocery shopping. The email was from Harvard. Whatever their decision was, he wanted his mother to be with him when he found out. He'd open the email, get the code, and wait until she came home. He clicked on the email. No code. Just congratulations and welcome to Harvard's freshman class.

He sat for a long time. He didn't shout or dance or speak. Finally he reached for his iPod and looked for something that could be a victory anthem. He played Soulja Boy's "Turn My Swag On." Above the music he heard the screech of metal—the sound of the worn brake pads on his mother's car—and rushed down the stairs. "Mom, Mom! I got into Harvard! The number one university in the U.S.!" He went to hug her, but she was clutching plastic bags from Food 4 Less.

"Okay," she said, "pero no me vas a ayudar con las bolsas (but aren't you going to help me with the bags)?" He took the grocery bags and carried them upstairs, and when she got to the top of the stairs she gave him an affectionate, perfunctory hug, the hug she'd give him for a good grade on a quiz. Back in Mexico, she'd gone only as far as eighth grade, and she didn't know much about colleges. He told her where Harvard was and how much money they were giving him in scholarship money. He didn't know what it meant to her until the fall.

She came to Cambridge for Freshman Parents Weekend. On Sunday she was eating with Jesse in Annenberg Hall, the enormous dining hall that Henry James described as "the great bristling brick Valhalla . . . that house of honor and hospitality which dispenses laurels to the dead and dinners to the living." She looked up at the hammerbeam trusses with their soaring central arch, and the colored light streaming through the stained glass windows. She was silent for a long time. Then she turned to her son and said, "I've seen all the old brick buildings. I've seen the beautiful architecture. I've worked very hard all my life. Por tus esfuerzos siento que mis sacrificios van a valer algo grande y mis suenos van a ser realizados (Your efforts make me believe that my sacrifices will have great value and my dreams will be realized)."

The afternoon that Jesse opened his email from Harvard, he'd be going to Reality Changers. The seniors would join the underclassmen after dinner that night to say where they were going in the fall. He'd announce it then. Right now he needed to hold it close to himself until he could believe it.

Stanford turned Karina down. New York University and UC San Diego and Santa Clara University offered her admission. NYU was out of the question; they didn't offer nearly enough in scholarship money. Walt the tutor told her about the Hurtado Scholarship at Santa Clara, a Jesuit university near Silicon Valley. More than twenty scholarships were awarded each year to undocumented students attending Santa Clara. She needed to get on it. The application was due in a week.

Daniel opened a thin envelope from Stanford. Thanks but no thanks. Another thin envelope, from Harvard. Sorry. He was looking at UC Santa Barbara, UC San Diego, and Northeastern Arizona. UCSB and Northeastern Arizona would mean living away from home for four years. His parents couldn't pay for that. He could go to UCSD, but he wouldn't get any scholarship help. Reality Changers would help with his first year, as it would for Karina. After that year, he'd be back in his old bedroom, riding three buses to get to campus, or one bus to San Diego City College. In the corner of the Senior Academy where he and Karina sat next to each other, their disappointment hung like a dark fog.

He looked at his email and flipped around friends' Facebook pages. He'd have to send a SIR to one of those schools, but not right now. In the break room he ate with Jesse and Fernando. Tamales for dinner tonight—chicken wrapped in masa and corn husks—plus cheese with jalapeño wrapped in banana leaves. He'd had swim practice this afternoon, and usually after practice he could eat three of them. Tonight he had no appetite. Jesse told them about a dance at his church this weekend. Fernando was interested, and he and Jesse talked about double-dating. Daniel barely listened. He didn't have a girlfriend—and anyway, getting to Jesse's church by bus would be a hassle.

Back at his desk in the Senior Academy, Daniel woke up the monitor and clicked on his email. One new message, from Dartmouth. He clicked it open. He was a member of Dartmouth's freshman class. Eighteen thousand applicants. One thousand places in the freshman class. He read the email over and over. Each time it said the same thing. It was from Dartmouth College. He was admitted to Dartmouth College.

He turned to Karina, and spoke softly, "I got in. To Dartmouth."

"Oh my god, that's so cool." She stood up and hugged him. Alessandra, next to her, looked up. "He got in to Dartmouth," Karina said to the whole room.

The seniors poured out of their chairs and surrounded him, high-fiving and fist-bumping and hugging him. Jesse crossed the room grinning. "Way to go, bro. They wait-listed me."

The wrestler and the swimmer hugged, eyes wet, powerful arms wrapped around each other. They were poor Mexican American kids whom others expected to become fry cooks or gardeners. They'd worked so hard, done everything Yanov and the tutors told them to do. Now they were claiming their places on the great American escalator.

At seven the seniors ambled down the hall to the large meeting room, talking and laughing. Last year and the year before, and the year before that at the iglesia, they'd sat and watched the seniors. Now they were the show. One by one they stood up and announced where they'd been admitted and where they'd be going next fall. They were going to Cal State San Marcos and San Diego State and UC Riverside and Dartmouth College and Point Loma Nazarene and Cal State LA and UC San Diego and Cal State Dominguez Hills and Harvard.

Students clapped and stomped for every senior, every announcement. The younger kids knew these guys; they'd sat here with them the previous year. Now the seniors were standing up in front of them with the news, barely believable, that kids just like them were really going to college. Yanov asked for one last cheer for all the seniors and then sent the younger students off to their tutoring groups.

Santiago Milagro stood in the hall, waiting for Yanov. "Chris! I got this essay I gotta write for English. I've gotta do it tonight."

He'd watched the seniors. Now he had to get himself into college. Tonight.

"Let's walk to your study group," Yanov said, and put a hand on his shoulder.

"I can't go home 'til I'm finished."

"Start working on it in your group. See how much you can get done."

Outside the Senior Academy room, Daniel sagged against the wall. His legs were jelly, and his shoulders heaved. His breath came in gulps, as though he'd swum a hundred-yard sprint. He slid down the wall and sat on the floor.

Yanov found him there, his head between his knees. "You okay?"

Daniel looked up and nodded. He was an undocumented Mexican kid who slipped off the city bus if the *migra* got on, and now he was a freshman at an Ivy League college. He couldn't connect the two pictures in his head.

Yanov knelt beside him and put a hand on his shoulder. "Don't worry. It'll still be true tomorrow and the day after that. You have some time to get your mind around it."

At nine o'clock, students finished their study groups, still high on the seniors' announcements. Santiago said, "I got to keep working on this essay, Chris. Can I stay 'til midnight?"

While Santiago wrote, Yanov waited in his office, replaying tonight's meeting. Daniel. Jesse. The looks on the younger students' faces. At eleven o'clock he told Santiago he'd have to wrap it up. In Yanov's truck Santiago slouched down in the seat and turned on the radio, old-school rock, freeway volume. Yanov rolled his eyes and drove. After a while Santiago said, "Chris. Can I read you my essay?" He backed the volume down a little and started reading.

He read a page. Turned the radio down some more.

He read, and backed the volume down again. By the time Yanov pulled up in front of Santiago's house, the radio was muted background noise and Santiago's new vision of himself was rising to full volume.

22 The Costs of Their Dreams

The journey takes the form of a quest, a search for
something of immense consequence but not necessarily
known, not necessarily found. The journey's import is not
in arriving at the destination but in knowing what it
means to arrive, and in knowing its cost.

Exie Abola, "Pilgrim of the Healing Hand"

At dinner in the break room the seniors were feeling good. Everyone was admitted somewhere, and even if they didn't all get their first-choice school, everyone was going to college. They still had homework and tests and papers to write, but they weren't worrying much about them.

In March, Senator Richard Durbin, who was a Democrat, introduced the DREAM Act for the eighth year, this time with cosponsorship from Senator Richard Lugar, a Republican from Indiana. The country had a new president and a new Congress, and hope for a better immigration law was running strong.

The nights were still cold, but now, in early April, the days were warm and getting longer, and today every senior was wearing shorts. Proms were coming up, and over dinner seniors talked about dresses and tuxes, where to eat, and what to do afterward. Robert Silva was happy. Parents brought pizza and pasta with sausage tonight, and Robert said, "Good food. And when it's good food, you know it's gonna be a good night."

Back in the Senior Academy room, Debbi Leto held up her hand for their attention. "I need to go over some things with you. Here's what you've got to do between now and graduation:

"Keep your grades up. One D or F can get your admission yanked. If you're having trouble with a class, let one of us know.

"Keep looking for scholarships. Money is *really, really* tight this year. You need to chase down every lead that Martha gives you.

"Bring in your parents' tax return as soon as they have it. FAFSA needs that update. If they don't have your parents' return, colleges won't even consider you for scholarship aid. They'll just put you in the 'deferred' pile, and by the time they get around to you, all the money will be gone.

"Remember that your SIR is binding. The minute you click on that, you're committed to that school. If you have any questions, talk to me. Talk to Chris. When you're ready to submit, do it here. We'll give you a drum-roll. Once you click for your SIR, right away get to work on housing. It's always a hassle, and you need to stay on top of it or you won't have a place to live.

"Sign up for orientation and placement tests and anything else your college tells you to do. Read your Gmail every day. Every day. You've got to stay on top of this stuff.

"Always, always, you need to tell us where you need help."

Getting into college was their holy grail. For years they'd dreamed of it, given up their nights and weekends for it, pushed themselves harder and reached higher than they thought they could to make it happen. They hadn't looked beyond getting in. Couldn't see that their quest for admission was only a short section on a very long road. Once they clicked on their SIR, their road turned a corner, and they saw that it stretched far out in front of them. Getting in wasn't even a guarantee they'd be going; they had to keep their grades up and keep looking for scholarships. Getting in didn't fix things in other parts of their lives. That lesson came home again and again.

Dartmouth invited Daniel to its spring weekend for prospective freshmen. There'd be parties and sports and campus tours and overnights in the dorms, a chance at last to see this campus on the other side of the country, which he knew only from its website.

How would he get to Hanover, New Hampshire? Fly to Boston, he knew that much. He'd never been on a plane. Debbi Leto explained that the price of the flight could vary a lot, depending on which airline, how far in advance he booked, and what day of the week. Even the time of day mattered. She explained what a red-eye was. Once he got to Boston, what would he do? She helped him find out about buses and trains. Even the red-eye wasn't cheap, and with bus fare and meals the trip was adding up to serious money. He called Dartmouth's admissions office to ask whether they could help with the cost. The woman he talked with was very nice, but she couldn't offer him any help.

His parents sat Daniel down at the kitchen table. They reminded him that not only would the trip cost a lot of money, but there was also real risk. Both ways, he'd have to show his ID at airport security. Maybe on the train or bus, too. His ID was a Mexican consulate card; it identified him as a Mexican citizen. What if airport security demanded to see a visa? His tourist visa expired when he was nine years old. What if they called *la migra?* He'd have to fly in the fall, they said. Don't push your luck with an extra trip now.

In his article "Learning to Be Illegal," immigration scholar Roberto Gonzales charts the painful transition that undocumented youth face as they launch into adulthood and learn that the protected status they enjoyed in high school has fallen away. By age sixteen most undocumented youth have begun to face this painful realization.[1] The fact of his immigration status wasn't news to Daniel, but the talk with his parents brought it home more forcefully than ever. He emailed the admissions office that he wouldn't be coming for freshman weekend. He was going to an Ivy League school, but to the government of his adopted country he was just one more undocumented immigrant, at risk for arrest and deportation.

He watched Jesse leave for a ten-day trip to Columbia and Harvard, no worries at airport security, and both schools providing financial help that covered his air fare. Getting into Dartmouth was a very good thing. But it didn't change anything about the biggest problem in his life.

This was the hardest year for scholarships that Debbi Leto had seen since she started the Senior Academy. The Cal States and some of the UC campuses were backing away from financial aid commitments they'd made only months earlier. The Lehman Brothers bankruptcy and the fallout from Wall Street that followed had gouged a huge chunk out of the universities' investments. Almost every week another senior came to her with a letter from a financial aid office that said it would not be able to deliver the full amount of a promised grant. Debbie or Martha followed up on every letter. They made calls and wrote appeals that explained students' financial situations. Sometimes it worked and a committee agreed to stand by the original amount or reduce the size of the hit. Sometimes it didn't. She felt like she was standing at the door of the Senior Academy with a shotgun, keeping the financial aid officers and their clawbacks at bay.

Then there were the glitches, unforeseen and anxiety-making for the seniors, unsurprising to their tutors and mostly fixable. Fernando Carrillo's high school dropped the ball. He was admitted to San Diego State, and his school didn't enter his first semester grades on the transcript they sent to SDSU. Without those first semester grades, SDSU wouldn't allow him to apply for housing. Debbi Leto called his guidance counselor, who pointed her to the district office. She was polite with the transcripts clerk at the district office, but relentless as a bulldog with its teeth sunk in a postman's ankle. She called every day until the clerk confirmed that, yes, she had entered Fernando's first semester grades on his transcript, and yes, as Mrs. Leto had insisted, she had hand-carried the transcript across town to San Diego State's admissions office. Then Debbi called SDSU's director of admissions every day until he decided it would be easier to allow Fernando Carrillo to apply for housing than to take another call from Mrs. Leto.

Karina took a plane, her first time, to San Jose, and met with people at Santa Clara University about the scholarships for undocumented students. She felt her interviews went well, but a week later an email from the school thanked her for her interest but said they would not be able to offer her a scholarship. She was admitted at Claremont-McKenna and NYU, but like Santa Clara, those places were expensive, and none offered her a financial aid package that came close to what she needed. She could go to UC Santa Barbara or UC Riverside or UC San Diego, but she couldn't get a scholarship or a Cal Grant or a Pell Grant. A year ago her father was making good money in construction, and her parents could have worked out something, but the recession had thrown the brakes on every kind of construction in Southern California. For months, her father had worked only on small jobs, a few days here and there.

Robert Silva was back in his grandmother's garage. He'd enlisted his mother and Marlon and Cathy, his younger sister, to work at a Reality Changers' service project, helping out at the Special Olympics. Even

Angel, now eight months old, came along in his stroller. It was a good day until they drove home late in the afternoon. His father stood in the doorway, red-faced and angry. "It's my house," he said. "You're all moving out tomorrow." The next day they left with not much more than a change of clothes, and diapers for Angel, and crowded into the garage.

After his parents had separated, Robert had worked to keep a connection with his father and an open mind about him. Now this craziness. His father asked his sister Cathy to go for a walk and told her that he was planning to move back to Honduras; would she like to move there with him? Cathy was committed to her mother and Angel. She said no. He asked Marlon. Marlon had his differences with Robert, but he couldn't imagine his life without his older brother. He said no. The parents had a court date the next week, and when the judge heard what Robert's father had done, he was furious. He gave him forty-eight hours to leave the house, move the RV, pay his back support and cease and desist all harassment. Robert and his family moved back to the house. That was a relief, but he felt whipsawed and helpless.

He said, "I thought about it. The one thing I have is my education. What I've learned is mine. Nobody can touch it. Nobody can take it away. I own it, forever."

Sony Entertainment had offices in San Diego, and Yanov had invited their senior executives to visit Reality Changers. In April they donated small, lightweight laptops, one for every graduating senior. The seniors would go to college with their own computers.

Kim wanted to live on campus at Cal State San Marcos. If she couldn't go to college in New York, she wanted to at least live on campus and see more of San Diego than her neighborhood of Logan Heights. She also wanted to step away, at least for a while, from the job of oldest daughter, the one who kept the household going and who looked after her sisters when her mother got depressed and retreated to her bedroom. But she was torn: living away felt like abandoning her family, yet she knew she needed to make a move; if she didn't do it now, would she ever? Her parents wouldn't talk about her going to college; when she brought it up, they changed the subject. Did they not get that she was really going? She and her sister Theresa, a year younger, talked endlessly about what their obligations were. They needed to take care of themselves; and they also needed to help their parents and, even more, Stephanie and Michelle, who were twelve and nine and looked to their older sisters as role models.

Kim took a break from her questions when the girls in Reality Changers learned about the Princess Project, a charity that organized donations of prom dresses and accessories from retailers and individuals and gave them away to girls who wouldn't be able to afford them. The Saturday of the giveaway, junior and senior girls met for breakfast at seven in the morning, then carpooled to the empty store where the giveaway was. A line already spilled out the door and wrapped around the building. The day was hot, and they waited for four hours in the sun for their chance. Inside, hundreds and hundreds of dresses hung on long racks, arranged by color. Girls with armfuls of dresses ran from rack to rack, shouting to their friends and texting photos of dresses to others who couldn't make it. The dressing rooms were packed, and everywhere girls and mothers were arguing. Lots of girls gave up on the dressing rooms and just tried on things between the racks. Kim knew just what she was looking for. She wanted a dress with a fitted top and a short poufy skirt, above the knee. She found it in the rack of purple and fuchsia dresses. The color was pretty intense, but it was the cut and the style she wanted. She walked out in triumph.

She couldn't get on-campus housing, but she found a Reality Changers student from the North County group who was going to San Marcos. She lived in Solana Beach, much nearer the campus, and her family had a room they could rent to Kim. For now, her plan was to work as many hours as she could throughout the summer, save her money, and keep reminding her parents that, come August, she'd be leaving for college.

Their ambitions and their families' needs were a difficult balancing act for the seniors. Many of them were the eldest children and, like Kim, carried a heavy burden of responsibility at home. They helped run the household, cared for younger siblings, worked and gave their earnings to their parents, and served as their parents' translators and cultural guides. Their departures would leave empty places in their families. Some, like Robert Silva, had a younger sibling who wasn't committed to the same ambitious path or who was veering toward trouble. Whether they stayed in San Diego or went to college far away, students stayed closely connected with their families and the problems that arose at home. Suzie Lozano, from the class of '05, went to UC San Diego. Through four years of college, an internship in Washington, DC, fellowships in Thailand and Brazil, and graduate school in Ann Arbor, no matter where she traveled, she always heard from her mother about what her younger brother was doing.

The seniors' parents were intensely proud of their children. That their children went to college was proof that the parents' long-ago decision to leave behind family and the life they knew, and to venture to *el Norte,* was worth the costs. Yet they also worried about how their families would manage without their firstborns. Who would help them as these eldest children had always done? And there was another worry, barely articulated but deeply felt. If their child went to college, how much would he or she change? Would he still want to be part of the family? If she got the good job and made a lot of money, would she look down on her parents? Would helping their children succeed in America mean losing them?

Karina sent her SIR to UC San Diego. She was disappointed. She'd made such good grades and she'd hoped to go to a private college. Staying in San Diego and going to UCSD felt like falling short of her goal. She couldn't get a Pell Grant or a Cal Grant; how would her family pay for it? Yanov told her that Reality Changers would pay her first year's tuition and her room and board in a dorm. He believed that living on campus was important for students who stayed in San Diego. He wanted them to have some distance from the strong pull of family. Karina could intern at Reality Changers this summer and next, and she and her parents would have her freshman year to figure how they would pay for the next three.

Then her father cut off his thumb. He was working construction, using a circular saw, and he lost his grip on the saw. Suddenly his left hand was in the blade's path. The blade spun through his thumb and cut it off clean. He picked his thumb up and wrapped it in a T-shirt, and carried it with him to the hospital. He was undocumented and he had no insurance. A hand surgeon said, Don't worry about paying now, let's see what we can do for your thumb. He came home from the hospital with his hand in bandages the size of a boxing glove. For a month, while ligaments and tendons and blood vessels regrew and knit his thumb back onto his hand, Karina cut up his food and pressed the TV remote and helped him button his shirts. She thought about all that her father nearly lost, and what that could have meant for him and for her family. She thought about what she'd accomplished and all that she had. "I saw that I have my family, and that I could go to UCSD," she said. "I made an intention that I was going to enjoy it."

23 Reckonings

*Santiago's got to resolve this for himself, and how he does
will shape the rest of his life.*

Chris Yanov

In May, stratus clouds form off the coast of Southern California, and
onshore winds carry them to San Diego, where they form a blanket of low
clouds that can linger for days. Locals call it May gray. The jacaranda trees
bloomed along University Avenue, and under the low gray sky their pur-
ple-blue panicles were luminous. The days grew longer, the air warmer,
and the end of the school year, which hardly felt possible a month ago,
now loomed a few weeks away. For Jenn Schadler and Jonny Villafuerte,
for Santiago Milagro and Chris Yanov, the shape of things became clearer
in the soft gray light: where the year had brought them, what they would
do next.

Jenn loved her work and she felt a deep connection to the students.
Debbi and Grace were the best colleagues she could imagine. She and
Grace had improved the program in so many ways, by making procedures
clearer, by making meeting nights run more smoothly, and especially by
advocating for girls. For months she'd thought about whether she could
work at Reality Changers another year. She could do a lot more good if
she stayed, but she would never have real authority. Coming into the
job, she'd hoped for a collegial relationship and a chance to learn from
Yanov. Instead, he called her the Challenger and stonewalled her when she

questioned his decisions; he insisted that she and Grace check all their plans with him. She couldn't see the situation getting any better.

Her longtime boyfriend, Alan, had gone to MIT, and now he had an offer to work with friends on a tech startup in Cambridge. He asked her to come with him. She'd grown up in the Bay Area and had gone to San Diego State; she had never lived outside of California. Here was a chance to see a new city, another part of the country. Leaving Reality Changers would be wrenching. Staying on would be intolerable.

She walked into Yanov's office. "Chris. I need to tell you that Alan and I are moving to Boston."

"You are? When?"

"I'll be here through the end of the school year and the scholarship banquet. We'll leave at the end of June."

"You could start a Reality Changers there."

He'd kept her on a short leash all year, dismissed her suggestions, and undone half her plans. Now he wanted her to found a new chapter three thousand miles away? "I don't think so, Chris."

"Well, thanks for all you've done."

That was all. No appreciation of her work, nothing about how he might replace her, no interest in how she was feeling. She felt as though he hadn't heard her.

Weeks passed. He never mentioned her upcoming departure to the students or the volunteers. She'd have to tell them herself. They'd need time to digest the news.

As the Senior Academy's session was winding down, Jenn walked in and stood at the front of the room. Her face was flushed and tears rolled down her cheeks. She looked at the seniors and beckoned to Jesse Sanchez. He stood beside her and draped his arm across her shoulders.

"You guys are the class I've gotten to know the best at Reality Changers. You're all going off to such terrific places, and . . ." Her voice broke. Jesse hugged her.

"I wanted to tell you I'm moving to Boston, about a mile from where Jesse's going to be, which is crazy."

Jesse wrapped both arms around her and said, "Let's give her a hug."

Twelve seniors jumped up and swarmed her, wrapping their arms around her and each other. They needed to feel their friends' arms around them as much as she did. So much was changing for them now. In a few months they'd be heading off to the new lives they longed to start, but when they imagined their leaving, they imagined that everything else would stay just the same. It's the fantasy we conjure whenever we move on, that the world we're leaving will stay just as we left it, as unchanged as the scene in a snow globe, always there for us to come back to. Now, here was Jenn, who'd been there since they joined, part of the heart of Reality Changers as much as Debbi or Chris or Grace, and she'd be leaving town before they did. It was another lesson of launching, that as much we want things to, nothing stays the same.

.   .   .   .   .

Jonny Villafuerte sat alone in the break room, hunched over the table as though a fifty-pound sack were slung across his shoulders. Point Loma Nazarene's graduation had been the previous weekend: pomp and circumstance, balloons, and speeches, and the air filled with mortar boards. His mother cried and took lots of pictures of him in his cap and gown. His father shook his hand. Then it was over, and seniors had to be out of the dorms by six that evening. He said a last good-bye to his girlfriend, Anna, and watched as her parents drove away, carrying her back to Los Angeles. His parents helped him haul his stuff out to the car. Now he was back in his old bedroom in their apartment.

His father told him he should have married Anna. If they'd gotten married, he'd be on his way to a green card now, finding a job wouldn't be a hassle, and graduate school would be a possibility.

He couldn't do it.

His life at Point Loma was over. He was a college graduate, but now he had to learn to be illegal. He'd left applications at ten restaurants where his father told him they wouldn't ask questions. Business was slow; his father had been out of work for three months. He told Jonny to take anything: bus boy, kitchen help, whatever. Jonny had always believed that his future was in God's hands, that God would show him the way. Could busing dishes be what God meant for him?

Driving home at night, Jonny turned the wrong way down a one-way street. The police car's red light filled his rearview mirror. He pulled over.

The officer asked for his license; Jonny said he couldn't provide one. He'd never had a license. He handed the officer his Point Loma ID. The officer didn't ask him any questions, just wrote him a ticket for driving without a license and told him that he'd have to impound the vehicle. Jonny walked home, shaky with relief. His friend Antonio had had the same thing happen to him a few months earlier. Antonio got deported.

He wondered if he'd ever get to be a guidance counselor.

·   ·   ·   ·   ·

Spring midterms, and Santiago Milagro made A's in every subject. Yanov cheered silently and braced himself for the blowback. Santiago got into a fight and was suspended from school for a week. Yanov told him he'd have to come to Reality Changers every day of his suspension, from noon until whenever Yanov went home. Santiago showed up well before noon, every day, wearing a black pinstripe suit with a white shirt whose untucked tails hung to his knees, and black-and-white patent leather wingtips. Yanov put him to work on his homework, found chores for him to do, and ate dinner with him. Santiago did everything Yanov assigned, complaining the whole time about how dumb everything was. His face was full of light and he was smiling.

Tuesday afternoon, when students arrived for the meeting, he stopped smiling. He sat through Hot Words, ate dinner, and sat through the lesson stone-faced. The lesson ended and students ambled off to their study groups. He waited in the hall for Yanov.

"Chris. You got anything you want me to do now?"

"It's Congress. You need to head on down to your group."

"Congress is dumb."

"It's where you're supposed to be, Santiago. That's part of your job here: be where you're supposed to be when you're supposed to be there."

Even Yanov's gentle limit-setting felt like an abandonment. The only way Santiago knew to help himself feel better was to provoke a fight. He took five minutes to walk thirty feet to the room where his tutoring group met, and walked in late. Bob, the lead tutor, handed him the Congress binder. "You're up, Santiago. It's your week to lead Congress."

"I don't know what I'm supposed to do." He shoved the binder back across the table at Bob.

Bob pushed it back to him. "Same thing we've done every week, all year. Read the Declaration of Purpose."

Santiago perched on the back of a chair, feet on the seat, and held the binder up in front of his face. He raced through the Declaration in a monotone.

"Okay. Now you need to go around the room and ask everybody their highs and lows."

Santiago flung his body across a table to shake Aldo's hand. The table wobbled under his weight.

He walked backward to where Marlon sat and shook his hand. He asked him his highs and lows with his back to him. He spoke to Bob and the other boys and sat down.

"You need to do highs and lows for everyone."

There were three girls in the group. He approached each of them as though she had a contagious disease. He mumbled the question, barely touched their hands, and wouldn't look at them.

Bob wasn't going to get into it with him. "Okay, thank you, Santiago. Now let's get to work." Santiago sat with a book in front of him, unopened. No fight, no distraction. Just missing Yanov.

In May, report cards came out again, and one of Santiago's teachers told Yanov that he'd put up a 4.0. His grade point average for the year would be higher than 3.5, good for a scholarship to Academic Connections. Attending would give him a taste of college. It could seal the deal. Yanov picked up a couple of fat carne asada burritos and drove over to Patrick Henry to surprise Santiago. He looked all over the campus. Santiago wasn't there. Hadn't been there for a couple of days, the attendance office said.

Santiago didn't come to Reality Changers that week. He didn't come the next week, for the night when every senior gave a speech. Their speeches were emotional, filled with testimonials about how Reality Changers had helped them. Yanov presented each senior with a sweatshirt for the college he or she would be going to. The seniors made a gorgeous showing of color in their new sweatshirts, bright, visible symbols of their achievement. Sweatshirt night packed a strong inspirational punch for the underclassmen. Yanov badly wanted Santiago to be there. He wished he could go find him and drag him back for the night.

Yet he knew that wouldn't work, even if he could find him. "It's up to him," he said. "Santiago's got to resolve this for himself, and how he does will shape the rest of his life."

Santiago showed up two weeks later. It was Tutor Appreciation Night, and in Hot Words the students worked in groups of three to come up with ways to show their appreciation for their tutors. Santiago and two other freshmen from his study group had to come up with an act of appreciation for Bob. Jesse Sanchez and Chris circulated among the groups, offering suggestions and coaching. Santiago folded his arms across his chest and stared out the window. It was as though he couldn't understand the task, as if everyone were speaking a language he didn't understand.

Had he ever had a birthday party? Had his family ever made a fuss over him, made him special?

The other two students in his group were working on a proclamation. Jesse insisted that Santiago had to do something. He could help write it. Santiago started printing in a crabbed gothic script. He finished half a sentence. It was his last time at Reality Changers.

He rode the bus for two days back to Rincón de Tlapita. The night that Yanov learned that Santiago had left, after the last parent drove away, after Debbi Leto wrote all her follow-up emails and Jenn and Grace checked the rooms where the study groups met, after the lights went out and everyone else rode down the elevator, he sat at his desk in the dark, staring out at University Avenue. What else could he have done? Would anything he could have done have changed things enough for Santiago?

This year Santiago learned that he could do the academics. That was the good news and the complication. Doing schoolwork and going to Academic Connections and all the other stuff that Reality Changers expected of him meant staying in San Diego, far away from his mother and his little sister. His *familia*. His aunt and uncle could give him a place to stay, and Yanov could give him fragments of what he needed, but it wasn't enough to live on. He wasn't even fifteen. He needed to go home.

·   ·   ·   ·   ·

Late in May, Yanov leaned back in his chair and talked about the year. It was the hardest year since he started the program. Having employees was more work than doing everything himself. He built a culture for the students, a collective vision that guided and supported them. He hadn't known that taking on paid staff meant that he needed to invest time with them, begin to build a culture with the staff, change how he operated. There was always too much to do; and even with fund-raising and dealing with difficult students—the tasks he knew best—he was overwhelmed. He could see that Grace and Jenn and the program had paid all year for his lapses.

Still, he felt he'd become a better manager this year. He'd learned to let them run with their assignments, and he didn't micromanage so much.

Santiago's leaving was still fresh. He didn't want to talk about it.

He talked about the year's gains. The program had doubled in size this year, serving 104 students at two sites and on three meeting nights. The graduating class of 22 was the largest in Reality Changers' history. While the national economy foundered in a brutal and deepening recession, he'd managed to raise more money than he ever had before. The program was in the black. A record 52 students were eligible for scholarships to Academic Connections this summer. Reality Changers' bill for them was $110,000, and he already had $70,000 in hand.

Even though he'd barely acknowledged Jenn's leaving to her, he thought a lot about it. She'd done what he most needed: written an operations manual that covered every aspect of the program. She was a great organizer, he said, excellent at details and implementation. He hadn't decided how he would replace her. He could bring in someone with experience at a higher salary or hire another new graduate, someone who'd tutored and knew the program, at a lower salary. He still saw Reality Changers as a small, hardscrabble startup; he couldn't imagine that anyone would want to work here. He remained sensitive to being told by anyone what to do. He mused, "Why bring in a fifty-year-old expert and have to listen to that person?"

Reality Changers made A's for the year in growth, fund-raising, and scholarships. It had succeeded in its core mission: helping students develop the skills, behaviors, and attitudes that would enable them to get to college. From the outside it looked very successful. Inside, less so. In building a management team and a supportive culture, in clarifying its priorities when choosing whom it would serve—the most vulnerable or the most determined—and in developing a succession plan, all of which are tasks that enable an organization's present and ensure its future, RC had blown off its homework and no-showed its exams. All these tasks are the work of more than a single year, but this year it didn't make a start. Its grade was an Incomplete. As it faced the future, questions remained about whether Yanov could help the program he'd built grow into a sustainable organization.

24 Scholarship Banquet

Don't give up. This program will never give up on you.

Rudy Torres, Reality Changers 2009

The Scholarship Banquet was Reality Changers' grandest celebration, its end-of-the-year party held on the roof of the parking garage to honor the accomplishments of the students, especially the seniors. The party started on the ramp that ran from the last parking floor up to the roof, in the long light of a June evening. Mariachi music played as the seniors; their parents and grandparents and brothers and sisters; alumni, tutors, and other volunteers; and donors from churches and corporations and foundations—more than six hundred people—walked up the gentle slope, past tables draped in royal blue, one for each senior. Each table held a nine-by-twelve-inch framed photo of the senior, clad in a sweatshirt from the college where he or she would be going in the fall, and a memory book where guests could write greetings and congratulations. Proud and hopeful, Reality Changers' class of 2009 smiled from their portraits at the arriving guests. With the names of their colleges right there, the photos were a powerful confirmation that these students had indeed changed their current realities and would change the shape of their futures.

The lines of attendees moved slowly, students' families mingling with donors and foundation officers as they moved together up the ramp. People stopped at tables whether they'd known those seniors all their lives, or not at all, and wrote their congratulations. Sometimes they took pictures. Little brothers and sisters and cousins moved the slowest. They stopped at every table, studied every picture. Spoke the names of the colleges. Turned the pages of the memory books, read every good word and message of congratulations. These children were very much in Yanov's mind when he and his team planned the night. They were Reality Changers' future, and tonight he would have their full attention.

Tonight was his most public opportunity to thank all his donors and show decision makers from foundations and corporations, from city government and school districts, what Reality Changers could accomplish. He would also honor the more than one hundred tutors and other volunteers whose work carried the program.

At the top of the ramp, guests strolled under a gently swaying arc of blue and white balloons and onto the roof. They settled at tables or stood talking, fathers in neatly pressed jeans and tooled leather belts and the occasional jacket; mothers in bright florals or crisp summer suits. All the parents looked proud and happy and sometimes a little stunned. Even though they'd driven their sons and daughters to meetings for years, woken them early on weekends for community service events, praised their report cards, and sent them to Academic Connections, their pride tonight was still tinged with amazement that they were here. That with their help and that of Reality Changers, their children had stepped onto the American ladder of success.

The seniors clustered with their friends, admiring their dressed-up selves: girls in short-skirted cocktail dresses, skintight or extravagantly ruffled, boys in dress shirts and ties and pants with creases. Robert Silva preened in white shirt and black tie, black vest and white pants. He and Jesse Sanchez would emcee a good part of the evening.

Jonny Villafuerte found Miguel Cerón talking with Suzie Lozano and Jorge Narvaez, all of them alumni of Reality Changers' first graduating class in 2005. Suzie was home from a semester's fellowship in Thailand. She'd graduate from UCSD next spring, and already she was working on applications to graduate school. Miguel had graduated from Harvard a week earlier, and he'd be flying to New York soon, to start a training program with Macy's in retail consulting. For now, he was happy to be home with his parents and younger brother Diego, who'd just finished his first year in Reality Changers. Miguel told a story about one of his best moments in Reality Changers: three years ago, home from Harvard on a break, he'd spoken to students at Patrick Henry High School about aiming for college. Afterward a student introduced himself. His name was Jesse Sanchez, he was a sophomore, and he wondered what he'd have to do to get into Harvard. Miguel had told him, "Go to Reality Changers. It'll help you get there." Tonight he was here to celebrate with Jesse. Jorge talked about his idea for a Reality Changers Alumni Association. It could be a way to keep in touch, a support network for RC graduates in college, and a way of communicating to alums about jobs and other possibilities.

Dinner, provided by students' families, was laid out on serving tables: platters of burritos and tamales, pots of barbacoa swimming in sauce, deep baking dishes of enchiladas, baskets of corn and flour tortillas. Bowls of orange and red and brown salsas that ranged from mild to volcanic, family recipes from every state and district in Mexico, filled the tables.

Yanov looked at the tables and kept walking. No time for eating tonight; he was working. He made his rounds to every table, congratulated every mother and father, every grandparent, made sure he was introduced to every younger brother and sister and cousin. He shook the hands of all of them in turn and welcomed them by name. He asked what grade they were in and told them he hoped they'd join Reality Changers when they started eighth grade. He greeted every person who'd donated to the program. He thanked them all and told them stories about the seniors, of setbacks overcome and bad influences defeated, of goals they'd reached and plans for college. He talked with city council members and staffers, representatives from the mayor's and from congresspeople's offices and thanked them for coming. He welcomed Judge Frank Devanney, who had given Eduardo Corona a second chance, and updated him on Eduardo's progress.

Clouds drifted in, softening the clear light. Down on the ground, a generator hummed and four enormous searchlights warmed up. The searchlights' white beams blazed and began their slow, dramatic sweeps across the twilight sky. Up on the roof, guests took notice and pointed. Yanov smiled. Everyone in City Heights and Golden Hill and all over San Diego could see those lights. This was Reality Changers' night.

Robert and Jesse stepped to the stage and welcomed everyone, families and guests. They invited up three underclassmen, who talked about their experiences at Academic Connections, how it made them sure they wanted to go to college. Yanov read out the names of a record fifty-two underclassmen who'd made a 3.5 or higher grade point average for the whole school year and would be going to Academic Connections in July. A video honored the program's volunteers, and Robert and Jesse gave gifts to those who'd served for five years or longer. Yanov made a pitch for donations. A video from the office of Congresswoman Susan Davis showed her standing on the House floor, telling Eduardo Corona's story. Eduardo came up on stage and thanked Judge Devanney for giving him a second chance.

Then it was the seniors' time. Yanov stepped forward and called the seniors to the stage, twenty-two of them, the largest graduating class in Reality Changers' history. He congratulated them, praised their courage and tenacity, their belief in themselves, and their service to their communities, and he thanked their parents for all that they had done to support them. He announced where each one would be going to college, and the amount of the scholarship each had earned, multiplied over four years. He handed each one a four-foot-long facsimile check for the amount of his or her scholarship. Carlos Solorio photographed each student holding the oversize check and shaking Yanov's hand while the audience cheered.

Yanov understood the importance of celebration. Reality Changers was a beacon of hope for its students. Now the seniors were part of that beacon, and their lives were lit with hope. That was only the first circle of light. Their achievements radiated through their families: after tonight, younger siblings would build their own dreams, that one day they would be the ones with the spotlights on them and their families cheering. The seniors' light would spread further, through their high schools, back to their middle schools, to kids they'd never met.

This year the seniors had learned that, as far as they'd climbed, from here on the road would only get steeper, their challenges harder. Tonight they weren't looking down that road or reckoning the costs of their dreams. Tonight was for celebrating with their families and with the friends who'd made the journey with them. Tonight they could watch the searchlights light the sky, and bask in the glow of their achievements, and be grateful for Reality Changers, the beacon of hope that helped them get to this night.

25 The Evolution of Reality Changers

When I talk about solutions that work, I hold up Reality Changers as the gold standard. You want to know how to do it, you watch Chris Yanov.

Cindy Marten, superintendent, San Diego Unified School District

By the time Yanov congratulated the seniors at the Scholarship Banquet, Reality Changers was serving more students in every successive year, and its reputation was growing, in California and around the country. It had the potential to become a national model. But Yanov couldn't make that happen by himself: he needed a strong staff. He would have to build a culture and institute practices that would develop his staff's skills, allowing them autonomy and holding them accountable. Building a strong organization was as necessary to his vision as fund-raising.

He didn't know how to do those things. This year he'd learned that they mattered, and that he and the program paid a steep price for neglecting them. Still he wasn't especially interested in the nuts and bolts of building an organization. That wasn't what he started Reality Changers to do. "My focus is on impact," he said. He was superb at making an impact in fund-raising, recruiting students, and program development, and that's where he'd always directed his energies. As Reality Changers grew, he continued to hire new college graduates, throw them into complex jobs, and expect them to learn on the fly. His young employees, many of them RC alumni, cared deeply about students and connected well with them, but often they lacked organizational and planning skills, and the quality of their work was uneven.

The solution came from an unexpected quarter. Yanov and his board were looking for innovative ways to expand the program's reach and to generate income. Yanov saw that a modified version of the Senior Academy could do both. Its model was scalable, portable, and marketable. Yanov and Debbi Leto designed College Apps Academy, a program that would meet in local high schools. It was designed for students who were aiming for college and were academically sound, but who, along with their parents, knew too little about the application process and needed a substantial helping of guidance. Too many students did not get the critical information and individualized guidance that they needed. In many of San Diego Unified's sixteen high schools, the student-to-counselor ratio hovered around five hundred-to-one. A counselor with a caseload that size, and a portfolio of other duties besides college counseling, often didn't even know the students he was charged with helping. College Apps Academy could change that.

College Apps would start with second-semester juniors and would guide them through their senior year in choosing colleges that were a good fit, help them with their applications, demand their best in their essays, look for scholarships, and prepare them and their parents for colleges' expectations. It would be priced on a sliding scale; no student would be turned away for lack of funds.

Mary Taylor applied for an instructor position with College Apps. Taylor grew up in East Los Angeles, and when her guidance counselor told her she shouldn't try to go to college, she got herself admitted to an elite private college-preparatory school. She went to UC San Diego, earned an M.Ed. at San Diego State, and completed UCLA's rigorous certificate program in college advising. As an assistant dean at UCSD she'd developed support programs for minority students. She'd also built her own advising practice, where she'd seen too many students and families who were floundering without guidance from schools. College Apps appealed to her as a means to provide students and parents with the same high-quality help that more prosperous families had.

Yanov was impressed with Taylor's fine-grained understanding of disadvantaged students' needs and her enthusiasm for the challenge. He also liked that she was an experienced manager: she understood the importance of a healthy organizational culture, and she knew how to build one. He offered her the directorship of College Apps Academy.

This move, hiring a senior manager who had expertise he lacked, marked a major change for Yanov. He'd always been the oldest staff member at Reality Changers, his authority unchallenged because he was the guy who knew the most. Taylor was seven years older, and she knew far more about college advising than he did. She would expect and deserve a larger measure of autonomy than he'd previously allowed any of his staff. He valued his young employees' energy and zeal, but he'd come to see the need for senior people with more education and experience.

As she built College Apps, Taylor continually presented her vision to Yanov of a program that was uniformly excellent in every aspect. She insisted on having the resources—time for program development and for staff training, and materials—that she knew were necessary to create it. She could explain to him the importance of what she asked for, and she wasn't intimidated. She was very clear that she had great respect for what he'd built. She could articulate how her position supported RC's values. She stood her ground. More often than not she got what she needed.

She recruited highly competent instructors and taught them principles of admissions advising. She laid out clear expectations and lines of accountability. She made the weekly staff meetings a time when her instructors could learn from each other and develop new skills. In the College Apps' work group, Taylor built the culture that all of Reality Changers needed.

Her work was a revelation for Yanov. He learned what an experienced manager could bring to the table—in her commitment to students, as passionate as his own, in her breadth of vision, and in her knowledge of the administrative structures and specific tasks required to make a program work. Although he hasn't written a formal succession plan, he's said that if something happened to him, he'd want Taylor to step into his position.

His experience with her convinced him that bringing on senior staff could make Reality Changers work better. He's since hired a vice president of organizational development to do for all of Reality Changers what Taylor has done for College Apps, in areas of staff development, supervision, evaluation, and culture-building. After fifteen years of looking for money, he's hired two seasoned fund-raisers and turned the job over to them.

Taylor's success in training her staff and building an organizational culture solved another problem for Yanov: how to replicate the programs as Reality Changers expanded. He'd built Reality Changers the only way he knew how, as an extension of his personal style. He recruited by intense personal engagement, ran meetings with his game-show-host persona, managed unruly students by getting tough and confrontational, and made all the decisions himself. His style worked for him; but few of his young employees could emulate it, and they were offered no other model. For Reality Changers to expand as Yanov wanted it to, its staff would need a set of guiding principles and practices that could accommodate a range of work and interpersonal styles, and against which staff could be measured. Taylor accomplished this with her work group, and she is now implementing her model with the core program's staff as well. For the first time since its founding, Reality Changers now provides its staff with a coherent set of principles, practices, and models that enable them to work more effectively from the outset.

College Apps Academy now operates at fourteen sites around San Diego County and serves more than six hundred students each year. It has greatly expanded Reality Changers' visibility in schools and the larger community. In the schools where it meets, administrators and faculty have watched College Apps staff help their students navigate the application process, and they've seen a significant increase in college acceptances. They're especially impressed with College Apps' ability to find scholarship funds. Martha Berner, who combed the Internet for scholarships, still produces a weekly list of scholarships for College Apps. Reality Changers markets College Apps to school districts as well as to individual students and parents. Two high school districts in northern San Diego County, San Marcos Unified and Vista Unified, have agreed to underwrite the cost the of the College Apps program for any senior at those two schools who wants to participate.

With the advent of College Apps Academy, a new name was needed for the core program to distinguish between the two. The core program is now called College Town.

As Yanov built the management team that Reality Changers needed, he significantly expanded its ambitions. He wants to grow College Town to serve a large enough cohort to make a difference for an entire community. He's partnered with San Diego Unified, the second-largest school district in California, to bring College Town and College Apps to hundreds more students within the district. He has a powerful ally in Cindy Marten, who was principal at Central Elementary when Eduardo Corona vandalized the school, and who now is San Diego Unified's superintendent. Her motto is "Dream Big," and she sees Yanov as a kindred spirit.

Marten is committed to expanding College Apps Academy throughout the district's sixteen high schools. A single College Apps cohort of twenty or so students doesn't begin to meet a high school's college counseling needs, but Marten sees the program as a lab and as a collaboration in which the district and Reality Changers can develop new solutions for helping students launch into college. She's seeking foundation support to make it happen.

Yanov and Marten are also working on a partnership to create a new home for the core program, College Town, and provide Reality Changers with the building that Yanov has always wanted. Their plan is for the district to provide a campus in City Heights, where Reality Changers will serve one thousand middle and high school students. This is Yanov's first large-scale collaboration with a publically funded entity; it will bring a higher level of visibility and public scrutiny to Reality Changers. The challenges in scaling up and in funding are substantial.

When he talks about the plan, Yanov speaks of the inspiration that a thousand determined students will draw from College Town, and of all the ways that students' hopes and energy will flow into City Heights and back to their own communities. One thousand students with new hope for their futures could catalyze hope and raise expectations in their own schools and in their communities. Parents would want more for their other children and expect more from their schools. Disadvantaged students succeeding in high school and going to college would no longer be an anomaly but could become a new norm.

Yanov continues to wrestle with the question of how to allot resources that are always scarce compared to the need. He's glad to have both College Apps Academy and College Town in Reality Changers' portfolio. College Apps serves students, many of them minorities or economically disadvantaged or both, who have already committed to changing their reality and need a time-limited scaffolding to help them launch into college.

He's insisted that College Town maintain its commitment to the low-performing, hard-to-engage young adolescents who require a commitment for the long haul. Every year, College Town admits another cohort from Wilson Middle School and Clark Middle School, drawn from eighth graders with the lowest grade point averages in the school. College Town also admits other low-performing, at-risk students, four-year-plan candidates, with the full knowledge that their progress will not be smooth, that they will tax the program's staff, and that not all will stay the course. Seeking out these students is crucial to his vision of Reality Changer; they are the ones that Yanov and others in the program want to prevent from ending up in a coffin, the ones he started the program for.

These are the latest mile markers on the long road from the iglesia in Golden Hill. Yet the vision that drives Reality Changers is the same as it was when a twenty-two-year-old substitute teacher brought his message of hope to a handful of eighth graders at the iglesia, to help students see what they're capable of and to provide the scaffolding to help them achieve it.

Epilogue

*The most important thing I got from Reality Changers is
the courage to try things.*

Kimberly Palafox

Since the seniors portrayed in this book graduated from high school, two changes have improved the lives of undocumented youth. The California Legislature passed the California DREAM Act (Development, Relief, and Education for Alien Minors), and now undocumented students who meet criteria for in-state tuition at California public universities can apply for Cal Grants, the state's financial aid program for low-income students. In 2012, after Congress had failed to act on immigration reform, President Obama wrote an executive order creating the Deferred Action for Childhood Arrivals program, DACA. It allows undocumented youth who were brought by their parents to the United States as children to register with the U.S. Citizenship and Immigration Services. Registration confers temporary legal status, allowing an undocumented youth to be in the country legally and to apply for a Social Security number, an essential, nonnegotiable credential for working. This status must be renewed every two years. In California and ten other states, whether immigrants are registered for DACA or not, they can apply for and receive a driver's license.

DACA has provided some sense of security for Karina, Daniel, Jonny, and others; they no longer feel at risk of arrest and deportation, and they're able to work legally. But DACA is a holding action, not a solution.

Its protections last for two years, and then an undocumented youth must reapply. It does not provide a path to citizenship, nor to permanent resident status, and it's not clear what will happen after President Obama leaves office.

Karina Vasquez graduated from UC San Diego with a major in psychology and a minor in law and society. Her last year in college, she took several electives in the school of education and became very interested in education policy. She hopes eventually to go to graduate school to study public policy with a focus on education, but for now she's taking a break from school. She registered with DACA, and she works for Reality Changers in operations and as a tutor in the College Apps Academy. Karina sees Reality Changers as a place to learn more about all aspects of helping disadvantaged students get to college, and how to support them once they're in college. Her voice is still soft, but she's become a more articulate and forceful advocate for herself.

Daniel Merced majored in anthropology at Dartmouth, and after he graduated he started work as a systems analyst for a large pharmaceutical company near Philadelphia. He's registered with DACA and he's gotten a driver's license and bought a car. He's grateful to be able to work and to have a good job, but the impasse on immigration reform leaves him anxious and discouraged. He feels that he can't count on ever becoming a citizen, and he worries what will happen to DACA after Obama leaves office. He's very interested in systems issues, and he'd like to go to graduate school in business, but the uncertainty about his immigration status hangs over his head: he feels he can't commit to any long-range plan. Despite his Ivy League education and an excellent job, he continues to feel an enforced orientation to the present.

While he was at Harvard, Jesse Sanchez worked as a mentor in the Crimson Summer Academy, Harvard's summer college-readiness program for disadvantaged youth in the Boston area. He developed an interdisciplinary major focusing on education policy, and for his senior thesis he proposed a comparative study of Reality Changers and Crimson Summer Academy, in which he aimed to identify the elements that contributed to the success of college-readiness programs. After his junior year he took a year's leave of absence from school and came home to San Diego, where he worked on his thesis and served as a site director for Reality Changers. He returned to Harvard, and during his senior year he cofounded the Harvard First Generation Student Union, the first organization at Harvard dedicated to building community, finding resources, and providing mentorship for first-gen students. He graduated with honors and was awarded a Fulbright Scholarship to teach for a year in Mexico. He taught English and organized leadership workshops at the Universidad Autónoma Metropolitana Iztapalapa, in Mexico City. He now works for the Future Project in San Francisco.

Kimberly Palafox, who wanted to go to New York, went to Cal State San Marcos, about twenty miles north of San Diego. After two years she was restless and wanted a change. She applied for, and was accepted into, a semester-long exchange program at Aarhus University in Denmark; she paid all of her expenses from her savings. When she first came to Aarhus, she was isolated and homesick. She made herself get out of her room and meet people, an experience that built her confidence in her ability to take care of herself. When she came home from Denmark, she found her mother deeply depressed, unable to work or care for Stephanie and Michelle, her younger sisters, who were still at home. As the oldest, Kim felt an obligation, she said, "to be the glue to hold things together, like I used to be." She took a year's leave from school and lived at home. She worked at the YMCA's after-school program and cooked and took care of the house and helped her sisters with school. She majored in global studies, and, she added with a smile, has a minor in French: a rebuttal to the high school teacher who discouraged her from taking AP French. She graduated in 2015 and now works full time for the YMCA in San Diego.

Her father stopped drinking and attends Alcoholics Anonymous meetings. He's taking English classes and asks Kim to speak English with him; he says he wants to keep up with his daughters. Kim's sister and confidant, Theresa, was awarded a Gates Millennium Scholarship and went to UC Riverside. She graduated in 2014 and is aiming for graduate school in political science. Their younger sister Stephanie also joined Reality Changers and now studies at Cal State Fullerton, near Los Angeles. Michelle, the youngest sister, belongs to Reality Changers. Kim's parents are proud of her, no longer ambivalent about her aspirations. When people ask about her, they say, "She's graduated from college."

Kim says, "The most important thing I got from Reality Changers is the courage to try things."

Robert Silva went to Cal State Los Angeles for two years, then left and worked as a bank teller for a year. His time away from college made him surer that he wants to finish. He's completed more than half of a bachelor's degree, with a major in philosophy, and is now supporting himself and carrying twelve units a semester. He's not sure when he'll graduate, because he's changed his major several times. He lives in Los Angeles and works as a waiter, and he also runs his own business, a bounce house, on weekends. His primary goals are to establish himself as an entrepreneur and to buy his mother a house. His little brother, Angel, is six years old; and seven years after her life-threatening diagnosis, his mother remains cancer-free. Marlon, his other brother, left Reality Changers after one year. He works and goes to community college part time, and he hopes to be a mechanical engineer.

Fernando Carrillo, who got beat up and lost his shoes because he wouldn't join a gang, went to San Diego State. He started as a business major, but figured out very quickly that business wasn't what he wanted. His second year he applied to, and was accepted in, the school of engineering. He's majoring in mechanical engineering and expects to graduate soon.

Robert, Daniel, Kim, Jesse, Fernando, and Karina are all continuing to launch into adulthood. They see college as an essential first step, the foundation that now enables them to move toward other goals and markers of adulthood: a good job, helping their parents, finding a partner, and making independent lives for themselves. Like their millennial peers, they're keenly aware of the twenty-first-century economic landscape, which offers fewer good jobs and less security than previous generations have enjoyed. Those goals and markers are important to them, but they recognize that their progress toward achieving them may be slower than for previous generations.

In the same week's time, Eduardo Corona started his freshman year at San Diego State and started as site director for the Wilson Middle School cohort at Reality Changers. When his parents ran into financial problems during the recession, he left school so that he could work a second job and help them out. He's continued to work for Reality Changers, and he's now director of College Town. He's reenrolled at San Diego State, majoring in psychology, and is on track to graduate. His story was featured in *The Graduates/Los Graduados,* a documentary about the challenges facing Latino students. He doesn't look like a gangbanger any more. He wears his hair in a brush cut, and dresses in plaid shirts with narrow ties; skinny jeans; and narrow, rectangular glasses. Reflecting on growing up in City Heights, and on the difference that Reality Changers made for him, he says, "All my friends are either in prison or in college."

The first group of Wilson students, whom he calls his kids, graduated from high school in 2015. He talks about how important it is to him to be there for all the Wilson students, "the way Reality Changers has been there for me."

Jonny Villafuerte has continued to work at Reality Changers. He's director of community opportunities, a part-time position that involves outreach and public speaking. He supplements his salary with some shifts as a waiter. He's also begun to market himself as an inspirational speaker, talking to groups about urban education and perseverance. When he was a student at Kroc Middle School, he noticed that the neighborhood around the school was much quieter than Golden Hill and had more trees. He promised himself that someday he'd live there. Now he lives in an apartment near Kroc.

He's registered with DACA, and although he's glad to have legal status and the authorization to work, he's uneasy about his future. Like other undocumented students, he doesn't know whether or when federal immigration policy will allow a path to citizenship; and like Daniel, he's reluctant to apply to graduate school without having any assurance about his long-term status. He's grateful for his education and for all the ways it's widened his world, but he feels unable to make long-term plans. As in the case of Daniel, his immigration status still forces an orientation to the present and undermines his hopes for the future.

Jorge Narvaez and Nancy separated, and shared custody of their two girls, who are now seven and ten. Now they've gotten back together and are exploring a future together. He graduated from UC San Diego with a major in ethnic studies. A YouTube video of him playing guitar and singing with his older daughter, Alexa, shot to viral fame, with more than 26 million views. He's been interviewed on national TV and National Public

Radio and has appeared in a commercial for Hyundai. He works for San Diego Dads Corps and continues to promote himself, sing, and make videos with his daughters.

Suzie Lozano completed her master's in information science at the University of Michigan and came back to San Diego, where she works as a user-experience designer for a large technology company. Her work involves ensuring that the company's products will be accessible for anyone to use, no matter their language or culture or education. She was married recently, to a man she'd known since college. She's amazed that she's reached all the goals—college, travel, graduate school, a good job—that loomed like impossibly distant mountains when she joined Reality Changers. She's not sure what she wants to do next, but she'd like to have work that allows both direct contact with people and a greater sense that her work is making a difference for people. For now, she plans to enjoy what she's accomplished, work hard at her job, and trust that new goals will emerge.

Perla Garcia, who came so close to graduating from UC Riverside, then was tripped up by the residuals of old trauma and deprivation, lives in San Diego. Her daughter, Salma, is three years old; and since Salma was born, Perla has not had much financial stability. She now works for a cosmetics chain, and she's been able to move out of her parents' house into her own apartment. She is two academic quarters short of her degree. Not finishing college eats at her; she wants better opportunities for herself, and she wants to be an example for her daughter. She's laying the groundwork of child-care arrangements and financial aid so that she can go to UC San Diego for those final two quarters and graduate. She invokes a vision of Salma working on her own college application: "I want her to be able to check the box that says 'mother is a college graduate.'" Her goal when she finishes her last two quarters and graduates is to tutor at Reality Changers and, in time, to lead a cohort.

Jenn Schadler moved to Boston with her longtime boyfriend, where she earned an M.Ed. in education policy and management at Harvard's Graduate School of Education. She and her boyfriend married and moved back to the Bay Area. They have a young daughter, and Jenn works as associate director of online courses at Stanford's Business School. She stays in touch with Grace Chaidez and Debbi Leto and many of the students she worked with at Reality Changers.

Grace Chaidez left Reality Changers to study nonprofit leadership and management at the University of San Diego, and she graduated with an MA. She served as assistant director of the Larry English LEAD Foundation in San Diego until the navy reassigned her husband to the Washington, DC, area. They live there now with their son, Giovanni. She stays in touch with Robert Silva and many other students.

Debbi Leto still tutors in the Senior Academy but has stepped down from leading it. One of her daughters has two small children and lives on the East Coast; Debbi decided that spending time with her grandchildren was her highest priority. She stepped away from running the Senior Academy, but she stays in touch with Jenn and Grace and dozens of former students.

Yanov is thirty-six, twice the age he was when he started hanging with the cholos in Golden Hill, and he's learned some hard lessons about what it takes to build an effective organization. After working with Mary Taylor, he's brought on additional senior managers, people whose competencies fill in the areas where he's weaker, and he's handed off large chunks of responsibility to them. It's what he intended to do when he hired Jenn and Grace; now he gets what they were saying. He's grateful to have people who know how to do things he doesn't. His staff sees less of Fort Chris.

Reality Changers remains the central focus of Yanov's life. Lately, after fifteen years of sixty-hour work weeks, he's decided that he wants to have more in his life—a relationship, maybe even a family of his own. He's reconnected with an old girlfriend and thinks their relationship is going somewhere. As he negotiates the plan for College Town with San Diego Unified's school board and city council members, he's frequently asked whether he's thought about running for office. The school board? City council? For now he's committed to getting a building and scaling up the program. After that . . . he shrugs and waves a hand in the air. He might be open to doing something new.

When Yanov was inventing Reality Changers, he aimed to build a scaffolding that would provide students with a sense of family. He couldn't foresee then what an enduring structure it would be. The sense of family was the heart of what held students in the program and what they valued most. It was easier for them to launch when they felt that they were pushing off from something solid, from people who knew them well and would go the distance with them. Now, as they launch past college into their adult lives, the Reality Changers family that held them, and their friendships with other students who were with them, have become part of their interior scaffoldings, their sense of their own worth.

Years after they've come through Reality Changers, its alumni maintain those friendships and continue to feel a strong connection to the program that helped them launch. A majority of alumni live in San Diego. Others come back for twice-yearly alumni reunions, where they catch up with friends and learn about new initiatives in the program. They volunteer for fund-raising events, and they come on program nights to visit, to talk with the current seniors, or to tutor. Even graduates who have no formal connection with the program become its advocates; their own lives and accomplishments are testimonies to how RC changes lives.

Reality Changers is integral to the structure of their lives; it acts as a scaffold for their efforts, and it enlarges their sense of what is possible. Alumni have learned that Reality Changers couldn't change their most difficult realities: not their immigration status, or illnesses, or family problems. It couldn't dissolve other people's prejudices, couldn't prevent the losses that inevitably come in the pursuit of ambitious goals. Still they call their experience in Reality Changers life-changing. It encouraged them to raise their expectations of themselves, of what they believed they could do, and it opened opportunities they didn't know existed. They all speak of their commitment to give back to their families and their community, and all say that Reality Changers enabled them to transform their lives and reach for their dreams.

Notes

INTRODUCTION

1. Roberto G. Gonzales, *Lives in Limbo: Undocumented and Coming of Age in America* (Oakland: University of California Press, 2015), p. 96.

2. Paul Tough writes about Geoffrey Canada and the Harlem Children's Zone in *Whatever It Takes: Geoffrey Canada's Quest to Change Harlem and America*, and in *How Children Succeed: Grit, Curiosity, and the Hidden Power of Character.*

3. Madeleine Blais, email communication with author, November 9, 2005.

4. Roberto G. Gonzales, *Young Lives on Hold: The College Dreams of Undocumented Students* (New York, College Board, 2009), p. 6, http://professionals.collegeboard.com/profdownload/young-lives-on-hold-college-board.pdf.

5. American Community Survey data for 2006, cited in Sandy Baum and Stella M. Flores, "Higher Education and Children in Immigrant Families," in "Immigrant Children," special issue, *Future of Children* 21, no. 1 (Spring 2011): 171–93, http://futureofchildren.org/futureofchildren/publications/docs/21_01_08.pdf.

6. Karl Alexander, Doris Entwisle, and Linda Olson, *The Long Shadow: Family Background, Disadvantaged Urban Youth, and the Transition to Adulthood* (Washington, DC: American Sociological Association, 2014), p. 178.

7. Rubén Rumbaut and Golnaz Komaie, "Immigration and Adult Transitions," in "Transition to Adulthood," special issue, *Future of Children* 20, no. 1 (Spring 2010): 63.

CHAPTER 3. LOOKING FOR A HOME

1. Victor Rios, *Punished: Policing the Lives of Black and Latino Boys* (New York: New York University Press, 2011), p. 108.

CHAPTER 4. INVENTING REALITY CHANGERS

1. Angela L. Duckworth, Christopher Peterson, Michael D. Matthews, and Dennis R. Kelly, "Grit: Perseverance and Passion for Long-Term Goals," *Journal of Personality and Social Psychology* 92, no. 6 (2007): 1087.

2. Greg J. Duncan and Katherine Magnuson, "The Nature and Impact of Early Achievement Skills, Attentions Skills, and Behavior Problems," in *Whither Opportunity? Rising Inequality, Schools, and Children's Life Chances*, ed. Greg J. Duncan and Richard J. Murnane (New York: Russell Sage Foundation, 2011), p. 68.

CHAPTER 6. UPHILL

1. Victor Rios, *Punished: Policing the Lives of Black and Latino Boys* (New York: New York University Press, 2011), p. 125.

CHAPTER 7. DOING RC

1. Victor Rios, *Punished: Policing the Lives of Black and Latino Boys* (New York: New York University Press, 2011), p. 40.

2. Prudence Carter, *Keepin' It Real: School Success beyond Black and White* (New York: Oxford University Press, 2005), p. 69.

3. Sean Reardon, "No Rich Child Left Behind," *New York Times,* April 16, 2013.

CHAPTER 10. UNDOCUMENTED

1. Roberto G. Gonzales, telephone interview with author, March 16, 2009.

2. Plyler v. Doe, 457 U.S. 202 (1982), https://supreme.justia.com/cases/federal/us/457/202/case.html.

3. Nicolas De Genova, "Migrant 'Illegality' and Deportability in Everyday Life," *Annual Review of Anthropology* 31 (2002): 427.

4. Roberto G. Gonzales, *Lives in Limbo* (Oakland: University of California Press, 2015), 56.

5. George Vernez, Richard Krop, and C. Peter Rydell, *Closing the Education Gap: Benefits and Costs* (Santa Monica, CA: Rand Center for Research on Immigration Policy, Rand Education, 1999), xxii, www.rand.org/content/dam/rand /pubs/monograph_reports/2007/MR1036.pdf.

CHAPTER 13. SANTIAGO MILAGRO AND THE FOUR-YEAR PLAN

1. Victor Rios, *Punished: Policing the Lives of Black and Latino Boys* (New York: New York University Press, 2011), p. 109.

CHAPTER 15. RESET

1. Angela L. Duckworth et al., "Grit: Perseverance and Passion for Long-Term Goals," *Journal of Personality and Social Psychology* 92, no. 6 (2007): 1098.

2. Edward Fergus, Pedro Noguera, and Margary Martin, *Schooling for Resilience: Improving the Life Trajectory of Black and Latino Boys* (Cambridge, MA: Harvard Education Press, 2015), p. 184.

CHAPTER 18. STARS AND PROJECTS AND EVERYONE ELSE

1. Edward Fergus, Pedro Noguera, and Margary Martin, *Schooling for Resilience: Improving the Life Trajectory of Black and Latino Boys* (Cambridge, MA: Harvard Education Press, 2015), p. 185.

CHAPTER 22. THE COSTS OF THEIR DREAMS

1. Roberto G. Gonzales, "Learning to Be Illegal: Undocumented Youth and Shifting Legal Contexts in the Transition to Adulthood," *American Sociological Review* 76, no. 4 (2011): 608.

Bibliography

Alexander, Karl, Doris Entwisle, and Linda Olson. *The Long Shadow: Family Background, Disadvantaged Urban Youth, and the Transition to Adulthood.* Washington, DC: American Sociological Association, 2014.

Arnett, Jeffrey J. "Emerging Adulthood, a Theory of Development from the Late Teens through the Twenties." *American Psychologist* 55, no. 5 (2000): 469–480.

Bailey, Martha J., and Susan M. Dynarsky. *Gains and Gaps: Changing Inequality in U.S. College Entry and Completion.* Working Paper 17633. Cambridge, MA: National Bureau of Economic Research, 2011. www.nber.org/papers /w17633on.

Baum, Sandy, and Stella M. Flores. "Higher Education and Children in Immigrant Families." In "Immigrant Children," special issue, *Future of Children* 21, no. 1 (Spring 2011): 171–193. http://futureofchildren.org/futureofchildren /publications/docs/21_01_08.pdf.

Carter, Prudence. *Keepin' It Real: School Success beyond Black and White.* New York: Oxford University Press, 2005.

Corwin, Miles. *And Still We Rise.* New York: HarperCollins, 2001.

De Genova, Nicolas. "Migrant 'Illegality' and Deportability in Everyday Life." *Annual Review of Anthropology* 31 (2002): 419–447.

Duckworth, Angela. "True Grit." *The Observer* (Association for Psychological Science) 26, no. 4 (April 2013). www.psychologicalscience.org/index.php /publications/observer/2013/april-13/true-grit.html.

Duckworth, A. L., and J. J. Gross. "Self-Control and Grit: Related but Separable Determinants of Success." *Current Directions in Psychological Science* 23, no. 5 (2014): 319–325.

Duckworth, Angela L., Christopher Peterson, Michael D. Matthews, and Dennis R. Kelly. "Grit: Perseverance and Passion for Long-Term Goals." *Journal of Personality and Social Psychology* 92, no. 6 (2007): 1087–1101.

Duncan, Greg J., and Richard J. Murnane, eds. *Whither Opportunity? Rising Inequality, Schools, and Children's Life Chances.* New York: Russell Sage Foundation, 2011.

Dweck, Carol. "Can Personality Be Changed? The Role of Beliefs in Personality and Change." *Current Directions in Psychological Science* 17, no. 6 (2008): 391–394.

———. *Mindset: The New Psychology of Success.* New York: Random House, 2006.

Fergus, Edward, Pedro Noguera, and Margary Martin. *Schooling for Resilience: Improving the Life Trajectory of Black and Latino Boys.* Cambridge, MA: Harvard Education Press, 2015.

Galla, Brian M., and Angela L. Duckworth. "More Than Resisting Temptation: Beneficial Habits Mediate the Relationship between Self-Control and Positive Life Outcomes." *Journal of Personality and Social Psychology* (February 2, 2015). Advance online publication, http://dx.doi.org/10.1037/pspp0000026.

Gonzales, Roberto G. "Learning to Be Illegal: Undocumented Youth and Shifting Legal Contexts in the Transition to Adulthood." *American Sociological Review* 76, no. 4 (2011): 602–619.

———. *Lives in Limbo.* Oakland: University of California Press, 2015.

———. "Wasted Talent and Broken Dreams: The Lost Potential of Undocumented Students." *Immigration Policy: In Focus* (Immigration Policy Center of the American Immigration Law Foundation, Washington, DC) 5, no. 13 (Fall 2007). www.immigrationpolicy.org/sites/default/files/docs/Wasted%20Talent%20and%20Broken%20Dreams.pdf.

———. *Young Lives on Hold: The College Dreams of Undocumented Students.* New York: College Board, April 2009. http://professionals.collegeboard.com/profdownload/young-lives-on-hold-college-board.pdf.

Gonzales, Roberto G., and Leo R. Chavez. "'Awakening to a Nightmare': Abjectivity and Illegality in the Lives of Undocumented 1.5 Generation Latino Immigrants in the United States." *Current Anthropology* 53, no. 3 (2012): 255–281.

Hauser, Brooke. *The New Kids.* New York: Free Press, 2011.

Klein, Malcolm. *The American Street Gang: Its Nature, Prevalence and Control.* New York: Oxford University Press, 1997.

Madera, Gabriela, Angelo A. Mathay, Armin M. Najafi, Hector H. Saldivar, Stephanie Solis, Alyssa Jane M. Titong, Gaspar Rivera-Salgado, Janna

Shadduck-Hernandez, Kent Wong, Rebecca Frazier, and Julie Monroe, eds. *Underground Undergrads*. Los Angeles: UCLA Center for Labor Research and Education, 2008.

Organization for Economic Cooperation and Development. *Strong Performers and Successful Reformers in Education, Lessons from PISA 2012 for the United States*. Paris: OECD Publishing, 2013. http://dx.doi.org/10.1787 /9789264207585-en.

Perez, William. *We ARE Americans, Undocumented Students Pursuing the American Dream*. Sterling, VA: Stylus Publishing, 2009.

Portes, Alejandro, and Rubén Rumbaut. *Immigrant America*. 4th ed. Berkeley: University of California Press, 2014.

Ralph, Laurence. *Renegade Dreams: Living through Injury in Gangland Chicago*. Chicago: University of Chicago Press, 2014.

Reardon, Sean. "No Rich Child Left Behind." *New York Times*, April 16, 2013.

———. "The Widening Achievement Gap between the Rich and the Poor: New Evidence and Possible Explanations." In *Whither Opportunity? Rising Inequality, Schools, and Children's Life Chances*, ed. Greg J. Duncan and Richard J. Murnane. New York: Russell Sage Foundation, 2011.

Rios, Victor. *Punished: Policing the Lives of Black and Latino Boys*. New York: New York University Press, 2011.

Rose, Mike. *Lives on the Boundary*. New York: Penguin Books, 1989.

Rumbaut, Rubén, and Golnaz Komaie. "Immigration and Adult Transitions." In "Transition to Adulthood," special issue, *Future of Children* 20, no. 1 (Spring 2010): 43–66.

Schorr, Lisbeth. *Within Our Reach*. New York: Anchor Press, 1988.

Shechtman, Nicole, Angela DeBarger, Carolyn Dornsife, Soren Rosier, and Louise Yarnall. *Promoting Grit, Tenacity, and Perseverance—Critical Factors for Success in the 21st Century*. Washington, DC: Office of Educational Technology, U.S. Department of Education, 2013. http://pgbovine.net /OET-Draft-Grit-Report-2-17-13.pdf.

Stetser, Marie C., and Robert Stillwell. *Public High School Four-Year On-Time Graduation Rates and Event Dropout Rates: School Years 2010–11 and 2011–12*. Washington, DC: National Center for Education Statistics, U.S. Department of Education, 2014. http://nces.ed.gov/pubs2014/2014391 .pdf.

St. John, Warren. *Outcasts United*. New York: Random House, 2009.

Thorpe, Helen. *Just Like Us*. New York: Scribner, 2009.

Tough, Paul. *How Children Succeed*. New York: Houghton Mifflin, 2012.

———. *Whatever It Takes: Geoffrey Canada's Quest to Change Harlem and America*. Boston: Houghton Mifflin, 2008.

———. "What If the Secret to Success Is Failure?" *New York Times Magazine*, September 14, 2011.

Tyler, John H., and Magnus Lofstrom. "Finishing High School: Alternative Pathways and Dropout Recovery." *America's High Schools* 19, no. 1 (Spring 2009). www.princeton.edu/futureofchildren/publications/journals/article/index.xml?journalid=30&articleid=49&sectionid=175.

Urrea, Luis Alberto. *Across the Wire.* New York: Anchor Books, 1993.

———. *The Devil's Highway.* New York: Back Bay Books, 2004.

Vernez, George, Richard Krop, and C. Peter Rydell. *Closing the Education Gap: Benefits and Costs.* Santa Monica, CA: Rand Center for Research on Immigration Policy, Rand Education, 1999. www.rand.org/content/dam/rand/pubs/monograph_reports/2007/MR1036.pdf.

Waters, Mary C., Patrick J. Carr, Maria J. Kefalas, and Jennifer Holdaway. *Coming of Age in America: The Transition to Adulthood in the Twenty-First Century.* Berkeley: University of California Press, 2011.

Index

223